BASIC FEDERAL INCOME TAX

FOURTH EDITION

Gwendolyn Griffith Lieuallen

Partner, Tonkon Torp LLP
Portland, Oregon

The *CrunchTime®* Series

Wolters Kluwer
Law & Business

Printed in the United States of America.

1 2 3 4 5 6 7 8 9 0

ISBN 978-1-4548-0920-3

Lieuallen, Gwendolyn Griffith, 1957-
  Basic federal income tax / Gwendolyn Griffith Lieuallen.—4th ed.
    p. cm.—(The crunchtime series)
  ISBN 978-1-4548-0920-3 (perfectbound)
  1. Income tax—Law and legislation—United States—Outlines, syllabi, etc. 2. Tax returns—
United States—Outlines, syllabi, etc. I. Title.
  KF6369.85.L55 2012
  343.7305'2—dc23
                                2012002137

This book is intended as a general review of a legal subject. It is not intended as a source of
advice for the solution of legal matters or problems. For advice on legal matters, the reader
should consult an attorney.

About Wolters Kluwer Law & Business

Wolters Kluwer Law & Business is a leading global provider of intelligent information and digital solutions for legal and business professionals in key specialty areas, and respected educational resources for professors and law students. Wolters Kluwer Law & Business connects legal and business professionals, as well as those in the education market, with timely, specialized authoritative content and information-enabled solutions to support success through productivity, accuracy, and mobility.

Serving customers worldwide, Wolters Kluwer Law & Business products include those under the Aspen Publishers, CCH, Kluwer Law International, Loislaw, Best Case, ftwilliam.com, and MediRegs families of products.

CCH products have been a trusted resource since 1913, and are highly regarded resources for legal, securities, antitrust and trade regulation, government contracting, banking, pension, payroll, employment and labor, and healthcare reimbursement and compliance professionals.

Aspen Publishers products provide essential information to attorneys, business professionals, and law students. Written by preeminent authorities, the product line offers analytical and practical information in a range of specialty practice areas from securities law and intellectual property to mergers and acquisitions and pension/benefits. Aspen's trusted legal education resources provide professors and students with high-quality, up-to-date, and effective resources for successful instruction and study in all areas of the law.

Kluwer Law International products provide the global business community with reliable international legal information in English. Legal practitioners, corporate counsel, and business executives around the world rely on Kluwer Law journals, looseleafs, books, and electronic products for comprehensive information in many areas of international legal practice.

Loislaw is a comprehensive online legal research product providing legal content to law firm practitioners of various specializations. Loislaw provides attorneys with the ability to quickly and efficiently find the necessary legal information they need, when and where they need it, by facilitating access to primary law as well as state-specific law, records, forms, and treatises.

Best Case Solutions is the leading bankruptcy software product to the bankruptcy industry. It provides software and workflow tools to flawlessly streamline petition preparation and the electronic filing process, while timely incorporating ever-changing court requirements.

ftwilliam.com offers employee benefits professionals the highest-quality plan documents (retirement, welfare, and non-qualified) and government forms (5500/PBGC, 1099, and IRS) software at highly competitive prices.

MediRegs products provide integrated healthcare compliance content and software solutions for professionals in healthcare, higher education, and life sciences, including professionals in accounting, law, and consulting.

Wolters Kluwer Law & Business, a division of Wolters Kluwer, is headquartered in New York. Wolters Kluwer is a market-leading global information services company focused on professionals.

To Spencer

Summary of Contents

Table of Contents

FLOW CHARTS

CAPSULE SUMMARY

EXAM TIPS

Preface

Thank you for buying this book.

This book is built on the foundation of the *Emanuel Law Outline* on *Basic Federal Income Tax*. The full-length *Outline* is intended as your guide as you study tax during the term. Then, as exams approach, this book can help you organize the large amount of material you've studied, as well as test yourself on your knowledge. In this book, the Capsule Summary is a bird's-eye view of the major concepts introduced in the basic tax course, and the problems and questions in this book will help you practice your test-taking skills. Use the Glossary to make sure you know tax terms and how to use them. The indexes in this book—Cases, Code, and Subject Matter—can help you as well. Use these to test your recall: Can you quickly identify what these statutes address? Can you recall the principles of the major cases?

The *CrunchTime* series is unique because it includes many flow charts. Many students find the "forest" of tax law daunting and get lost in the trees of all the statutes and regulations that they must study. Let the flow charts help you get oriented in tax. Take a look at the first chart (Figure 1) and last chart (Figure 18) to see the major issues that will appear on any tax exam: income, deductions, character, timing, and rates/credits. Then, use the individual charts to see the specific issues that arise in each area. You can use the charts to review what you've learned throughout your course and to help you see how all the concepts you've studied fit together. You can see how this is done in the Essay Exam Answers, which guide you through the applicable charts.

To use the flow charts to solve problems, you should first determine which charts are applicable to a particular problem. Many problems will require reference to multiple charts. Then you can use the flow charts to guide yourself through the "right questions to ask" in analyzing typical tax problems. If you develop the habit of asking these tax questions in the order in which they appear in the flow charts, you will be less likely to miss an important issue on the exam. (Of course, some of the detailed analysis, such as special rules or exceptions, is necessarily omitted from the charts, and you should refer to the full-length *Emanuel Law Outline* on *Basic Federal Income Tax*, your class notes, and the Code and Regulations for this detail.)

A few words about using the charts: Each flow chart is a series of choice questions, which are in rectangles or squares connected by straight lines. Sometimes the choice questions lead to a need for a calculation, and these are indicated with a triangle; curved lines direct you to the results of the calculation. The final conclusions are in circles or ovals. When you see dotted lines, you will be "netting" two calculations. Dashed lines lead to related questions that must be asked even after a conclusion is reached.

Each choice question is numbered with brackets, like this: [#]. The bracketed number allows you to identify the choice question as you make notes. It also makes it easier to discuss these guiding questions with your study partners. Some choice questions have endnote numbers attached to them. The endnote numbers reference explanatory notes following the chart, which give supplementary information and cross-references to the text and to material in the *Emanuel Law Outline* on *Basic Federal Income Tax*. The first time a term of art is used in a chart, it is italicized.

No book can replace the hard work of studying for exams, but the Wolters Kluwer Law & Business editors and I hope that the *CrunchTime* series will make the process just a little easier. Of course, no book is ever brought to press without a patient and understanding editor on the other end of the telephone. Many thanks to Barbara Lasoff, especially for tackling all these flow charts with such enthusiasm.

Good luck on your tax exam!

Gwendolyn Griffith Lieuallen
Portland, OR
October 2011

FLOW CHARTS

SUMMARY OF CONTENTS

FLOW CHART KEY

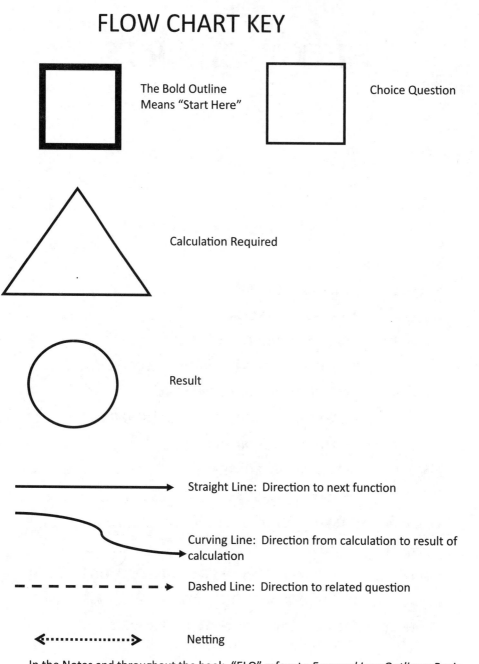

The Bold Outline
Means "Start Here"

Choice Question

Calculation Required

Result

Straight Line: Direction to next function

Curving Line: Direction from calculation to result of
calculation

Dashed Line: Direction to related question

Netting

In the Notes and throughout the book, "ELO" refers to *Emanuel Law Outlines: Basic
Federal Income Tax*, 4th ed., written by Gwendolyn Griffith Lieuallen and published
by Wolters Kluwer Law & Business. "CT" refers to this *CrunchTime* book.

FIGURE 1

THE BIG PICTURE

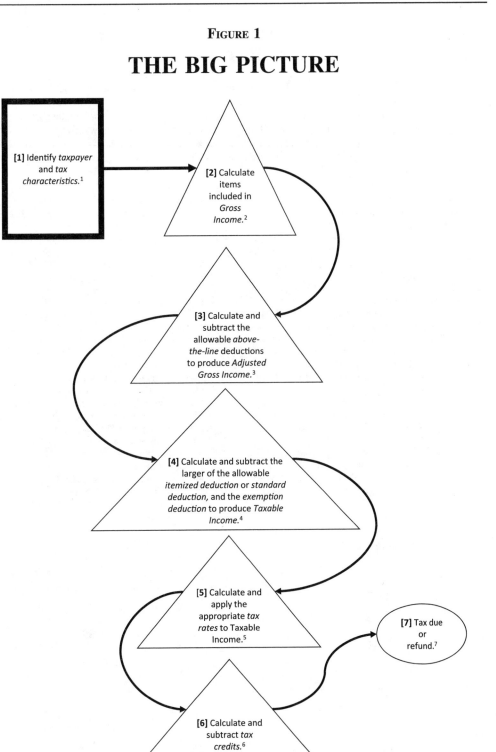

Notes to Figure 1
THE BIG PICTURE

This figure will help you get started in Federal Income Tax. Tax law is all about computing a number: the tax owed by a particular taxpayer. This figure shows the computation required to get there. Tax professors aren't usually very interested in that number. Instead, they are fascinated by the legal issues presented at each step along the way—and want you to be as well. These legal issues are explored in the other figures. (You might also take a look at Figure 18 at this point, which summarizes the eight questions any professor might ask on an exam.)

[1] The starting place is the proper identification of the basic facts about the taxpayer in question. Because tax problems usually involve more than one taxpaying person or entity, the first task is to identify *which taxpayer's* tax consequences are relevant to the problem. See Griffith Lieuallen: *Emanuel Law Outlines: Basic Federal Income Tax*, Fourth Edition, © 2011, published by Wolters Kluwer Law & Business (hereinafter "ELO"), Chap. 14; this book [Griffith Lieuallen: *CrunchTime: Basic Federal Income Tax*, Fourth Edition, © 2012, published by Wolters Kluwer Law & Business (hereinafter "CT")] pp. 96–97. The second task is to identify that taxpayer's tax characteristics that are important in the analysis of his or her income and deductions: the taxpayer's tax status, taxable year, and method of accounting. See ELO, Chaps. 11 & 13; CT, pp. 86–88.

[2] Gross Income includes all income from whatever source derived. §61. See Figure 2 (Analyzing Income) and Figure 12 (Gain/Loss on Property Dispositions). See ELO, Chaps. 2–4; CT, pp. 62–66.

[3] The first set of deductions available to a taxpayer are the so-called above-the-line deductions, i.e., those that are subtracted from Gross Income to produce Adjusted Gross Income. See Figures 3 (Personal Deductions) and 4–9 (Deductions and Losses), 11 (Capital Recovery), and 12 (Gain/Loss on Property Dispositions). See ELO, Chaps. 6–8; CT, pp. 71–73.

[4] A taxpayer must choose between claiming the standard deduction and the itemized deduction, and a rational taxpayer will choose the larger of the two. See Figures 3–5 (Deductions) and 6–9 (Losses). See ELO, Chaps. 5–6; CT, pp. 73–74. Almost every taxpayer may claim a personal exemption, depending on his or her family status and other factors. Subtracting these deductions from Adjusted Gross Income will produce Taxable Income.

[5] Once Taxable Income has been computed, the taxpayer must apply the appropriate rates of tax, considering the rates on ordinary income and capital gain and the alternative minimum tax (AMT). See ELO, Chaps. 12 & 13; CT, pp. 93–94. See Figures 15–17.

[6] A credit is a dollar-for-dollar reduction in the amount of tax owed and, in some cases, may reduce the tax liability below zero, resulting in a refund. See ELO, Chap. 13; CT, pp. 94–95

[7] The point of this exercise is to calculate the amount of tax owing or the refund due the taxpayer. But in most law school tax classes, this calculation is of relatively minor importance. Instead, most professors focus on the legal questions inherent in each of the previous steps.

Figure 2

ANALYZING INCOME

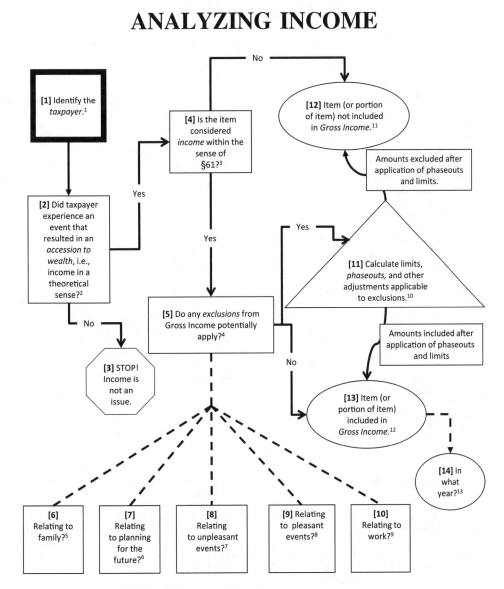

Consider all of these potential exclusions.

NOTES TO FIGURE 2
ANALYZING INCOME

This figure will help you with the most basic problem that appears on any tax exam: identifying whether a taxpayer has Gross Income. Because this is the starting place in basic tax, it is a question that appears on most tax exams in some form.

[1] In any given problem, there is usually more than one taxpayer involved in a transaction, and it is important to identify the relevant taxpayer. The relevant taxpayer is the one who experienced the accession to wealth, regardless of what he or she did with that wealth. See ELO, Chaps. 2 (III), 14 (III); CT, pp. 96–97. Usually, each taxpayer's tax consequences are analyzed separately. However, situations do exist in which the tax consequences of the relevant taxpayer may be entwined with others in the problem, such as when a gift occurs (e.g., the donee takes the donor's basis in the gifted property).

[2] An accession to wealth is an event that causes the taxpayer to be better off even if he or she doesn't end up with cash in hand. For example, if someone else pays a debt of the taxpayer, the taxpayer is better off and has therefore experienced an accession to wealth. See ELO, Chap. 2 (III); CT, pp. 62–63.

[3] Section 61 refers to *"income* from all sources," requiring a definition of income. There are five kinds of benefits that are not considered income in the sense used in §61: 1) imputed income; 2) loan proceeds; 3) the capital that one has invested in property; 4) noneconomic benefits; and 5) certain general welfare payments. See ELO, Chap. 2 (IV); CT, p. 63. In addition, the income must be "realized." See ELO, Chap. 9 (II); CT, p. 81.

[4] In order to be excluded from Gross Income, a specific statute must apply and its requirements must be strictly met. Construe exclusions narrowly. See ELO, Chap. 4 (II); CT, p. 66.

[5] Consider these potentially applicable exclusion statutes: §§71 (child support, but not alimony), 102 (gifts), and 1041 (transfers of property between spouses/former spouses). See ELO, Chaps. 4 (IV) & (XI), 10 (V); CT, pp. 65–67, 70-71.

[6] Consider these potentially applicable exclusion statutes: §§103 (interest on state/local bonds), 135 (interest on savings bonds used for education), 408 (Roth IRAs), 529/530 (distributions from certain college savings accounts), and especially 72 (defines includible portion of distribution from annuity, regular IRA distribution). See ELO, Chaps. 3 (V), 4 (V) & (X); CT pp. 64, 66–68.

[7] We might quibble about what constitutes an unpleasant event versus "good things happening" (Boxes [8]–[9]), but consider these potentially applicable exclusion statutes: §§101 (life insurance received on account of death of insured), 104 (personal injury settlements, but not punitive damages), and 108 (discharge of debt when taxpayer is insolvent or in bankruptcy, and in certain other situations). See ELO, Chap. 4 (III), (VI), (VII); CT, pp. 66–68.

[8] Consider these potentially applicable exclusion statutes: §§74 (prizes and awards), 102 (gifts), 111 (tax benefit recoveries), 117 (scholarships), 121 (sale of personal residence), and 1202 (sale of qualified stock). See ELO, Chaps. 4(IV), (VIII), (X), (XII); 11 (II); CT, pp. 66–68, 86.

[9] Consider these potentially applicable exclusion statutes: §§79 (group term life insurance), 106 (health and disability insurance), 119 (food and lodging), 120 (group legal services), 127 (education assistance), 129 (child care assistance), 132 (other fringe benefits), and 137 (adoption assistance). See ELO, Chap. 4 (IX); CT, pp. 68–70. Consider also that a taxpayer may deduct the unreimbursed expenses of employment, but these are subject to the 2% floor of §67. See ELO, Chap. 6 (X); CT, p. 74.

[10] It is common for the benefit of exclusions to be phased out, usually based on a taxpayer's Adjusted Gross Income level. See, e.g., §135(b)(2). Other exclusions apply only to a certain amount of a benefit received. See, e.g., §129 (maximum $5,000 dependent care assistance). As a result of these phaseouts and limits, some portion of the amount of the taxpayer's actual expenditure may be excluded from Gross Income, and some portion may be included in Gross Income. See ELO Chap. 4 (II).

[11] If an item of income is excluded from Gross Income, it never enters the computation of Taxable Income and thus is never taxed. Compare a deduction, which has the same net effect but appears as a subtraction in the computation of tax. See ELO, Chap. 5 (II); CT, p. 71.

[12] If an item of income is included in Gross Income, it is potentially subject to tax, even though it may be offset by a deduction. The amount included in Gross Income is the amount of money or the fair market value of property received.

[13] Figure 2 addresses only *whether* an amount is included in Gross Income. It doesn't address *when* (in what taxable year) that should occur, which depends on the taxpayer's taxable year, method of accounting, and special rules for some kinds of income. See ELO, Chap. 11; CT, pp. 86–88.

ANALYZING INCOME

A Congressman, upon retiring from public service, becomes a consultant to a Washington lobbying firm. An old friend offers him the free use of a car-and-driver service for the next two years. The former Congressman accepts. What are the tax consequences of this transaction to the former Congressman?

Box Number in Figure	Analysis
[1]	The former Congressman is the relevant taxpayer, not the friend (who may have deduction or gift tax issues).
[2]	The receipt of a car-and-driver service increases the former Congressman's wealth (otherwise, he would have to make other arrangements for which he would have to pay—driving himself, paying for a car-and-driver service, or taking a cab or the subway).
[4]	Although not all accessions to wealth are "income" within the sense of §61, the use of a car-and-driver service is not one of the excluded categories of potential income.
[5]	The former Congressman would very much appreciate you finding an exclusion for this accession to wealth.
[9]	The former Congressman probably thinks of this as a "gift," and therefore excludable under §102. Is this a gift? A gift is a transfer made with "detached and disinterested generosity." We do not know sufficient facts to understand the motivation for the transfer. If any facts suggest that this transfer is business related or a quid pro quo for future or past activities, and not merely a personal gesture of generosity, the IRS will claim that it is not a gift and therefore not excludable under §102, (And it certainly is a hefty gift. . . .)
[10]	The former Congressman might try to exclude this as a working condition fringe benefit under §132(d). However, that won't apply because it is not the employer making the car-and-driver service available to the former Congressman; it is the friend.
[11]–[13]	If the former Congressman cannot establish that the transfer is a gift, he must include the fair market value of the car-and-driver service in gross income. There are no phaseouts or limits that apply, so the entire amount must be included.
[11]–[12]	If the former Congressman could establish that this is a gift, then he could exclude it from gross income, and there are no limits on the amount excluded.
[14]	The proper year for inclusion is the year of receipt of the services.

FIGURE 3

PERSONAL DEDUCTIONS

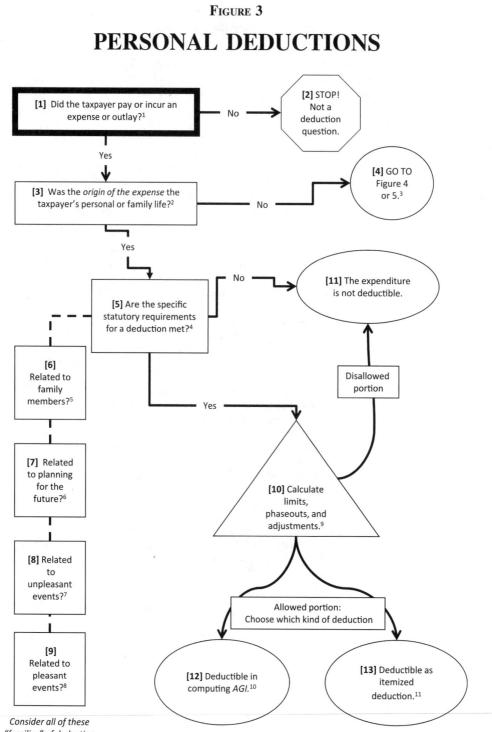

NOTES TO FIGURE 3
PERSONAL DEDUCTIONS

This figure will help you when faced with an individual who makes expenditures associated with his or her personal life and wants to know if he or she can deduct them. Remember: If in doubt, deny the deduction, because deductions are construed narrowly.

[1] The starting place is to determine whether the taxpayer has made an expenditure that could potentially generate a deduction. Look for outflows, and since most individuals are cash method taxpayers, they will be making actual payments, by cash, check, or credit card. For losses, see Figures 6–9.

[2] It is the origin of an expense—not the effect of making the expenditure—that determines deductibility. See *United States v. Gilmore*, 372 U.S. 39 (1963). See ELO, Chap. 5 (III); CT, p. 78.

[3] If the origin of the expense is not the personal or family life of the taxpayer, go to Figure 4 or 5 to determine if the expense is deductible as a trade or business or investment expense.

[4] As a general rule, personal or family expenses are not deductible. §262. However, the Code provides a deduction for certain personal expenses, if the taxpayer meets every requirement of the applicable statute. Construe deductions narrowly. See ELO, Chap. 5 (II); CT, pp. 71–72.

[5] Consider these potentially applicable deduction statutes: §§71 (alimony); 151, 152 (personal and dependent exemptions). See ELO, Chap. 6 (II) & (XI); CT, pp. 72, 74.

[6] Consider these potentially applicable deduction statutes: §§219 (IRA contributions), 162 (health insurance for self-employed), 223 (medical savings account contributions), 221 (student loan interest), 163 (home mortgage interest), 164 (investment interest), and 408 (retirement planning). See ELO, Chap. 6 (II) & (V); CT, pp. 73–74.

[7] Consider these potentially applicable deduction statutes: §§1211 (capital losses; see Figure 17), 165 (losses; see Figures 6–9), 172 (net operating loss), 164 (taxes), and 213 (medical expenses). See ELO, Chap. 6 (VI), (VII), (VIII); CT, pp. 72–74, 88.

[8] Consider these potentially applicable deduction statutes: §§170 (charitable contributions); 151, 152 (relating to dependency exemptions). See ELO, Chap. 6 (IX) & (XI); CT, pp. 73–74.

[9] The deduction statutes are riddled with limitations and phaseouts, which can result in some or all of an otherwise deductible expenditure not being deductible. See, e.g., the AGI limitations contained in §221 on the deduction for student loan interest. See ELO, Chap. 5 (VII).

[10] Taxpayers generally prefer above-the-line deductions (those deductible in computing AGI) because (1) AGI is used as a limitation on many itemized deductions; and (2) the taxpayer may not have sufficient deductions to make itemizing a sensible choice. Only certain deductions are allowable in computing AGI. Consider these potentially applicable deductions: §§62; 71; 165; 172; 217; 221; 223; 1211. See ELO, Chap. 6 (II); CT, pp. 72–73, 88. In addition, although technically not part of the traditional "above-the-line" deductions, the standard deduction (in lieu of the itemized deduction) and personal exemptions are deductible from AGI in computing Taxable Income. In other words, they do not become part of the itemized deduction.

[11] Some deductions are allowed only if the taxpayer itemizes, i.e., claims the itemized rather than the standard deduction. Consider §§163, 164, 165, 212, and 213. See ELO, Chaps. 5 (II), 6 (IV); CT, pp. 73–74.

EXAMPLE TO FIGURE 3

PERSONAL DEDUCTIONS

Emily, a cash method taxpayer, has an AGI of $35,000. This year, she made the following expenditures that she would like to deduct. May she deduct them?

Medical expenses for herself:	$15,000
Contribution to §529 plan for nephew:	$500
Cash contribution to Red Cross:	$600
Vet expenses for her cat (on credit card):	$1,000
Purchase of "coffee cart" for starting new business:	$10,000

Box Number in Figure	Analysis
[1]	Emily has a number of outlays or expenditures, as listed. For the vet expense, it doesn't matter that she paid with a credit card; as a cash method taxpayer, this is still her "expenditure."
[3], [4]	All of the expenses related to Emily's personal life, except for the purchase of the coffee cart, which is potentially a business expenditure. Analyze that expenditure using Figure 4.
[5]	Emily's question to you is precisely this: Does she qualify for a deduction for any of the expenditures other than the coffee cart?
[6]–[9]	These boxes are designed to get you thinking about possible deductions Emily might claim.
[6]	*Family members:* Although Emily may think of her cat as a family member, she cannot claim a deduction for its medical expenses. The §529 plan for the nephew is possible (see below).
[7]	*Planning for the future:* Emily's contribution to the §529 plan is not deductible for federal tax purposes, although it may be for state purposes.
[8]	*Unpleasant events:* Emily's medical expenses, assuming they are qualifying medical expenses, will be partially deductible. (The cat's will not be deductible, of course.)
[9]	*Pleasant events:* Emily's charitable contribution, assuming it is to a qualifying charity, will potentially be deductible.
[10]	There are limits potentially applicable to the charitable deduction and the medical expenses. Emily may potentially make a charitable contribution of up to 50% of her contribution base. Emily's medical expenses are deductible to the extent that they exceed 7.5% of her AGI.
[11]	Emily's AGI is $35,000, so 7.5% of that amount is $2,625. This is the nondeductible portion.
[12]–[13]	The rest of the medical expense ($12,375) is deductible. The charitable contribution and medical expenses are allowed as itemized deductions, if Emily "itemizes,"i.e., claims the itemized deduction rather than claiming the standard deduction. (If she does not itemize, they are nondeductible.)

FIGURE 4

TRADE OR BUSINESS DEDUCTIONS

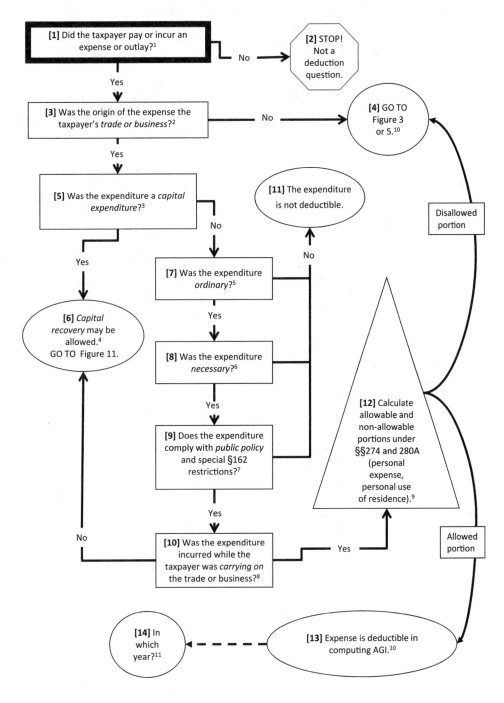

TRADE OR BUSINESS DEDUCTIONS

This figure will help you when you are faced with a sole proprietor or business entity that incurs expenses associated with the business. The question is whether any particular expense is deductible. Pay special attention to Box [5]: whether the expenditure is a capital expenditure or a potentially deductible expense.

[1] Look for outflows: expenses paid (cash method taxpayers) or accrued (accrual method taxpayers). But for losses, see Figures 6–9.

[2] The origin of the expense, not the effect of making it or not making it, determines whether it is a trade or business expense. See ELO, Chap. 7 (II), CT, p. 78. Although there is no specific definition of a "trade or business," the term generally means holding oneself out as being in the business of selling goods and services for profit. (If an activity is not for profit, a portion of the expenses—generally up to the income from the activity—will be deductible, but no loss can be generated from the activity. See ELO, Chap. 8 (IX); CT, pp. 78–80.) If the *origin* of the expense is not the taxpayer's trade or business, go to Figure 3 or 5 to determine if the expense is deductible as personal expense (Figure 3) or investment expense (Figure 5). Remember: (1) an employee is in the trade or business of providing services to an employer; and (2) a person can have more than one trade or business, in which case it is important to allocate expenditures to the correct activity.

[3] A capital expenditure is an expenditure that creates a separate asset or creates a significant benefit that lasts beyond the close of the taxable year. See *Indopco v. Commissioner,* 503 U.S. 79 (1992), and ELO, Chap. 7 (IV); CT, p. 77.

[4] No deduction is allowed for a capital expenditure. §263. However, a taxpayer will be allowed capital recovery, either during ownership of the asset, or at disposition. See Figure 11; ELO Chap. 7 (IV); CT, pp. 76–78. When a taxpayer makes a capital expenditure, the taxpayer acquires a "basis" in the property acquired. See Figure 10.

[5] "Ordinary" means usual in business, even if unique in the taxpayer's experience. See ELO, Chap. 7 (II); CT, p. 75.

[6] "Necessary" means appropriate and helpful, and sufficiently connected with the trade or business. See ELO, Chap. 7 (II); CT, p. 75.

[7] See, e.g., §162(c) (bribes), (f) (fines), (g) (treble damages). See ELO, Chap. 7 (II); CT pp. 76, 164.

[8] The taxpayer must be "open for business" in order to deduct an expense. See ELO, Chap. 7 (II); CT, p. 76. If an otherwise deductible expense is incurred prior to opening, it may be amortizable under §195 as a pre-opening expense. See Figure 11.

[9] Sections 274 and 280A potentially disallow deductions for all or a portion of certain expenses that are of a mixed business/personal nature. Consider: meals (50% deductible), significant restrictions on entertainment deductions, home offices, and rental of personal or vacation residences. See ELO, Chap. 8; CT, pp. 78–80.

If §280A or §274 disallow all or a portion of a deduction as a trade or business expense, this expense might still be deductible as a personal or investment expense. To determine this, go to Figure 3 or 5.

[10] Trade or business expenses are generally deductible from Gross Income in computing AGI. A sole proprietor computes business income and deductions on Schedule C, and the net profit is included, or the loss deducted, "above the line." See ELO, Chap. 3 (III); CT, p. 64.

[11] This figure addresses only *whether* an item is deductible, not *when* it is properly deductible, which will depend on the taxpayer's taxable year, method of accounting, and special rules. See ELO, Chap. 11; CT, pp. 86–88.

EXAMPLE TO FIGURE 4

TRADE OR BUSINESS DEDUCTIONS

Rocco owns a residential painting business. This year, he incurred the following expenses:

Purchase of new sprayers:	$15,000
Insurance and business fees:	$2,000
Parking fines incurred by trucks illegally parked:	$200
Pledge to contribute to local school baseball team:	$3,000

Of these expenses, which are deductible this year? Rocco is a cash method taxpayer.

Box Number in Figure	Analysis
[1]	Rocco made an outlay or expenditure for all of the expenses except for the pledge. The pledge is not deductible in the current year.
[3]	All of the remaining expenses are related to his trade or business.
[5]	The new sprayers are a capital expenditure. Go to Figure 11 to see how capital recovery will be allowed.
[7]–[8]	The other expenditures (insurance, fees, and fines) are ordinary (Box [7]) and necessary (Box [8]).
[9], [11]	Deduction of the fines would violate public policy (as well as §162(f)), and therefore, they will not be deductible.
[10]	The other expenses (insurance and fees) were incurred in the carrying on of the business.
[12]	These are no expenditures for which a deduction is limited by §274 or §280A, and therefore no limitations will be imposed by either section.
[13]–[14]	The insurance and fees are deductible as trade or business expenses, in the year that Rocco paid for them.

FIGURE 5

FIGURE 5

INVESTMENT DEDUCTIONS

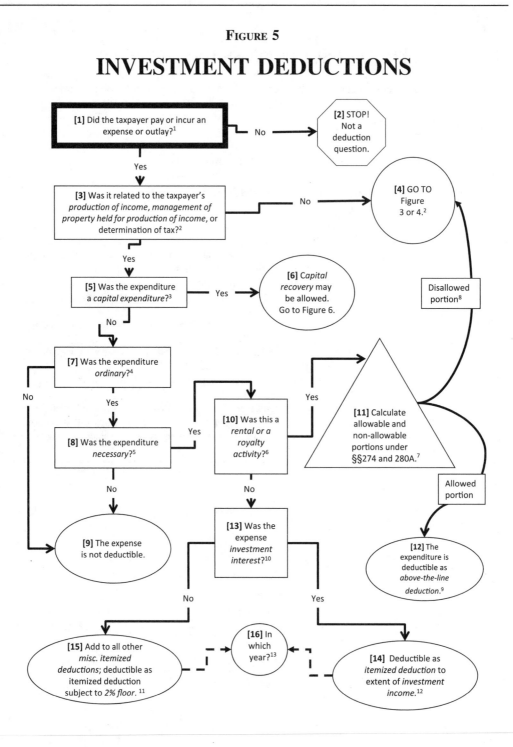

NOTES TO FIGURE 5

INVESTMENT DEDUCTIONS

This figure will help you analyze deductions that are potentially allowable when a taxpayer pays or incurs expenses in connection with an activity that the taxpayer engages in for profit, but which does not rise to the level of a trade or business. Rentals and royalties and investments fall into this category.

[1] The starting place is to determine whether an event has occurred that could potentially generate a deduction. Look for outflows: expenses paid (for cash method taxpayers) or accrued (for accrual method taxpayers). For losses, see Figures 6–9.

[2] This figure addresses profit-seeking expenditures that are associated with activities that do not rise to the level of a trade or business, but are not purely personal. Examples include investing in stocks and securities or owning a rental home. The "origin of the expense" rule applies. If the origin of the expense is not the taxpayer's investment activities, go to Figure 3 or 4 to determine if the expense is deductible as personal expense (Figure 3) or a trade or business expense (Figure 4).

[3] An expenditure that creates a separate asset or has a significant benefit that lasts beyond the close of the taxable year is a capital expenditure, which cannot be deducted. A capital recovery deduction may be available. See ELO, Chap. 7 (IV); CT, pp. 77–78; Figure 11.

[4] "Ordinary" has the same meaning in this context as it does in the context of trade or business deductions: usual in the income-producing activity, even if unique in the taxpayer's experience. See ELO, Chap. 7 (II) & (V); CT, p. 75.

[5] "Necessary" has the same meaning as in trade or business deductions: appropriate and helpful, and sufficiently connected with the income-producing activity. See ELO, Chap. 7 (II) & (V); CT, p. 76.

[6] Expenses of rental and royalty activities are generally deductible from Gross Income in computing AGI. The taxpayer computes his or her income and deductions from such activities on Schedule E, and the net income

is included, or the net loss is deducted, "above the line."

[7] Sections 274 and 280A disallow deductions for all or a portion of certain expenses arising from mixed personal and business activity. Consider meals (50% deductible), entertainment deductions, home offices, and rental of personal or vacation residences. See ELO, Chap. 8; CT, pp. 79–80.

[8] If §274 or §280A disallows all or a portion of a deduction as an investment expense, the disallowed portion may still be deductible as a personal (itemized) expense. To determine this, go to Figure 3, which addresses deductions for personal expenses.

[9] This figure is about whether a particular expenditure is deductible. If, when added together, all the expenditures result in a loss, go to Figure 8 to determine the deductibility of the loss and its particular components.

[10] Investment interest is interest incurred on a debt to acquire investment assets, such as stocks or bonds. §163(d)(3)(A). See ELO, Chap. 6 (V); CT, p. 74.

[11] The 2% floor of §67 allows a deduction for miscellaneous expenses only to the extent that they, in the aggregate, exceed 2% of the taxpayer's AGI. See ELO, Chap. 6 (X); CT, p. 74.

[12] Investment interest is deductible only to the extent of net investment income. §163(d)(2). See ELO, Chap. 6 (X); CT, p. 74. The 2% floor does not apply to investment interest.

[13] This figure addresses only *whether* an item is deductible, not *when* it is properly deductible, which will depend on the taxpayer's taxable year, method of accounting, and loss restrictions, such as §§465 and 469.

EXAMPLE TO FIGURE 5
INVESTMENT DEDUCTIONS

Shannon borrowed $10,000 at 7% interest, and used the proceeds to purchase shares of XYZ stock. This year, Shannon paid $700 as interest on the loan and had the following investment income:

Dividends from XYZ:	$200
Other investment income:	$300

May Shannon deduct the interest paid on the loan?

Box Number in Figure	Analysis
[1]	Shannon made a payment for interest.
[3]	The interest related to her purchase of investment property, i.e., the XYZ stock.
[5]	The interest is not a capital expenditure.
[7]–[8]	Interest expense is considered both ordinary (usual in the activity) and necessary (appropriately connected to the investment activity).
[10]	This is not a rental or royalty activity.
[13]	It is investment interest, i.e., interest incurred to purchase or carry investment property.
[14] – [16]	Shannon may deduct the interest to the extent of her investment income, or $500, in the year paid. The remaining $200 carries forward to future years, in which she can deduct the amount to the extent of her investment income.

FIGURE 6

LOSSES OF INDIVIDUALS—IN GENERAL

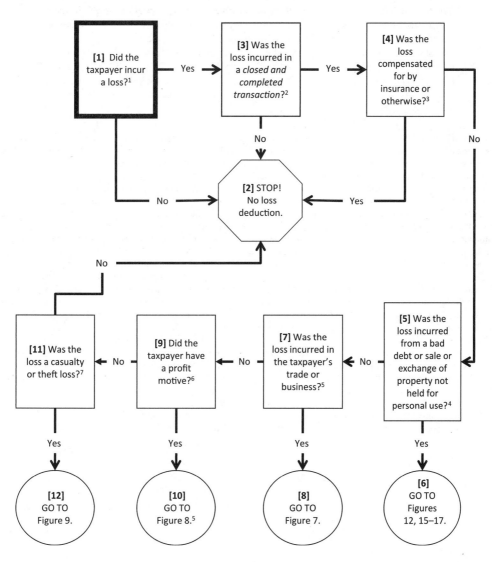

NOTES TO FIGURE 6

LOSSES OF INDIVIDUALS—IN GENERAL

This figure will help you when faced with an individual who experiences a "loss." Remember: Losses for individuals are specially limited by §165(c). Only certain kinds of losses are potentially deductible for individuals: losses incurred in a trade or business (see Figure 7), or losses incurred in an activity engaged in for profit that doesn't rise to the level of a trade or business (investment losses, see Figure 8), and personal casualty losses (see Figure 9). A taxpayer experiencing any other kind of loss is just plain out of luck. For example, a loss incurred on the sale of a personal residence at a loss is not deductible because the house is viewed as property held for personal use.

[1] The starting place is to identify an individual taxpayer incurring a loss. Losses occur when a taxpayer's deductions exceed his or her income, in an activity that generates income and deductions. Or a loss can occur when a taxpayer's property is destroyed, or is sold, or is exchanged for something less valuable. Taxpayers bear the burden of establishing the fact and amount of the loss, as well as the proper year for claiming the loss. In a theft situation, for example, it is necessary to establish the year of the theft. For a mugging, that's easy. For embezzlement, on the other hand, it can sometimes be quite difficult.

[2] If there is a realistic possibility that the taxpayer may recoup the loss, the transaction is not closed for purposes of assessing loss. A mere decline in value, for example, is not a realized loss for tax purposes. See ELO, Chap. 6 (II); CT, p. 81.

[3] Watch for situations in which the taxpayer's loss is covered by insurance or a private arrangement that substitutes for insurance, even if the taxpayer decides not to file a claim or seek indemnification. In these situations, there is no deductible loss for tax purposes.

[4] If the loss is from the worthlessness of a debt or from the sale or exchange of property, it will generate a capital or §1231 loss. Losses from the worthlessness of a debt (a bad debt) or from the sale or exchange of property are analyzed in Figures 12 and 15–17. See ELO, Chap. 12 (III); CT, pp. 89–90.

[5] A taxpayer must be carrying on a trade or business in order to deduct a loss attributable to that activity. While the Code does not define a "trade or business," the courts have defined it as holding oneself out as selling goods or services in order to generate a profit. Cf. §183 (hobby losses). See Figure 4 for an analysis of trade or business losses. See ELO, Chap. 7 (II); CT, pp. 75–76.

[6] A taxpayer has a profit motive if he or she has the actual and honest objective of making a profit. This can be contrasted with activities and transactions entered into for personal motives, i.e., not to make a profit. For losses from activities entered into for profit, but that do not rise to the level of a trade or business, see Figure 8. See ELO, Chap. 8 (IX); CT, pp. 78–80.

[7] A personal casualty loss (PCL) is a loss from events such as a fire, storm, flood, or earthquake. §165(c)(3). Figure 9 analyzes personal casualty losses. See ELO, Chap. 6 (VII); CT, pp. 74.

[8] If a loss doesn't fit within any of these categories, the individual incurring the loss may not deduct it.

LOSSES OF INDIVIDUALS—IN GENERAL

Peggy was shocked to discover this year that termites had eaten away the foundation under her house. She had the foundation repaired at a cost of $25,000. May she deduct this loss?

Box Number in Figure	Analysis
[1]	Peggy has definitely incurred a loss.
[3]	This is a closed and completed transaction because she is not likely to recover either the foundation or the outlay.
[4]	There is no mention of insurance or any other source for reimbursement.
[5]	This is not a bad debt or investment property.
[7]	This property was not held for use in Peggy's trade or business.
[9]	Holding and repairing the property is a personal activity, not a profit-seeking activity, even though, at least in the past, taxpayers have viewed their homes as profit-generating investments.
[11]–[12]	Peggy may try to argue that this is a casualty loss, but the IRS has disagreed, saying that the "suddenness" requirement is not met for the kind of damage that occurs over an indefinite period.
[13]	This is not likely to be a deductible loss.

FIGURE 7

TRADE OR BUSINESS LOSSES

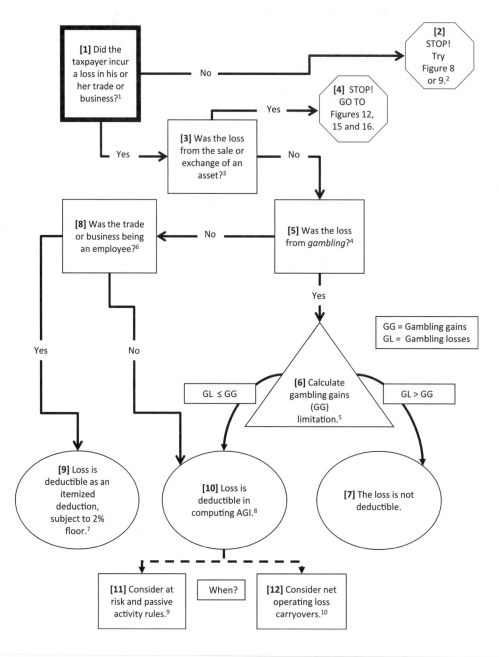

NOTES TO FIGURE 7
TRADE OR BUSINESS LOSSES

This figure will help you when you are faced with a taxpayer carrying on a trade or business who may have incurred a loss. In the basic tax course, the businessperson you will see is usually a sole proprietor. That person will have income from business (see Figure 2) and may deduct many (but not all) of the costs of producing that income (see Figure 4). If the net result is a loss, that loss may be deductible. In addition, the taxpayer may have specific events that generate a loss, such as a theft. See also Figure 12.

[1] The starting place is to identify a taxpayer in a "trade or business" because the taxpayer must be carrying on a trade or business in order to deduct a loss attributable to that activity. While the Code does not define a "trade or business," the courts have defined it as holding oneself out as selling goods or services in order to generate a profit. See ELO, Chap. 7 (II); CT, pp. 75–76.

[2] If the loss does not occur in connection with a taxpayer's trade or business, see if it is an investment loss (Figure 8) or a personal casualty loss (Figure 9).

[3] If the loss is from the sale or exchange of property, calculate the gain or loss using Figure 12, and then determine the character of the gain or loss (Figure 15), paying special attention to the rules of §1231, which apply to real and depreciable property used in a trade or business. See Figure 16.

[4] While a professional gambler is not in the business of selling goods and services, which is central to the usual definition of a "trade or business," the Supreme Court has ruled that gambling can be a trade or business. *Commissioner v. Groetzinger*, 480 U.S. 23 (1987). See ELO, Chap. 8 (X).

[5] Special limitations apply to the trade or business of gambling. See §165(d). Gambling includes all the usual wagering activities and games, and also includes sweepstakes and tournaments. Gambling losses of a gambler engaged in the trade or business of gambling are deductible only to the extent of gambling gains in the year incurred. Any excess loss is not deductible and does not carry over to future years. §165(d). The professional gambler's losses are allowed as a deduction from Gross Income only to the extent of gains; no excess loss is allowed as a deduction. (A nonprofessional gambler would not deduct his or her losses above the line as a trade or business loss, but would instead deduct gambling losses as an itemized deduction, subject to the limitation that losses can be deducted only to the extent of gambling gains.)

[6] An employee is in the trade or business of being employed. See ELO, Chap. 7 (II). As a result, the unreimbursed expenses of that trade or business are potentially deductible. Remember: A person may have more than one trade or business, such as when an employee moonlights. If so, it is necessary to allocate expenses appropriately.

[7] Some expenses, such as unreimbursed employee business expenses, are deductible as itemized deductions, but only to the extent that these expenses, in the aggregate, exceed 2% of AGI. §67(a). See ELO, Chap. 6 (X).

[8] The taxpayer includes all the income from the business in Gross Income and claims the appropriate deductions on Schedule C. If the net effect is a loss, it is deductible from Gross Income in computing Adjusted Gross Income, subject to at-risk and passive loss restrictions.

[9] Taxpayers typically want to deduct their losses in the earliest year possible. However, a number of Code provisions limit the deduction of a loss in the current year and require the deduction of the loss to be deferred into the future. For some activities, a taxpayer's loss may be restricted to his or her amount "at risk," i.e., the amount for which the taxpayer is personally liable. §465. In addition, if the loss is a passive loss (such as a trade or business in which the taxpayer does not materially participate), §469 will restrict the deduction of the loss to the taxpayer's passive income. If §465 or §469 disallows a loss for a year, it is carried forward until the taxpayer is eligible to deduct the loss. See ELO, Chap. 11 (II); CT, p. 88.

[10] Section 172 allows a taxpayer to carry over an operating loss to other years: 2 years back and 20 years forward. See ELO, Chap. 11 (II); CT, p. 86.

Example to Figure 7

TRADE OR BUSINESS LOSSES

Tillie is an employee of BigLaw, a law firm. Evenings and weekends, however, she is a hypnotherapist who helps clients stop smoking, lose weight, and achieve their other goals. Tillie incurred the following income and expenses this year:

Salary from BigLaw:	$50,000
Fees from hypnotherapy business:	$11,000

Expenditures for the following:

(1) Continuing education courses for improving word processing skills: $500
(2) Continuing education courses for hypnotherapy licensure: $1,000
(3) Ordinary and necessary business expenses associated with $12,000
    hypnotherapy:

Tillie has two trades or businesses, one of which is her employment and the other of which appears to be a sole proprietorship. Her expenses must be allocated to each activity. Expenses in category (1), above, are properly allocable to her trade or business of being an employee. Categories (2) and (3), above, are properly allocable to her hypnotherapy business. Figure 4 would be used to determine what deductions are allowable. The result would be that Tillie has a $1,000 loss in her hypnotherapy business. Is this loss deductible, and if so, how?

Box Number in Figure	Analysis
[1]	Tillie incurred a loss in her trade or business.
[3]	The loss was not from the sale or exchange of an asset.
[5]	The loss was not from gambling.
[8]	This loss was not from the trade or business of being an employee.
[10]	The loss is deductible "above the line," i.e., in computing AGI.
[11]	The loss would be deducted in the year incurred, and there is no evidence that the passive loss rules would apply.
[12]	As Tillie has plenty of other income against which to deduct the loss, it will not generate a net operating loss carryover.

FIGURE 8

INVESTMENT LOSSES

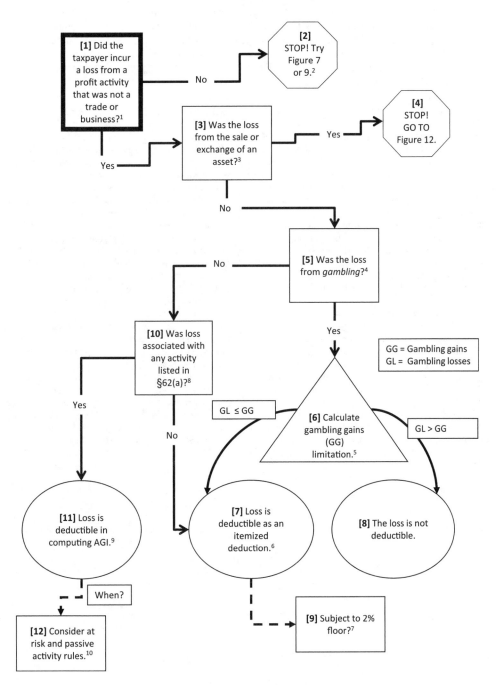

NOTES TO FIGURE 8

INVESTMENT LOSSES

This figure will help you when faced with a taxpayer who is carrying on an activity for profit, but that activity doesn't rise to the level of a trade or business. It is related to Figure 5, which addresses the individual deductions that can make up such a loss. This figure will help you analyze gambling questions and questions in which the taxpayer incurs a loss from rental or royalty activities. For losses on the sale or exchange of assets, see Figure 12.

[1] The starting place is to identify "investment activities." In these situations, the taxpayer has a profit motive, but the extent of his or her activities do not rise to the level of a trade or business. For example, no matter how extensive a taxpayer's activity, investing in stocks or securities for his or her own account is not a trade or business. See ELO, Chap. 7 (X); Section 212 allows deductions for this kind of activity, and if these expenses exceed income, the taxpayer has a potentially deductible loss.

[2] If the loss doesn't arise from an investment or similar activity, see if it is a trade or business loss (Figure 7) or a personal casualty or theft loss (Figure 9).

[3] If a loss arises from the sale or exchange of an asset, it should be analyzed separately due to the need to analyze the restrictions on capital losses and the nonrecognition provisions. See Figures 12 and 14–17.

[4] A nonprofessional gambler typically has a profit motive, but the activity doesn't constitute a trade or business.

[5] Gambling losses are deductible only to the extent of gambling gains. §165(d). Any excess is not deductible in the year incurred and does not carry over to any future year. Nonbusiness gambling losses are deductible as an itemized deduction, not subject to the 2% floor. See ELO, Chap.7 (X); CT, p. 80.

[6] If a loss becomes part of the itemized deduction, it is available only if the taxpayer "itemizes," rather than claiming the standard deduction. It is deductible from AGI in computing Taxable Income. See ELO, Chap. 5 (II), 6 (IV); CT, pp. 71, 73–74.

[7] Some itemized deductions are subject to the 2% floor of §67, which means that they are deductible only to the extent that, in the aggregate, they exceed 2% of the taxpayer's AGI. For investment activity, these include tax preparation fees, safety deposit box fees, and fees associated with investment accounts not properly added to the basis of the securities. See ELO, Chap. 6 (X).

[8] Section 62(a) lists the deductions that are deductible from Gross Income in computing AGI (the so-called above-the-line deductions). Many of these are personal deductions (see Figure 3) or those relating to a trade or business (see Figure 4). Some, however, are expenses of profit-seeking activities that do not rise to the level of a trade or business, such as rentals, royalties, or forfeitures relating to early withdrawals of savings.

[9] If a loss is deductible in computing AGI, it is subtracted from Gross Income in computing AGI. See ELO, Chap. 5 (II).

[10] For some activities, a taxpayer's loss may be restricted to his or her amount "at risk," i.e., the amount for which the taxpayer is personally liable. In addition, if the loss is a passive loss (such as a loss from a rental of real estate), §469 will restrict the deduction of the loss to the taxpayer's passive income. If §465 or §469 disallows a loss for a year, it is carried forward until the taxpayer is eligible to deduct the loss. See ELO, Chap. 11 (II); CT, p. 88.

EXAMPLE TO FIGURE **8**

INVESTMENT LOSSES

Perry became concerned about the condition of his bank. Despite his banker's assurances that FDIC insurance would protect his funds, he withdrew funds from certificates of deposit before those certificates matured. He incurred $1,200 of penalties for early withdrawal. May he deduct this loss?

Box Number in Figure	Analysis
[1]	Perry's investments are motivated by an intention to make a profit, but he is not in the trade or business of investing. He incurred a $1,200 loss from that activity.
[3]	This did not involve the sale or exchange of an asset.
[5]	This loss was incurred in a gambling activity.
[10]	This activity is described in §62(a)(9).
[11]	These penalties may be deducted in computing AGI, i.e., "above the line."
[12]	The at-risk and passive activity rules do not apply, as this is not a trade or business.

FIGURE 9

PERSONAL CASUALTY LOSSES

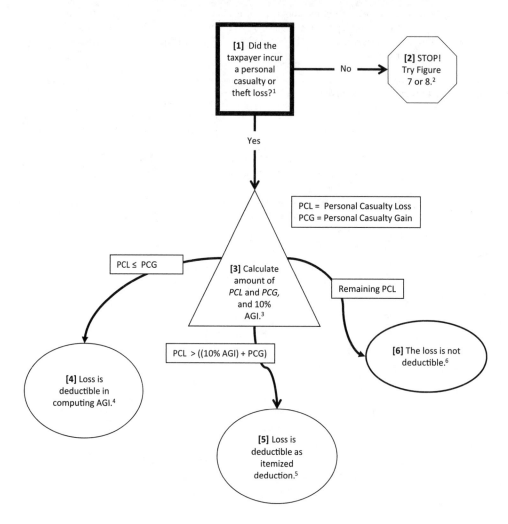

[1] Did the taxpayer incur a personal casualty or theft loss?[1]

No → **[2]** STOP! Try Figure 7 or 8.[2]

Yes

PCL = Personal Casualty Loss
PCG = Personal Casualty Gain

PCL ≤ PCG

[3] Calculate amount of *PCL* and *PCG,* and 10% AGI.[3]

Remaining PCL

PCL > ((10% AGI) + PCG)

[4] Loss is deductible in computing AGI.[4]

[6] The loss is not deductible.[6]

[5] Loss is deductible as itemized deduction.[5]

Notes to Figure 9

PERSONAL CASUALTY LOSSES

This figure will help you when you are faced with an individual who has experienced a natural disaster. (Remember: There have been many of these in recent years, so the fact pattern is likely on the minds of many professors.) It applies only to losses; if the taxpayer experiences a "gain" (receives insurance or other proceeds in excess of his or her basis in the property destroyed), you should analyze the gain using Figure 13. If the loss is incurred in a trade or business, or from investment property, you should analyze it with Figure 7 or 8.

[1] The starting place is to determine whether the taxpayer has experienced a property loss from a casualty, with respect to property that is held for personal use. Typical casualty losses occur from storms, earthquakes, and similar disasters, or from theft. See ELO, Chap. 6 (VII); CT, p. 74.

[2] If a loss doesn't qualify as a personal casualty loss, check to see if it qualifies as a deductible loss under other provisions of §165(c): as a loss incurred in a trade or business (see Figure 7) or a loss in an investment activity (see Figure 8).

[3] The amount of the personal casualty loss (PCL) is limited to the lower of the fair market value (FMV) of the property immediately before the event or the taxpayer's adjusted basis in the property. In addition, each loss must be reduced by $100 (think of it as a "deductible"). A personal casualty gain (PCG) occurs when the taxpayer's property is destroyed in a casualty event, and the insurance proceeds received exceed the taxpayer's basis in the property destroyed. See ELO, Chap. 6 (VII).

[4] A taxpayer must include PCGs in gross income; PCLs are deductible to the extent of these gains. If PCLs are deductible against PCGs, this deduction is above the line, i.e., in computing AGI. If PCGs exceed PCLs in any particular year, both PCGs and PCLs are treated as capital. §165(h). See ELO, Chap. 6 (VII).

[5] After allocation of PCLs against PCGs, the rest of the PCL (if any) is deductible as an itemized deduction, but only to the extent that the remaining PCLs exceed 10% of AGI. §165(h). See ELO, Chap. 6 (VII); CT, p. 74.

[6] All remaining amounts of PCLs (the amount less than 10% of AGI) are not deductible.

PERSONAL CASUALTY LOSSES

Sally's sailboat was destroyed by a hurricane. It was worth $250,000, and her basis in it was $100,000. She had insurance on the boat, and her insurance company paid her the FMV, or $250,000. Flooding from the hurricane also destroyed her home, but unfortunately, she did not have flood insurance. It was worth $500,000, and her adjusted basis in it was $280,000. Her AGI, without considering either of these events, was $120,000.

Box Number in Figure	Analysis
[1]	Sally has experienced one tax loss (the flood loss of her home). Although the loss of her boat is a loss in the "real world," in the tax world, she has a gain equal to the difference between what the insurance company paid her and her adjusted basis in the boat. The flood is a closed and completed transaction unless there is some evidence to suggest that Sally's insurance company will change its mind or she will receive FEMA assistance.
[3]	PCG = $150,000. PCL = $280,000 (basis) − $100 = $279,900. 10% of AGI = $12,000.
[4]	The PCG and PCL included and deducted from Gross Income, respectively, are capital in nature. Loss deductible in computing AGI = $150,000.
[5]	Loss deductible as an itemized deduction = $279,900 − $150,000 − $12,000 = $117,900.
[6]	The amount of PCL that is not deductible is $12,100.

FIGURE 10

BASIS

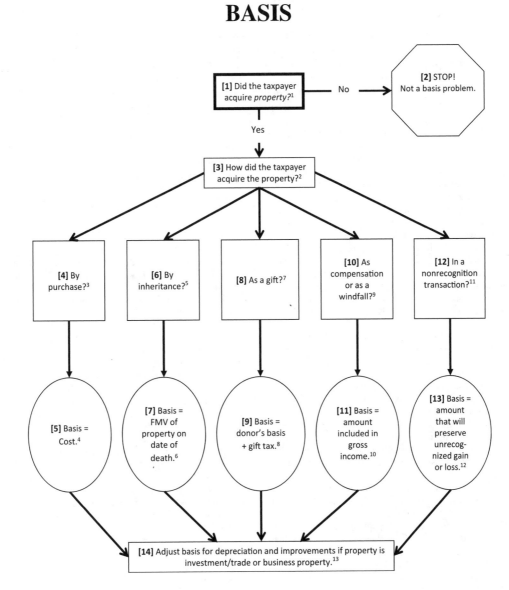

NOTES TO FIGURE 10

BASIS

This figure will help you get ready to learn about gains and losses from the sale or exchange of property. When a taxpayer acquires an asset, he or she must acquire a "basis" in that asset: the taxpayer's unrecovered economic investment (or deemed investment) in the property. For a purchase, for example, the basis of a purchased item is the cost of the item. Make sure you know the rules governing the different computations of initial basis before going on to consider capital recovery (Figure 11) or sales and exchanges (Figure 12).

[1] The starting place is to determine whether the taxpayer has acquired "property" because basis is a concept that is only relevant to property—tangible or intangible. If a taxpayer acquires a piece of property—such as land, a building, or a copyright—he or she must determine the basis of the property. Basis is relevant to capital recovery (see Figure 11) in the form of depreciation or amortization, and to the determination of gain or loss on disposition. See ELO, Chap. 9 (V); CT, p. 81.

[2] The most important question in determining the initial basis of property is *how* the taxpayer acquired the property. In most cases, this will be by purchase (see Box [4]). Remember, however, that a taxpayer may acquire property partially by one method and partially by another, such as a bargain sale. See ELO, Chap. 9 (V); CT, p. 81.

[3] "Purchase" includes a purchase in the usual sense of the word, as in a purchase for money. But it also includes purchase by an exchange of one property for another (unless a nonrecognition rule applies).

[4] If a taxpayer purchases property, the initial basis of the property will be the purchase price: the amount of money, plus the fair market value of property, plus the amount of liabilities of the seller assumed by the buyer. §§1012, 1016. If a taxpayer takes out a loan to purchase property, the basis of that property will include the amount of the borrowed funds used to purchase the property. See ELO, Chap. 9 (V) & (VI); CT, p. 82.

[5] A taxpayer receives property by inheritance when he or she receives it because of someone's death, i.e., through a will, trust, or estate settlement.

[6] If a taxpayer receives property through inheritance, the initial basis of the property will be the fair market value on the date of death or, if elected by the executor, on the alternate valuation date. §1014. This is often referred to as a "stepped-up basis" because the basis of the property in the hands of the decedent is often much lower. But if the property is worth less at death than the decedent's basis, then the basis to the recipient will be a "stepped-down" basis. See ELO, Chap. 9 (V); CT, p. 81.

[7] A taxpayer receiving a gift of property does not include it in his or her gross income. §102. A gift is a transfer made with detached and disinterested generosity. *Commissioner v. Duberstein,* 363 U.S. 278 (1960). See ELO, Chap. 4 (IV); CT, p. 67.

[8] The basis of the property received by gift will be the donor's basis, plus any gift tax paid by the donor. But if, at the time of the gift, the donor's basis exceeded the fair market value of the property, and upon sale by the donee this basis would generate a loss, then the basis will be the fair market value at the date of the gift. §1015. See ELO, Chap. 9 (V); CT, p. 81.

[9] Sometimes a taxpayer performs services and receives property in exchange. Or, a taxpayer may win property on a game show. Or, a taxpayer may find property, such as finding a diamond ring inside a purse purchased at a thrift store. If, under state law, the taxpayer is entitled to keep the property, he or she must report the value of the property as income. See *Cesarini v. Commissioner,* 296 F. Supp. 3 (N.D. Ohio 1969), aff'd per curiam, 428 F.2d 812 (6th Cir. 1970).

[10] In these fairly unusual cases, the basis of the property is its "tax cost basis," i.e., the amount the person must include in gross income. This would be the fair market value of the property received.

[11] In a variety of transactions, Congress has determined that the time is not ripe for recognition of gain or loss. These include like-kind exchanges (§1031), involuntary conversions (§1033), and transfers of property between spouses or former spouses incident to a divorce (§1041). See ELO, Chap. 10; CT, pp. 85–86.

[12] Each nonrecognition rule contains its own special basis calculation. All of these have a common thread: the basis of the "new" property must preserve, as of the moment of the exchange, the realized gain or loss that went unrecognized in the transaction. See ELO, Chap. 10; CT, p. 84. Consider also §267, which provides a special basis rule for the purchaser when a loss property is transferred between related parties. See ELO, Chap. 11 (VII).

[13] Once the initial basis is determined, basis is adjusted upward for improvements, and downward for depreciation or amortization. See §1016 and ELO, Chap. 9 (V); CT, p. 81.

EXAMPLE TO FIGURE **10**

BASIS

David is a broker specializing in helping people locate and purchase businesses. He usually takes a commission equal to 10% of the purchase price upon the closing of a successful sale. This year, he assisted his friend Charlene in purchasing a business for a price of $1,000,000. He agreed with her that, instead of taking his usual commission, he would accept 1,000 shares of stock in the business. When she purchased the business, he received the shares. There are no restrictions on the shares.

What is David's basis in the shares?

Box Number in Figure	Analysis
[1]	Stock is property, so David received property that must be assigned a basis.
[3]	To determine basis, you must determine how the taxpayer acquired the property.
[10]	Boxes [4]–[12] guide you through the usual ways that people acquire property, until you find the one that works best. In this case, David earned a fee for services. Instead of taking 10% of the purchase price ($100,000) in cash, he agreed to take the 1,000 shares of stock. This is compensation income.
[11]	David's compensation is equal to the fair market value of the stock. That fair market value must be included in David's gross income and becomes his basis in the shares. It is difficult to determine the fair market value of the shares, but it could be determined by appraisal of the shares.
[14]	Intangible, non-wasting property like stock is not the kind of property the basis of which is adjusted for improvements or depreciation.

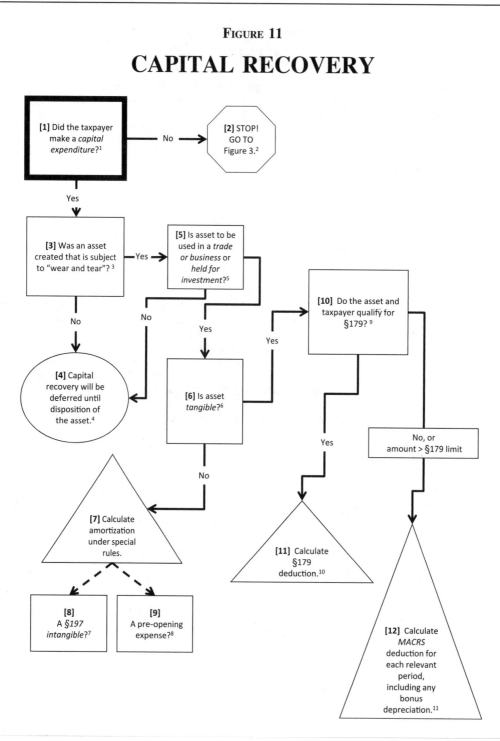

FIGURE 11

CAPITAL RECOVERY

Notes to Figure 11

CAPITAL RECOVERY

This figure will help you understand depreciation and amortization, as well as the other ways that a person may claim capital recovery for his or her investment in an asset. Make sure you understand "basis" (Figure 10) before tackling capital recovery. Many professors aren't particularly interested in the computations associated with the Modified Accelerated Cost Recovery System (MACRS) but are interested in seeing that you understand the theory of the three ways to recover capital: (1) at the beginning of the investment, (2) during the investment as it produces income, or (3) at the end of the investment (at sale).

[1] The starting place is to identify whether the taxpayer has made a "capital expenditure," which is one that either creates a new asset or is expected to generate benefits beyond the close of the taxable year. See ELO, Chap. 7 (IV); CT, pp. 76–77. If in doubt, treat an expenditure as capital rather than allowing a current deduction.

[2] If the taxpayer has made an expenditure, but it is not a capital expenditure, it may be deductible. See Figures 3–5.

[3] In order for a taxpayer to claim deductions for amortization or depreciation of an asset, it must be of a kind that is "used up" as it generates income in order to be depreciable. Example: Buildings are depreciable, but collectible art is not. Land is never depreciable. See ELO, Chap. 7 (IV); CT, pp. 76–77.

[4] If capital recovery is deferred until disposition of the asset, the gain or loss will be determined by subtracting the taxpayer's basis in the property from the amount realized. See Figure 12.

[5] If the taxpayer holds an asset exclusively for personal use, capital recovery through §179, MACRS, and related provisions is not allowed. Property that is partly for business use and partly for personal use is governed by §280A, so that capital recovery may be allowed only for a portion of the property. See ELO, Chap. 8 (VII) & (VIII); CT, p. 80.

[6] Capital recovery for intangible assets, such as trademarks or goodwill, is called "amortization," not "depreciation." Amortization is allowed under special rules that vary from asset to asset. Only two of the most commonly encountered rules are described here; there are many others as well. See ELO, Chap. 7 (IV).

[7] These assets include goodwill, covenants not to compete, licenses, franchises, and permits. See ELO, Chap. 7 (IV); CT, p. 78. The recovery period is 15 years, and is calculated on a straight-line basis, beginning with the month the property is placed in service. See ELO, Chap. 7 (IV); CT, p. 78.

[8] Section 195 allows up to $5,000 of deductions in the year of opening, but this amount must be reduced by the amount by which the taxpayer's pre-opening expenses exceed $50,000. See ELO, Chap. 7 (IV); CT, p. 76.

[9] Section 179 requires that property be §1245 property held for use in a trade or business, and the deduction cannot exceed the taxable income of the taxpayer, determined without regard to the deduction.

[10] The amount of the deduction is the cost of the property up to $500,000 (as of 2012), and the expense deduction is phased out if the taxpayer places in service more than $2,000,000 of assets during the year. See ELO, Chap. 7 (IV); CT, p. 77. Section 280F may also impose a limit on this deduction for luxury autos or business property also used for personal purposes. The asset's basis is reduced by the capital recovery deduction. See ELO Chap. 8 (VIII), CT p. 80.

[11] Computing the MACRS deduction requires determining the applicable recovery period for the particular asset, the applicable convention, the cost, and the date placed in service. Section 280F may also affect the MACRS deduction for luxury autos or business property also used for personal purposes. The Code contains a wide variety of special statutes that assign cost recovery periods or methods to certain kinds of property. See ELO, Chaps. 7 (IV), 8 (VIII). In addition, the taxpayer may be eligible for bonus depreciation, depending on the kind of assets, the date purchased, and the date placed in service. The asset's basis is reduced by the capital recovery deduction.

EXAMPLE TO FIGURE 11
CAPITAL RECOVERY

Sia purchased a laundry business. She paid $100,000 for equipment and $45,000 for the goodwill associated with the business. When may she deduct the cost of these purchases?

Box Number in Figure	Analysis
[1]	Sia's expenditures are capital in nature.
[3]	Both assets are potentially subject to amortization or depreciation as they are both "used up" as the taxpayer uses them to generate income.
[5]	Both assets are used in the trade or business.
[6]	Sia has purchased one tangible asset (equipment) and one intangible asset (goodwill).
[7], [8]	The goodwill is a §197 intangible. Sia will deduct $3,000 ($250/month) per year as amortization deductions attributable to the goodwill.
[10], [11]	Sia's business should be eligible for the §179 deduction for the purchase of the equipment, up to the whole amount, but more facts are necessary to determine how much. Specifically, the new business may not generate sufficient taxable income in the year of purchase to justify the full §179 deduction.
[12]	Any amount that is ineligible for the §179 deduction will be eligible for MACRS deductions. How much the MACRS deduction will be will depend on the appropriate recovery period and the method Sia chooses. She may also be eligible for bonus depreciation.

FIGURE 12

GAIN/LOSS ON PROPERTY DISPOSITIONS

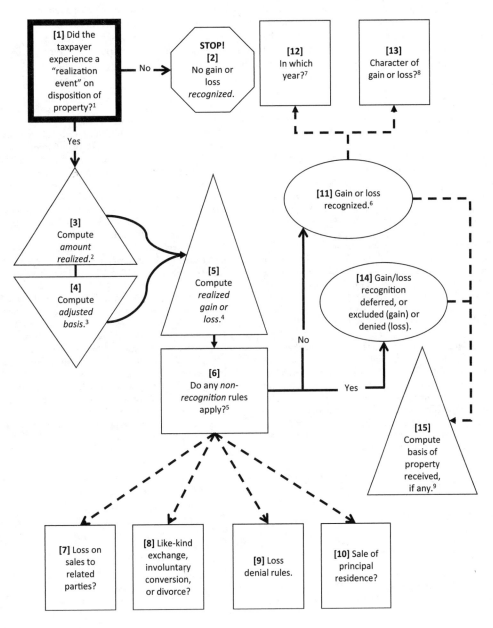

Notes to Figure 12

GAIN/LOSS ON PROPERTY DISPOSITIONS

This figure will help you with a frequently tested area of tax law: the sale or exchange of property. The typical tax question focuses on the sale of land or stock in a corporation, but may also include personal property or buildings. Make sure you understand basis (Figure 10) and capital recovery (Figure 11) before tackling sales and other dispositions. When reviewing, make sure you understand that the gain or loss on sale or exchange must be characterized as capital or ordinary (see Figures 15–17).

[1] The starting place is to identify a "realization event." This is a transaction in which the taxpayer gives up property and receives property that is different in kind or quality from property surrendered. See *Cottage Savings Ass'n v. Commissioner*, 499 U.S. 554 (1991), and ELO, Chap. 9 (III) & (IV); CT, p. 81.

[2] A taxpayer's amount realized is equal to the sum of what he or she receives in the transaction, i.e., (1) the amount of money, plus (2) the fair market value of property, plus (3) liabilities that the taxpayer assumes as part of the transaction. See ELO, Chap. 9 (V); CT, p. 81.

[3] The taxpayer's adjusted basis in the property depends on how he or she acquired the property, as well as subsequent events affecting the property's basis. See Figure 10 and ELO, Chap. 9 (V); CT, p. 81.

[4] Realized gain or loss is equal to the difference between the taxpayer's amount realized and his or her adjusted basis in the property transferred. §1001. See ELO, Chap. 9 (V); CT, p. 81.

[5] Generally, realized gains and otherwise deductible losses (see Figures 6–9) are recognized (included in income or deducted) in the year of realization, absent a specific statutory provision deferring the gain or loss recognition. Consider whether any nonrecognition rules apply. Some nonrecognition rules are exclusion statutes (e.g., §121 for excluding gain on the sale of a principal residence, Box [10]) or statutes limiting an otherwise

deductible loss (e.g., §267, Box [7]). Others are deferral statutes, such as those listed in Box [8], §§1031 (like-kind exchanges, see Figure 14), 1033 (involuntary conversions, see Figure 13), and 1041 (transfers of property between spouses and incident to a divorce). Finally, §165(a) allows the recognition of only certain types of losses by individuals. See Figure 6 and ELO, Chap. 10; CT, pp. 83–86.

[6] The portion of the gain or loss that is recognized is either included in gross income or is deducted. This assumes that the loss is otherwise deductible. See Figures 6–9.

[7] If gain is recognized, it may nevertheless be deferred under the installment method of reporting income. See ELO, Chap. 11 (IV); CT, p. 87. The installment method doesn't apply to losses.

[8] If gain or loss is recognized, it is important to characterize the gain or loss as an ordinary, capital, or §1231 gain or loss. See Figures 12–17.

[9] If the taxpayer received property in an exchange, it is critical to compute properly the taxpayer's basis in the property received. Property received in a fully taxable transaction will take a basis equal to its fair market value. Each tax deferral statute (e.g., §§1031, 1033, and 1041) contains its own approach to calculating the basis of the property received in the transaction, using substituted basis as a means to preserve unrecognized gain or loss for later potential recognition.

GAIN/LOSS ON PROPERTY DISPOSITIONS

Jack and Jill lived in identical houses on the same street. This year, both Jack and Jill sold their homes for $250,000 in cash after living in them for some years. Jack had purchased his home several years ago for $300,000. Jill had purchased her home many years ago for $125,000. Will Jack and Jill recognize the gain or loss on their sales?

Box Number in Figure	Analysis
[1]	Both Jack and Jill have a realization event upon the sale of their homes.
[3]	The amount realized for both Jack and Jill is $250,000.
[4]	The adjusted basis for Jack is $300,000. For Jill, it is $125,000 (no facts suggest additional investments in the homes) under §1012.
[5]	Jack's realized loss is $50,000. Jill's realized gain is $125,000.
[6], [9], [14]	Jack's loss is not deductible by reason of §165, which allows only certain kinds of losses to be recognized by individuals. Because a principal residence is personal use property, a loss on its sale does not fit within any of the allowed categories.
[6], [10], [14]	Jill's gain is excluded from Gross Income under §121.
[15]	Because both Jack and Jill received cash, it is not necessary to determine the basis of property received.

FIGURE 13

INVOLUNTARY CONVERSIONS (IRC §1033)

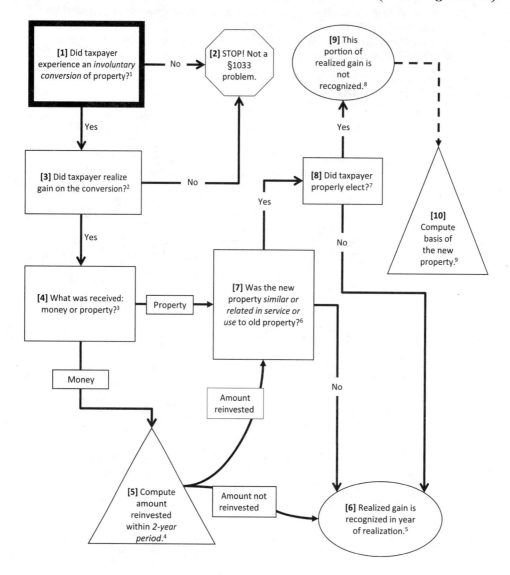

NOTES TO FIGURE 13

INVOLUNTARY CONVERSIONS (IRC §1033)

This figure will help you when you are faced with a taxpayer who has experienced a condemnation action or a natural disaster (and there have been so many disasters these days, professors are likely to have the fact pattern on their mind). Taxpayers that might take advantage of deferral under §1033 have experienced a gain—they have received proceeds in excess of their basis in the property destroyed or condemned. For losses, see Figure 9 (for personal casualty losses) or 12 (other losses).

[1] The starting place is the identification of an "involuntary conversion." An involuntary conversion occurs when property is destroyed or condemned. Examples include natural disasters (floods, earthquakes, hurricanes, etc.) and eminent domain proceedings. When the value of what is received (usually money in the form of insurance proceeds, but sometimes property) is different from the adjusted basis of the property that is destroyed or condemned, the taxpayer realizes gain or loss on the transaction. See ELO, Chap. 10 (IV); CT, p. 85.

[2] Section 1033 applies only to realized gains; for losses, see §§165 (personal and investment property) and 1231 (business property). See ELO, Chaps. 6 (VII), 12 (IV); CT, pp. 72–73.

[3] In an involuntary conversion, the taxpayer may receive other property to replace the converted property (as in some condemnation actions), but is more likely to receive insurance proceeds. See ELO, Chap. 10 (IV); CT, p. 85.

[4] The taxpayer must reinvest the money received in new property within two years of the close of the taxable year in which the conversion occurred. §1033(a)(2)(B). Special rules apply to certain disasters, where a taxpayer is given a longer time period to reinvest. §1033(h). In some cases, the taxpayer will reinvest only a portion of the proceeds in new property, and in that situation, a portion of the realized gain will be recognized.

[5] Realized gain is recognized only to the extent of the proceeds not reinvested in qualifying property. §1033(a)(2). See ELO, Chap. 10 (IV); CT, p. 85.

[6] "Similarity" depends on function and use by the owner; the replacement property does not need to be identical to the converted property. Special rules apply to real property used in a trade or business and livestock. See ELO, Chap. 10 (IV); CT, p. 85.

[7] The taxpayer makes the election by including only the amount of the gross income required to be included (Box [6]) and by providing information about the circumstances of the conversion and replacement.

[8] If the taxpayer receives qualifying property, or reinvests money into qualifying property, this portion of the realized gain will not be recognized in the year of conversion. §1033(a)(1). See ELO, Chap. 10 (IV); CT, p. 85.

[9] If §1033 applies to the exchange of property, the taxpayer's basis in the replacement property must be computed. The basis of the replacement property is equal to the basis of the converted property, plus any gain recognized, minus any proceeds not reinvested in similar property. §1033(b)(2). This usually means that the basis of the replacement property will be equal to the basis of the converted property. See ELO, Chap. 10 (IV); CT, p. 85.

INVOLUNTARY CONVERSIONS (IRC §1033)

Roxanne's property was condemned by the city in order to make way for a new freeway. She received $500,000 for the property, in which her adjusted basis had been $100,000. She immediately used those proceeds, plus $100,000 of her savings, to purchase a new property. The new property was identical in every respect to the condemned property, except that it was, she hoped, far away from any future freeway site. Assume Roxanne will make all the proper elections. How should Roxanne report this transaction for tax purposes?

Box Number in Figure	Analysis
[1]	A condemnation is an involuntary conversion.
[3]	Roxanne realized $400,000 of gain on the conversion, which is equal to her amount realized ($500,000) minus her adjusted basis of $100,000.
[4]	Roxanne received money, not property.
[5]	She immediately invested all the money received.
[7]	The new property is identical to the old, except for the location.
[8]	Assume that Roxanne will make the proper election.
[9]	None of Roxanne's realized gain is recognized.
[10]	The basis of the new property is equal to the basis of the old property, plus Roxanne's additional investment of $100,000. This produces a basis of $200,000.

FIGURE 14

LIKE-KIND EXCHANGES OF PROPERTY (IRC §1031)

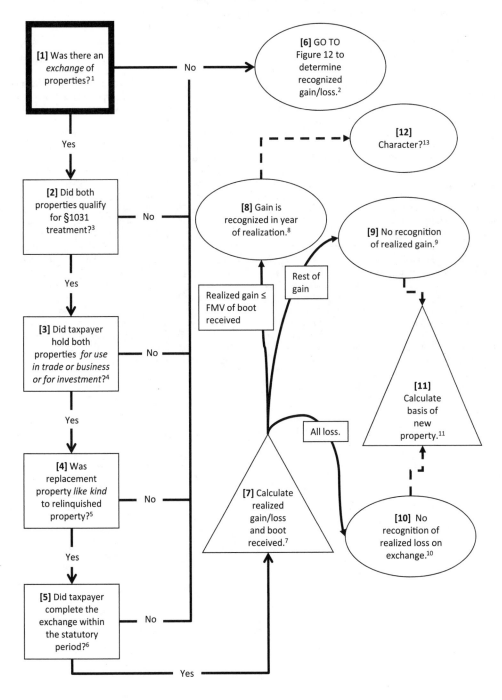

[1] Was there an *exchange* of properties?[1]

No → [6] GO TO Figure 12 to determine recognized gain/loss.[2]

Yes

[2] Did both properties qualify for §1031 treatment?[3]

No

[3] Did taxpayer hold both properties *for use in trade or business or for investment*?[4]

No

[4] Was replacement property *like kind* to relinquished property?[5]

No

[5] Did taxpayer complete the exchange within the statutory period?[6]

No

Yes

[12] Character?[13]

[8] Gain is recognized in year of realization.[8]

[9] No recognition of realized gain.[9]

Rest of gain

Realized gain ≤ FMV of boot received

[11] Calculate basis of new property.[11]

All loss.

[7] Calculate realized gain/loss and boot received.[7]

[10] No recognition of realized loss on exchange.[10]

LIKE-KIND EXCHANGES OF PROPERTY (IRC §1031)

This figure will help you when faced with any exchange of properties that could potentially qualify as a §1031 exchange. This is a topic quite frequently tested on tax exams, so you should be ready to answer the question, "Does this transaction qualify under §1031?" No matter what the answer to that question, follow up with an explanation of the tax consequences.

1 The starting place is the identification of an "exchange" because §1031 applies only to exchanges (trades) of property, not to sales. See ELO, Chap. 10 (III); CT, p. 83.

2 If any of the requirements of §1031 are not met, the gain will be recognized in the year of realization. If a loss is realized, it may be recognized if allowed by the loss deduction rules. See Figures 6–9.

3 Inventory, partnership interests, stocks, bonds, and notes are not eligible for §1031 treatment. In addition, personal use property is not eligible for §1031.

4 The taxpayer must use both the relinquished property and the replacement property in a trade or business or hold them for investment. Each taxpayer in the exchange is analyzed independently

5 "Like kind" means similar in character and nature. Most real estate is like kind to other real estate, but personal property is separated into classes.

6 Some exchanges will not be simultaneous, and may involve parties. There are strict statutory periods for completing deferred exchanges and strict rules for the participation of facilitators. If a taxpayer engages in a deferred exchange, he or she must comply with the identification (45 days) and receipt (180 days) requirements of §1031(a)(3) in order for the exchange to qualify.

7 The calculation of realized gain or loss is made under the usual rules. See Figure 12 and ELO, Chap. 9; CT, p. 81. "Boot" is any nonlike-kind property, including cash, nonqualifying property, and the assumption of liabilities by the other party to the exchange.

8 Realized gain will be recognized to the extent of the fair market value of the boot received. In other words, the recognized gain will be the lesser of the fair market value of the boot or the realized gain. See ELO, Chap. 9 (III); CT, p. 84.

9 The amount of realized gain in excess of the fair market value (FMV) of the boot received will be deferred until the taxpayer disposes of the property—if ever. The whole point of entering into a like-kind exchange is to defer all or part of the recognition of gain on the exchange of properties.

10 No loss is recognized on the exchange of properties in a qualifying §1031 exchange.

11 The basis of the property received is equal to the basis of the property transferred, plus the gain recognized, minus the FMV of the boot received, minus the loss recognized, plus any additional investment by the taxpayer. The basis of any boot will be its FMV, a type of cost basis. §1012.

12 If gain is recognized, its character as capital or ordinary must be determined. See Figures 15–17.

EXAMPLE TO FIGURE **14**

LIKE-KIND EXCHANGES (IRC §1031)

Mike owns Property A, which is farmland. Mike has a basis of $100,000 in Property A, and he holds it for investment. Mike trades Property A for Property B, which was owned by an unrelated party. Property B is a parking lot. Mike also receives $10,000 in cash. Property B is worth $80,000. Mike intends to use Property B in his business. What are the tax consequences of this transaction to Mike?

Box Number in Figure	Analysis
[1]	Mike exchanged Property A for Property B.
[2]	Property A and Property B are real property, both of which qualify for §1031 treatment.
[3]	Mike held Property A for investment and intends to hold Property B for use in his trade or business.
[4]	These properties are both real estate, and therefore are like kind.
[5]	This was a simultaneous exchange, not a deferred exchange, so the time limits do not matter.
[7]	Realized gain or loss: Mike had an adjusted basis of $100,000 in Property A. His amount realized was $90,000 ($10,000 in cash and $80,000 in the form of Property B). His realized *loss* is $10,000.
[10]	No loss is recognized on the transaction, even though he received boot. (Mike should have sold Property A and then purchased Property B in order to maximize his chances of recognizing the loss.)
[11]	Mike's basis in Property B equals $90,000, as follows:

His basis in Property A	$100,000
+ Gain recognized	+0
− FMV boot received	− $10,000
Basis of Property B	$90,000

FIGURE 15

CHARACTER OF GAIN OR LOSS
AS CAPITAL OR ORDINARY

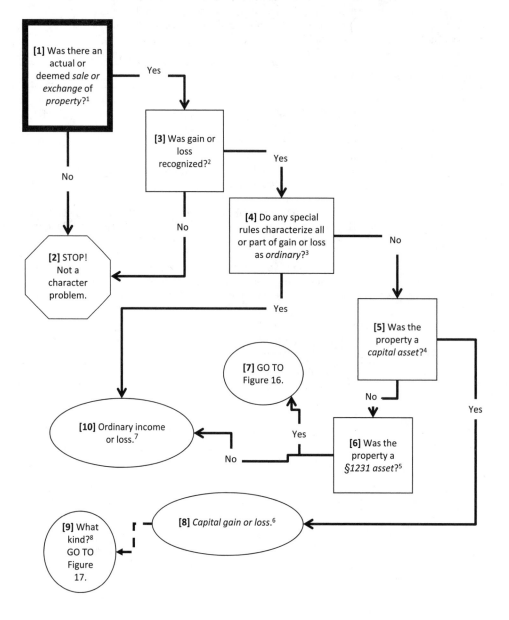

NOTES TO FIGURE 15

CHARACTER OF GAIN OR LOSS AS CAPITAL OR ORDINARY

This figure will help you characterize gain or loss as capital or ordinary. If you are faced with some sort of transaction in property, you will first quantify the realized and recognized gain or loss. See Figures 12–14. Then, for recognized gain or loss, you must characterize it as capital or ordinary. This matters because capital gain is taxed at preferential rates and the deduction of capital losses is limited.

[1] The starting point is whether a "sale or exchange" has occurred. This requires a giving, a receipt, and a connection between the two. The Code "deems" a sale or exchange to occur in a number of situations. For example, worthlessness of a security is a deemed sale/exchange under §165(g). In addition, the transaction must involve "property," not just a substitute for ordinary income. See ELO, Chap. 12 (III); CT, p. 89.

[2] The character of a gain or loss is only relevant if the gain or loss is recognized. If, for example, one of the nonrecognition rules applies to defer recognition of gain, character would not be relevant for the unrecognized gain. If the transaction resulted in partial recognition of gain, however, character is relevant for that portion.

[3] Consider whether §1245 or §1250 (recapture) or §1244 (small business stock) would recharacterize as ordinary what would otherwise be capital gain or loss. See ELO, Chap. 12 (III); CT, p. 91.

[4] A capital asset is *any* asset other than the nine enumerated categories listed in §1221. Although defined by exclusion, capital assets generally are those that are outside the daily scope of business operations, such as investment or personal assets. See ELO, Chap. 12 (II) & (III); CT, pp. 89–90.

[5] A §1231 asset is real or depreciable property used in a trade or business (not property held for investment). See Figure 16 and ELO, Chap. 12 (IV); CT, pp. 90–91.

[6] Capital gain is taxed at lower rates than ordinary income; capital losses are subject to significant restrictions on deduction. Taxpayers prefer *capital gain* to ordinary income and *ordinary loss* to capital loss. See ELO, Chap. 12 (II); CT, pp. 90–91.

[7] Ordinary income is generally taxed at higher rates than capital gain, and ordinary losses are generally more usable for taxpayers than capital losses. However, qualified dividend income is taxed at the same rates as 15% capital gain. See ELO, Chap. 13 (II); CT, p. 93.

[8] Capital gains and losses must also be categorized into four types of gain or loss. This process is illustrated in Figure 17. See ELO, Chap. 12 (V); CT, p. 93.

EXAMPLE TO FIGURE 15

CHARACTER OF GAIN OR LOSS
AS CAPITAL OR ORDINARY

Justin exchanged Blackacre, a parcel of raw land he held for investment, in a qualifying §1031 exchange in which he realized $100,000 of gain and recognized $20,000 of that gain. What is the character of that gain?

Box Number in Figure	Analysis
[1]	There was a sale or exchange of property.
[3]	The exchange resulted in partial recognition of gain, so the character of the $20,000 is relevant. The character of the nonrecognized portion of the gain is not relevant.
[4]	No special rules apply. (Blackacre was raw land and therefore could not be depreciated, so there would not be any recapture.)
[5], [8]	Blackacre was a capital asset in Justin's hands, and therefore the gain is capital.

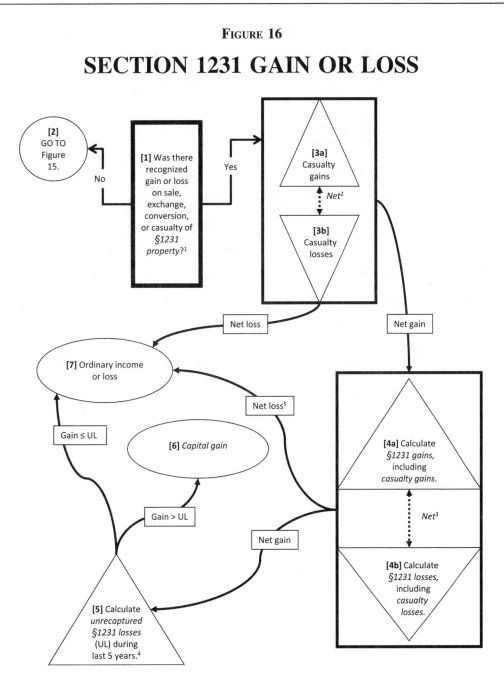

FIGURE 16

SECTION 1231 GAIN OR LOSS

NOTES TO FIGURE 16

SECTION 1231 GAIN OR LOSS

This figure will help you when you are faced with the sale or other disposition of depreciable property used by a taxpayer in his or her trade or business. This kind of transaction can produce a special kind of gain or loss—called a §1231 gain or loss—that will be subject to special, taxpayer-friendly characterization rules. Remember: Net §1231 gain is capital in nature; net §1231 loss is ordinary.

[1] The starting place is the identification of a §1231 asset. A §1231 asset is real or depreciable property held for more than one year and held for use in a taxpayer's trade or business (not for investment or personal use). When such assets are sold, exchanged, or involuntarily converted, the recognized gain or loss may be §1231 gain or loss. See ELO, Chap. 12 (IV); CT, pp. 90–91. Notice, however, that any recapture is taken into account before the §1231 analysis. See Figure 15, Box [4].

[2] Compute all of the taxpayer's casualty losses and casualty gains on §1231 property, and net them. "Netting" means comparing losses with gains and coming up with a net figure of net loss (losses exceed gains) or net gain (gains exceed losses). If losses exceed gains, all of those losses and gains will be considered ordinary income. If losses do not exceed gains, then all the losses and gains are put into the netting process in the next step. See ELO, Chap. 12 (IV); CT, pp. 90–91.

[3] Add up all of the taxpayer's gains on the sale or exchange of §1231 assets, along with net casualty gains from Boxes [3a] and [3b] with respect to §1231 assets. ELO, Chap. 12 (IV); CT, pp. 90–91. Add up all of the taxpayer's losses on the sale, exchange, or conversion of §1231 assets with casualty losses. Net the gains and losses to produce a net gain or a net loss.

[4] If the result is a net gain, the gain is capital in nature, except to the extent of unrecaptured (UL) §1231 losses during the last five years. See ELO, Chap. 12 (IV); CT, pp. 90–91.

[5] If the result is a net loss, the loss is ordinary in nature. See ELO, Chap. 12 (IV); CT, pp. 90–91. Taxpayers prefer losses to be ordinary, as they offset ordinary income.

EXAMPLE TO FIGURE 16

SECTION 1231 GAIN OR LOSS

Debi is in the business of growing and selling heritage vegetables. This year, she experienced the following events:

Sale of equipment #1:	$5,000 loss
Sale of equipment #2 (net of depreciation recapture):	$2,000 gain
Business furniture destroyed by fire (uninsured):	$6,000 loss
Grant of easement to county under threat of condemnation:	$13,000 gain
Sale of stock held for investment:	$10,000 gain

Debi held all of the items described above for more than one year. Debi had $500 of unrecaptured §1231 loss in prior years. What are the tax consequences of these events to Debi?

Box Number in Figure	Analysis
[1]	Debi has recognized gain or loss from the sale, conversion, and casualty of §1231 property—real or depreciable property used in her trade or business (equipment, furniture, and easement).
[2]	The stock is not §1231 property. Go to Figure 15 to analyze this sale.
[3a], [3b]	Debi's casualty losses on §1231 property ($6,000) do not exceed casualty gains on such property ($13,000). She has a net casualty gain of $7,000, so all of the casualty gains and losses are included in the next step.
[4a], [4b]	Total §1231 gains: $15,000. Total §1231 losses: $11,000. Therefore, she has a net §1231 gain of $4,000 ($15,000 − $11,000).
[5], [6], [7]	Debi's unrecaptured loss is $500. Therefore, of her net gain of $42,000, $3,500 will be capital and $500 will be ordinary.

FIGURE 17

UNDERSTANDING CAPITAL GAINS AND LOSSES

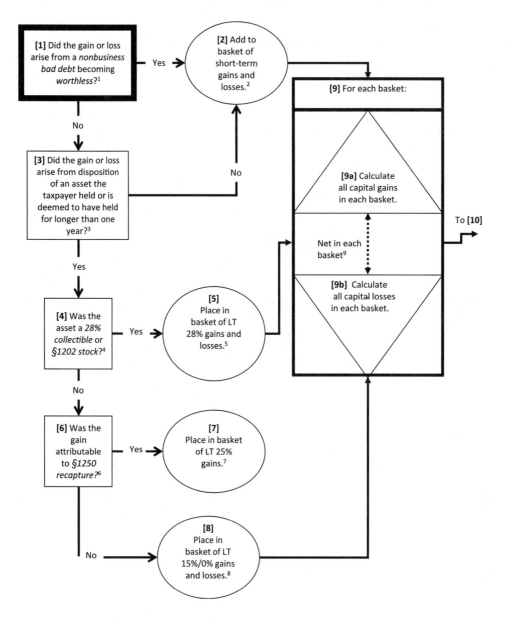

FIGURE 17 *(cont.)*

UNDERSTANDING CAPITAL GAINS AND LOSSES

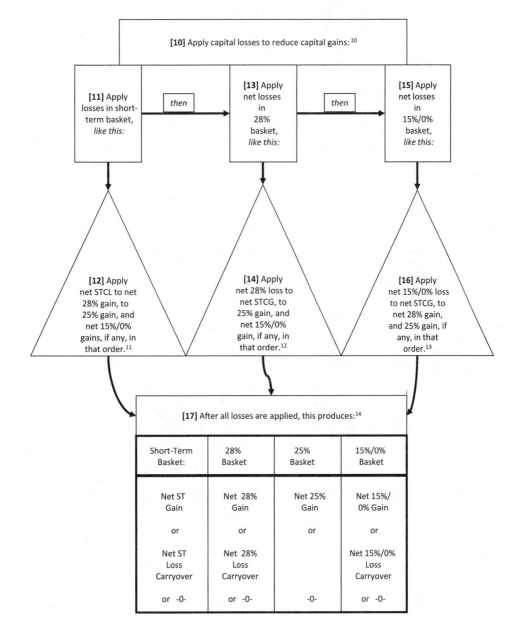

[10] Apply capital losses to reduce capital gains: [10]

[11] Apply losses in short-term basket, *like this:*

then

[13] Apply net losses in 28% basket, *like this:*

then

[15] Apply net losses in 15%/0% basket, *like this:*

[12] Apply net STCL to net 28% gain, to 25% gain, and net 15%/0% gains, if any, in that order.[11]

[14] Apply net 28% loss to net STCG, to 25% gain, and net 15%/0% gain, if any, in that order.[12]

[16] Apply net 15%/0% loss to net STCG, to net 28% gain, and 25% gain, if any, in that order.[13]

[17] After all losses are applied, this produces:[14]

Short-Term Basket:	28% Basket	25% Basket	15%/0% Basket
Net ST Gain	Net 28% Gain	Net 25% Gain	Net 15%/ 0% Gain
or	or	or	or
Net ST Loss Carryover	Net 28% Loss Carryover		Net 15%/0% Loss Carryover
or -0-	or -0-	-0-	or -0-

NOTES TO FIGURE 17

UNDERSTANDING CAPITAL GAINS AND LOSSES

This figure will help you understand how the four types of capital gain/loss are combined to produce the result of net capital gain or net capital loss. This computation occurs after you have computed recognized gain or loss (see Figures 12–14) and characterized gain or loss as capital or ordinary (see Figures 15 and 16). The process in Figure 17 matters because it produces "net capital gain," which is taxed at a lower rate than ordinary income, and "net capital loss," the deduction of which is limited to capital gains and $3,000 of ordinary income. *Note: This complex area of tax law is sometimes ignored by professors and may be destined for tax simplification.* Therefore, make sure you understand the emphasis placed on this material by your own professor.

[1] There is no perfect starting place for this analysis, but as good a starting place as any is to determine whether the gain or loss arises from a "nonbusiness" bad debt. See ELO, Chap. 7 (III). A nonbusiness bad debt is treated as a short-term capital gain (STCG), regardless of the period of time the taxpayer held the debt. §166(d)(1)(B).

[2] The "basket" approach requires that capital gains and losses be categorized and placed in a basket with all similar gains and losses. For example, all the short-term capital gains and losses will be placed in the "short-term basket" for the netting process and application of capital losses. There will be four baskets: (1) short-term, (2) 28%, (3) 25%, and (4) 15%/0%. See ELO, Chap. 12 (V); CT, p. 92.

[3] A taxpayer's holding period is the period of time he or she actually owned the property, plus the period of time another person owned the property if that person's holding period can be "tacked" on to the taxpayer's holding period. For example, the recipient of a gift tacks the donor's holding period to his or her own. See ELO, Chap. 12 (V).

[4] A collectible is an item such as a painting, an antique, a stamp collection, or the like. IRC §1202 excludes from gross income a percentage of the gain on the sale of certain qualifying stock, and the included percentage is also a 28% gain. See ELO, Chap. 12 (V); CT, pp. 92, 177.

[5] All of the gains and losses from 28% property are combined into the 28% basket.

[6] A 25% long-term capital gain is gain from the sale or exchange of real property attributable to prior depreciation that has not been recaptured as ordinary income under §1250. See ELO, Chap. 12 (V); CT, p. 92.

[7] The 25% basket will only have gains, not losses, so netting will not be required.

[8] A 15%/0% capital gain or loss is capital gain or loss that does not fall into any other category. Most capital gains and losses encountered in the basic income tax course will be this kind of gain, e.g., gain or loss from the sale of stocks, raw land, etc.

[9] The netting process requires that all of the gains and losses in each "basket" be computed and compared. More losses than gains in a category will produce a net loss in that basket. More gains than losses in a basket will produce a net gain in that basket.

[10] Capital gains are deductible only to the extent of capital losses and, for individuals, $3,000 per year of ordinary income. §1211(b). Therefore, the losses in each category are applied to reduce the gain in each category in the specified order. See ELO, Chap. 12 (V); CT, p. 92.

[11] The amount of short-term capital loss (STCL) reduces on a dollar-for-dollar basis the net gain in the 28% basket, if any. If there is no 28% gain, or if any STCL is left over after application to the 28% basket, it is then applied to reduce gain in the 25% basket, if any. If there is no 25% gain, or if any STCL is left over, it is applied to reduce gain in the 15%/0% basket. See ELO, Chap. 12 (V); CT, p. 92.

[12] The amount of 28% capital loss (CL) reduces on a dollar-for-dollar basis the net gain in the short-term basket, if any. If there is no STCG, or if any 28% CL is left over after application to the short-term basket, it is then applied to reduce gain in the 25% basket, if any. If there is no 25% gain, or if any 28% CL is left over, it is applied to reduce gain in the 15%/0% basket. See ELO, Chap. 12 (V); CT, p. 92.

[13] The amount of 15%/0% CL reduces on a dollar-for-dollar basis the net gain in the short-term basket, if any. If there is no STCG, or if any 15%/0% CL is left over after application to the short-term basket, it is then applied to reduce gain in the 28% basket, if any. If there is no 28% gain, or if any 15%/0% CL is left over, it is applied to reduce gain in the 25% basket. See ELO, Chap. 12 (V); CT, p. 92.

[14] After the netting processes in Boxes [12], [14], and [16] are complete, the taxpayer will have the results in this figure. Net capital gain will be taxed at the applicable rate. A net loss in a category carries over to future years, retaining its nature as short term, 28%, or 15%/0%, to be applied against future years' capital gain in the various categories. See ELO, Chap. 12 (V); CT, p. 92.

EXAMPLE TO FIGURE 17

UNDERSTANDING CAPITAL GAINS AND LOSSES

Ron experiences the following tax events this year:

- His ZZZ stock, in which he had a basis of $100,000, became worthless.
- He sold a collectible painting, in which he had a basis of $250,000, for $50,000.
- He sold ABC stock, in which he had a basis of $120,000, for $300,000.
- His former friend, Ken, reneged on a debt to him of $60,000.

Ron had held the ZZZ stock, the painting, and the ABC stock for longer than one year.
What are the tax effects of these events to Ron?

Box Number in Figure	Analysis
[1], [2]	The debt to Ken is a nonbusiness bad debt and is placed in the basket of short-term gains and losses.
[3]	All the rest of the assets were held for longer than one year.
[4], [5]	The painting is a collectible. The loss is a 28% LTCL.
[6], [8]	The sales of stock are in the 15%/0% category.
[9]	Netting: STCL: $60,000 28% LTCL: $200,000 15%/0% LTCG: $80,000 ($180,000 gain on ABC stock netted against $100,000 loss on ZZZ stock)
[10]	Applying capital losses to reduce capital gains:
[11], [12]	Apply STCL to reduce LTCG to $60,000.
[13], [14]	Apply 28% loss to reduce LTCG to zero.
[17]	Net result: $180,000 28% to carry forward to future years, retaining its character as 28% gain.

FIGURE 18

THE EIGHT TAX QUESTIONS ON ANY EXAM

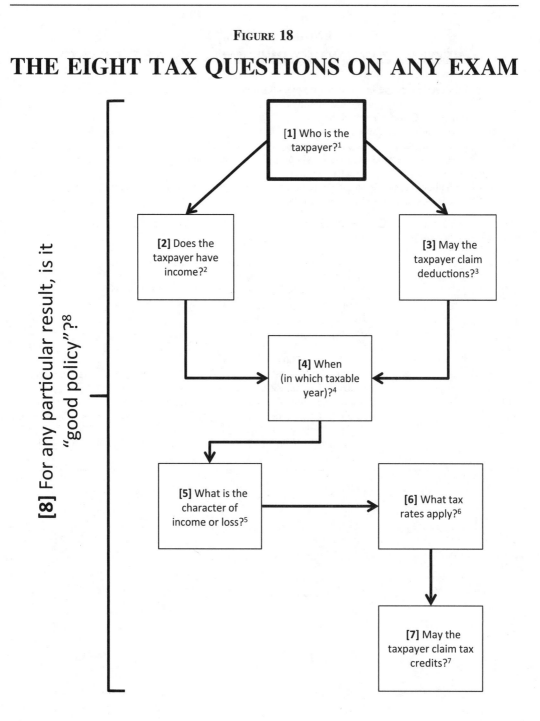

[8] For any particular result, is it "good policy"?[8]

[1] Who is the taxpayer?[1]

[2] Does the taxpayer have income?[2]

[3] May the taxpayer claim deductions?[3]

[4] When (in which taxable year)?[4]

[5] What is the character of income or loss?[5]

[6] What tax rates apply?[6]

[7] May the taxpayer claim tax credits?[7]

THE EIGHT TAX QUESTIONS ON ANY EXAM

This figure will help you just before you take an exam, or any time that you find yourself "lost" in the sea of tax law. Addressing the questions in this figure will ensure that you spot all of the issues.

[1] **Who is the taxpayer?** Tax is a transactional subject, typically involving two or more taxpayers. Identifying the relevant taxpayer is crucial. In whose tax consequences is the professor interested? Also, do you see related taxpayers acting in ways that benefit the group (usually a family or related entities) but direct income or deductions in ways that seem inconsistent with the tax principles you know? This might indicate assignment of income issues. See ELO, Chaps. 13, 14; CT, pp. 96–97.

[2] **Does the taxpayer have income?** The federal income tax is concerned with a tax on income, and therefore, the starting place is whether the taxpayer has items of income that will be included in his or her gross income. This requires an understanding of the concept of income. It also requires a grasp of the myriad tax statutes that include particular items of income in, or exclude particular items of income from, a taxpayer's gross income. See ELO, Chaps. 2, 3, 4, 9, and 10; CT, pp. 62–71; 83–85.

[3] **May the taxpayer claim deductions?** Because the income tax is a tax not on gross income but on something less, *deductions* constitute an essential step in the computation of the tax base. Deductions may be business related or personal, but whatever their nature, they are a matter of legislative grace: A taxpayer must be able to point to a specific statute as justification in order to claim a deduction. See ELO, Chaps. 5–8; CT, pp. 71–82.

[4] **In which taxable year should the taxpayer include items in gross income or claim deductions?** Federal income tax law uses a system of measuring income and collecting tax on an annual basis. Therefore, it becomes important to determine when (in which year) a taxpayer must include an amount in gross income or may claim a deduction. For many items, the proper reporting year is clear. But for transactions that occur over several years, selection of the proper year can have important tax implications for the taxpayer. Moreover, taxpayers invoke

timing rules in the *income deferral* and *deduction acceleration* strategies that they use to save taxes. See ELO, Chaps. 10, 11, and 15; CT, pp. 86–88.

[5] **What is the character of the taxpayer's income or loss?** The federal income tax differentiates among some types of income and loss, giving tax preference to some types and imposing limits on others. Principal among these is the distinction between *ordinary income* or *loss* and *capital gain* or *loss. Net capital gain* is subject to a preferential rate compared to the rates for *ordinary income,* and the *deduction* for *capital losses* is limited to an individual's *capital gains,* plus $3,000 of ordinary income. Thus, characterizing income and loss as capital or ordinary can have a significant impact on tax liability. See ELO, Chap. 12; CT, pp. 88–93.

[6] **To what tax rate is the taxpayer subject?** The particular tax rate(s) to be applied to a taxpayer depends on the taxable income and status of that taxpayer. The tax rate multiplied by the taxpayer's taxable income produces the tentative tax. But remember: There are two tax systems at work—the regular tax and the alternative minimum tax—as well as the preferential rates on capital gains. See ELO, Chap. 13; CT, pp. 93–94.

[7] **Is the taxpayer entitled to any tax credits?** *Tax credits* are subtracted on a dollar-for-dollar basis from the taxpayer's tentative tax. Increasingly, Congress uses tax credits to achieve nontax goals, such as energy or job-creation incentives. See ELO, Chap. 13; CT, pp. 94–96.

[8] **Is it a "good idea" from a policy point of view?** Any particular result can be analyzed from a tax policy point of view. Does it make the system "fairer"? Does it result in a rational administrative system? Does it create the intended (or unintended) economic results? Increasingly, professors are interested in tax policy, so be ready to answer these questions for all of the principal tax statutes studied in your basic tax course.

CAPSULE SUMMARY

SUMMARY OF CONTENTS

This Capsule Summary is intended for review at the end of the semester. Use it to confirm your understanding of basic concepts and to direct you to areas in which you need further review.

CHAPTER 1

GETTING STARTED IN FEDERAL INCOME TAX

I. UNDERSTANDING THE BIG PICTURE

The process of computing tax liability is summarized below and can be traced in Form 1040, included in the Outline. See Figure 1.

Gross Income
– Certain Deductions
—————————————
  Adjusted Gross Income
– Standard Deduction *or*
  Itemized Deduction
– Personal Exemption
—————————————
  Taxable Income
×Tax Rate(s)
—————————————
  Tentative Tax
– Tax Credits
—————————————
  Tax Due or Refund

A. Gross income—§61: Gross income includes all income from whatever source derived. §61(a). Income from compensation, dividends, gains from dealings in property, and discharge of debt are common types of income. However, particular Code sections exclude certain types of income from gross income.

B. Deductions: Deductions are subtractions from income when computing taxable income. There are two types of deductions available when computing taxable income:

   1. Deductions from gross income when computing adjusted gross income: Certain expenditures are deducted (subtracted) from gross income when computing adjusted gross income (AGI).

   2. Deductions from AGI when computing taxable income: The taxpayer subtracts his or her personal exemptions and subtracts the larger of the standard deduction or the itemized deduction. The standard deduction is a statutorily set amount, and the itemized deduction is the sum of all allowable itemized deductions.

C. Multiply taxable income by the tax rate(s): The taxpayer's tax rate, which depends on his or her filing status, is multiplied by taxable income to produce the "tentative tax." The tax rates applicable to individuals range from 10% to 35% for ordinary income and 15% (sometimes even 0%) to 28% for capital gain. §1. The alternative minimum tax (AMT) is a separate tax imposed on some taxpayers, with tax rates of 26% and 28% of alternative minimum taxable income (AMTI). Unless Congress acts, tax rates are scheduled to increase in 2013.

D. Subtract available tax credits: A tax credit is a dollar-for-dollar reduction in the amount of tax due. Available tax credits are subtracted from the tentative tax to produce the actual tax due.

E. Seven fundamental tax questions: Substantive (as opposed to policy) tax problems—and the material in any tax course—can be summarized in seven fundamental tax questions.

1. **Who is the taxpayer?** Identifying the right taxpayer is critical. Families often try to rearrange income and deductions so as to minimize the tax on the family as a whole, while the Internal Revenue Service (IRS) seeks to match income and deductions to the "right" taxpayer.

2. **Does the taxpayer have income?** To begin the analysis of a taxpayer's tax liability, it is necessary to identify his or her income in a theoretical sense and in the sense of §61. Always construe income broadly.

3. **What deductions may the taxpayer claim?** The income tax is a tax on net income, not gross income. Therefore, taxpayers are entitled to reduce gross income by certain deductions, principally personal and business deductions. Always construe deductions narrowly.

4. **In which taxable year should the taxpayer include items in gross income or claim deductions?** Once income and deductions are identified, the next question is when—that is, *in which taxable year*—a taxpayer must include an item of income in gross income and when a taxpayer may claim a deduction. Taxpayers seek to defer income as far into the future as possible and accelerate deductions to the earliest possible year.

5. **What is the character of the taxpayer's income and loss?** When income or loss arises from the sale or exchange of property, it is necessary to characterize it as ordinary or capital. Taxpayers prefer capital gain to ordinary income because capital gain is subject to preferential, lower tax rates. Taxpayers prefer ordinary loss to capital loss because the deductibility of capital losses is restricted.

6. **To what tax rate is the taxpayer subject?** The particular tax rate(s) to be applied to a taxpayer depends on the taxable income and status of the taxpayer. The tax rate multiplied by the taxpayer's taxable income produces the tentative tax.

7. **Is the taxpayer entitled to any tax credits?** The final step in calculating a taxpayer's tax liability is determining and subtracting available tax credits. Tax credits can be refundable (they can result in a refund to the taxpayer) or nonrefundable (the credit can only reduce tax to zero).

II. SOURCES OF TAX LAW

Title 26 of the U.S. Code is the statutory base for all federal tax law, including the federal income tax. The Department of the Treasury, through the IRS, and the courts offer guidance on the interpretation of various provisions of the Code.

A. Administrative interpretation: The Department of the Treasury issues regulations (temporary, final, or proposed) interpreting various Code provisions as well as revenue rulings, revenue procedures, notices, announcements, private letter rulings, and technical advice memoranda on various issues.

B. **Judicial interpretation:** The U.S. Tax Court, the U.S. District Courts, the U.S. Court of Federal Claims, and the U.S. Bankruptcy Courts are trial courts for tax matters. Cases are appealed to the appellate court for the circuit in which the taxpayer lives, and then to the U.S. Supreme Court.

   1. **U.S. Tax Court—litigate without first paying tax:** A taxpayer may adjudicate tax matters in the U.S. Tax Court without first paying the tax, if the taxpayer files a petition within 90 days of the date of the Statutory Notice of Deficiency (90-day letter).

   2. **U.S. Bankruptcy Court:** A bankruptcy court has jurisdiction over tax matters of the debtor and may stay proceedings in the U.S. Tax Court regarding tax matters.

   3. **Other courts—pay first, then litigate:** To litigate in the U.S. District Court or the U.S. Court of Federal Claims, the taxpayer must first pay the tax and file a claim for refund. If that claim is either denied or ignored, the taxpayer can sue for refund.

C. **Deference to IRS interpretation:** As in all areas of law, the courts interpret statutory material in cases properly brought before them. A court will properly give deference to an IRS-published, prelitigation interpretation of a Code provision. This means that the court will adopt the IRS's interpretation of a Code provision if it is a "reasonable" interpretation of the statute. The IRS's interpretation need not be the only reasonable interpretation, or even the "best" interpretation. It need only be a reasonable interpretation. If, however, there is no published, prelitigation interpretation by the IRS, the courts need not give deference to the IRS's interpretation and may select the interpretation that seems most reasonable.

III. TAX ETHICS

A taxpayer has a responsibility to file an accurate tax return, and a lawyer can advise a client to take a return position only if he or she abides by the applicable ethical rules imposed by the state bar association. The IRS itself regulates practice before it by imposing certain standards on tax practitioners. Both tax preparers and taxpayers are subject to certain penalties if they do not comply with applicable statutes.

IV. READING TAX STATUTES

Consider using a five-step process—called *parsing*—to understand an unfamiliar statute.

A. **The general rule:** Find the statute's general rule and underline it in red.

B. **Definitions:** Find the statute's terms of art and definitions and highlight these in yellow.

C. **Exceptions and special rules:** Find the statute's exceptions and special rules and mark them with a green "X."

D. **Related statutory material:** Find the statute's explicit and implicit references to related material and circle these in blue.

E. **Know when this statute is typically implicated:** Note the kinds of transactions in which the statute becomes relevant.

V. TAX POLICY

The wisdom of a particular tax statute can be evaluated using three criteria: fairness of the system, its administrative practicality, and its economic effects. These goals are often at odds with each other.

A. **Fairness:** The U.S. income tax burden is intended to be allocated among taxpayers based on their "ability to pay." A "fair" system imposes similar taxes on those with similar abilities to pay (horizontal equity). It is impossible to measure directly each taxpayer's ability to pay, and thus taxable income is the surrogate for a taxpayer's ability to pay. If a tax statute causes taxable income to distinguish more accurately among various taxpayers' abilities to pay, it is more "fair" than a provision that does not do so.

B. **Administrative practicality:** A good tax statute will assess and collect tax in a cost-effective manner and will not require undue governmental interference with a taxpayer's life.

C. **Economic effects:** Taxpayers change their behavior in response to tax statutes, and proponents of a taxing measure must consider the effects (both intended and unintended) that the measure likely will have on taxpayer behavior.

CHAPTER 2

IDENTIFYING GROSS INCOME

I. SECTION 61—INCOME

The linchpin of the Code, §61, defines gross income as "all *income* from whatever source derived" (emphasis added). Thus, it is important to define "income" in order to determine what is included in gross income (even if it is excluded by another statute later). See Figure 2.

II. DEFINITIONS OF INCOME

A. **Haig-Simons definition—theoretical approach:** Under this approach, income is the sum of (1) the market value of rights exercised in consumption, plus (2) the change in the value of the store of property rights between the beginning and end of the period in question (usually a taxable year). The Haig-Simons definition defines a comprehensive tax base, but difficulties may arise in measuring all consumption and in valuing assets each year.

B. "Economic benefit"—a more practical approach: Under this approach, income is the value of any economic benefit received by the taxpayer regardless of the form of the benefit.

INCOME

1. **Tangible items:** The receipt of cash or other property generates income under this approach, even if it comes from an unusual source, such as a windfall.

2. **Barter:** The exchange of services for services constitutes income to both service providers. See Rev. Rul. 79-24, 1979-2 C.B. 60.

3. **Intangible benefits:** The receipt of an intangible benefit would be included in gross income under this approach. For example, if one taxpayer satisfies another taxpayer's legal obligation, the latter has income in the amount of the satisfaction. *Old Colony Trust Co. v. Commissioner,* 279 U.S. 716 (1929). But noneconomic benefits (such as a sunny day in Oregon) are not income under this principle.

III. CERTAIN ITEMS THAT ARE NOT INCOME

Certain items are not considered income by general understanding of that term in federal tax law, even though they might qualify as "income" under a theoretical definition of income.

A. Imputed income: The value of any services one performs for oneself or one's family and the value of any property used that one owns are imputed income, which is not considered income for purposes of federal income tax.

B. Capital recovery: A taxpayer's income from the sale or exchange of property is his or her profit on the transaction, not the total amount received. A taxpayer is entitled to receive his or her capital investment in the property tax-free, although the timing of this recovery is a matter for legislative determination.

C. Loans: Neither the creation nor the repayment of a loan is a taxable event. However, forgiveness or discharge of a loan may generate income to the debtor.

D. General welfare exclusion: As a matter of IRS practice, governmental payments made to a person as part of a system of general welfare are not included, unless specifically addressed by the Code.

CHAPTER 3

SPECIFIC INCLUSIONS IN GROSS INCOME

I. SECTION 61

Section 61 provides that gross income includes "all income" from all sources. Courts construe §61 broadly to include most types of income in gross income, unless they are specifically excepted by statute.

II. SPECIFIC ITEMS

Section 61(a) provides a nonexclusive list of types of income specifically included in gross income.

A. Compensation income—§61(a)(1): Compensation income is the consideration transferred for the performance of services, whether in the form of salary, fees, commissions, or fringe benefits, and whether in the form of cash, property, or other services.

   1. **Amount included:** The amount of compensation income is the amount of cash received or the fair market value of the property or services received.

   2. **Timing issues:** The taxable year in which a taxpayer will include an amount of compensation income will depend on the taxpayer's method of accounting and, if restricted property is involved, the rules of §83.

   3. **Character:** Compensation income is ordinary income, potentially taxable at the highest tax rate.

B. Gross income from business—§61(a)(2): A taxpayer engaged in business as a sole proprietor will include his or her gross income from business and will subtract available deductions from that amount, reporting the net result (income or loss) on the tax return.

C. Gains derived from dealings in property—§61(a)(3): When a taxpayer sells, trades, or otherwise disposes of property, the taxpayer may realize and recognize gain or loss. Gain is included in gross income unless there is a specific statutory exception.

D. Investment income—§61(a)(4)–(7): Various types of investment income are included in gross income, including dividends, interest (both explicit and imputed), rents, royalties, and income from annuities.

   1. **Imputed interest—OID rules, §§483, 7872:** Most loans explicitly provide for interest to be paid. Some, however, provide for no interest or a below-market rate of interest, and the Code often will recharacterize these loans or investments to impute interest to the transactions.

   2. **Annuities—§§61(a)(9), 72:** A taxpayer receiving a regular annuity payment is receiving a partial return of his or her invested capital, and the balance of the payment is income. To determine the amount of a payment that is excluded from gross income, multiply the payment by the exclusion ratio. The exclusion ratio is the following fraction:

$$\frac{\text{Investment in the contract}}{\text{Total expected return under the contract}}$$

The amount of the payment in excess of the excluded amount is included in the gross income of the taxpayer, subject to certain limitations.

E. Alimony—§§61(a)(8), 71: A taxpayer receiving alimony must include it in his or her gross income. The federal definition of alimony governs the tax consequences of alimony payments, regardless of the label used under state law for the payment.

1. **Definition of alimony:** For a payment to qualify as alimony, it must meet six requirements: (1) it must be paid in cash, not in property or services; (2) the payment must be received by or on behalf of the spouse or former spouse pursuant to a divorce decree or separation instrument; (3) the decree must not designate the payment as nondeductible and nonincludable; (4) the payor and recipient must not be members of the same household at the time of the payment; (5) there must be no obligation to make a payment after the death of the recipient spouse; and (6) the payment must not be, in substance, support for the child of the payor (there is an incentive to characterize child support as alimony because alimony is deductible to the payor and child support is not).

2. **Front-end-loaded alimony:** If alimony payments vary by more than $15,000 in the first three years, and the payments are greater in the beginning than at the end of the three-year period, they will be "front end loaded." In that case, the "excess alimony amount" is included in the gross income of the payor spouse and is deducted from the income of the recipient spouse in the third post-separation year.

3. **Property settlements:** If an amount payable in divorce is not alimony or child support, it may be a property settlement.

F. Discharge of indebtedness income—§61(a)(12): Creation of a loan is not a taxable event to either the creditor or the debtor, for neither has a net economic benefit. If, however, the creditor forgoes collection under the debt, the debtor will have a benefit equal in amount of the debt forgone. This is discharge of indebtedness income and must be included in the debtor's gross income.

1. **Enforceable debt:** To have discharge of indebtedness income, there must be an enforceable debt. See *Zarin v. Commissioner,* 916 F.2d 110 (3d Cir. 1990).

2. **Identifying discharge:** A discharge occurs when the creditor agrees to (or is forced to) take something less than he or she originally agreed to take in satisfaction of the loan. Payment of a debt is not discharge, nor is payment of a debt by another, or payment deferral. If the creditor receives what he or she bargained for, even if that amount is different from the amount loaned, there is no discharge.

3. **Contested liability doctrine:** If a taxpayer in good faith disputes the amount of the debt, a subsequent settlement of the debt is treated as the amount of the debt for tax purposes.

4. **Possible exclusion—§108:** Certain types of discharge of indebtedness income are excluded from the gross income of the taxpayer. The newest of these—ripe for testing—is the exclusion of gain on certain home foreclosures. In general, if a taxpayer excludes discharge of indebtedness income, he or she may also be required to reduce his or her "tax attributes."

III. PRIZES, AWARDS, HELPFUL PAYMENTS, EMBEZZLEMENTS, AND DAMAGES

Code sections other than §61 provide for specific inclusions in gross income, and judicial doctrines also include some amounts in gross income.

A. Prizes and awards—§74: Prizes and awards are included in gross income unless the recipient did nothing to be selected, the recipient is not required to render substantial future services as a condition of receiving the prize, and he or she immediately transfers the prize to charity.

B. Helpful payments—§§82, 85, 86: Various types of helpful payments are included in gross income, such as unemployment compensation, and a portion of Social Security benefits received, depending on the income of the recipient.

C. Embezzled funds: Embezzlers must include the proceeds of their embezzlements in their gross income unless they can show that the transaction is akin to a loan. See *Gilbert v. Commissioner,* 552 F.2d 478 (2d Cir. 1977).

D. Damages: Damages received for injury are includable in a taxpayer's gross income, unless specifically excluded under §104.

CHAPTER 4

SPECIFIC EXCLUSIONS FROM GROSS INCOME

I. EXCLUSIONS—IN GENERAL

The Code includes a number of statutes providing that items that are otherwise income will not be included in gross income. See Figure 2. An item must fit within the precise requirements of an exclusion statute in order to be excluded from gross income. Always construe exclusions narrowly.

II. DEATH BENEFITS—§101

Amounts received under a life insurance policy by reason of the death of the insured are excluded from gross income. Life insurance has its own vocabulary, so make sure you are familiar with the principal terms.

A. Transfer for valuable consideration: The exclusion does not apply to payments made under policies that were transferred for valuable consideration; in that case, the exclusion is limited to the purchaser's purchase price under the contract.

B. Chronic or terminal illness: The exclusion extends to amounts paid to or for the care of chronically or terminally ill insureds.

III. GIFTS—§102

The recipient of a gift or an inheritance may exclude the cash or value of the property received from gross income regardless of amount.

A. Definition: A gift is a transfer made with detached and disinterested generosity. See *Duberstein v. Commissioner,* 363 U.S. 278 (1960). Most intrafamily transfers are gifts.

B. Exceptions

    1. Income from property: The exclusion does not apply to the income derived from property received by gift.

    2. Employee gifts: The exclusion does not apply to any transfer made by an employer to an employee; these amounts are considered compensation income, not gifts.

C. Basis—§1015: A recipient of property by gift or inheritance must determine the basis he or she has in the property.

    1. Property received by gift: The recipient of property by gift takes the donor's basis in the gift, plus a portion of any gift tax paid on the transfer. However, if, at the time of the gift, the fair market value of the property was less than its basis, for purposes of determining loss on subsequent sale or disposition, the donee takes the fair market value of the gift on the date of the gift. §1015(a).

    2. Property received by inheritance—§1014: The recipient of property through inheritance takes as his or her basis in the property the fair market value of the property on the date of the decedent's death or the alternate valuation date if that date is elected.

IV. INTEREST ON STATE AND LOCAL BONDS—§103

A taxpayer may exclude the interest paid to the taxpayer on qualifying state and local bonds.

V. COMPENSATION FOR PERSONAL INJURY OR SICKNESS—§104

Section 104 excludes from gross income amounts received as a result of personal *physical* injury or sickness. This excludes compensatory damages from suit or settlement of personal physical injury actions (in lump sums or in structured settlements), but does not exclude punitive damages (except in very limited situations), previously deducted medical expenses, and pre- or post-judgment interest.

VI. DISCHARGE OF INDEBTEDNESS INCOME—§108

Certain types of discharge of indebtedness income may be excluded from gross income. The exclusion is generally conditioned on the taxpayer giving up certain tax benefits.

A. Types of discharge of indebtedness income excluded: Only certain types of discharge of indebtedness income are excluded under §108. Of these, the principal types are the following:

1. **Bankruptcy—§108(a)(1)(A):** If the discharge occurs in a Title 11 (bankruptcy) case, the discharge of indebtedness income is excluded from gross income.

2. **Insolvency—§108(a)(1)(B):** If the discharge occurs at a time the taxpayer is insolvent, the discharge of indebtedness income is excluded from gross income to the extent of the insolvency. Insolvency is the amount of the taxpayer's debts over the fair market value of his or her property.

3. **Certain farm debt—§108(a)(1)(C):** If the discharge is of "qualified farm indebtedness" the discharge of indebtedness income will be excluded from gross income.

4. **Qualified principal residence indebtedness—§108(a)(1)(E):** If the discharge is of acquisition indebtedness for a taxpayer's principal residence, the discharge will generally be excluded from gross income if the discharge occurs before January 1, 2013. The limit on this exclusion is $2,000,000.

5. **Student loans—§108(f)(1):** Gross income does not include any discharge of a student loan if the discharge is the result of the former student working for a period of time in a nonprofit or governmental setting.

B. "Paying the piper"—§108(b): Each dollar of exclusion generally requires a reduction in the taxpayer's tax benefits, i.e., net operating losses, tax credits, capital loss carryovers, and other carryovers. The taxpayer may elect in some circumstances to apply the exclusion amount to reduce the basis of depreciable property. The result of this reduction is that the taxpayer will have a greater amount of income in the future.

VII. EXCLUSION FOR GAIN ON SALE OF PRINCIPAL RESIDENCE—§121

Section 121 allows a taxpayer to exclude from gross income $250,000 ($500,000 for joint returns) of gain on the sale of a principal residence, if the taxpayer has owned *and* used the dwelling as a principal residence for at least two of the past five years.

VIII. EMPLOYMENT-RELATED EXCLUSIONS

The Code provides a variety of employment-related exclusions.

A. Meals and lodging—§119: An employee may exclude from gross income the value of meals and lodging provided by an employer if the meals or lodging are provided for the convenience of the employer, are provided on the business premises of the employer, and in the case of lodging, the employee is required to accept the lodging as a condition of employment.

1. **Convenience of the employer:** "Convenience of the employer" means that the employer has a "substantial noncompensatory business reason" for supplying the meals and lodging, considering all the facts and circumstances of the situation.

2. **Business premises:** The business premises of an employer are the grounds of the employer's place of business. The circuits have split on whether the business premises for state police include all public roads and contiguous restaurants.

3. **Condition of employment:** The condition of employment requirement is generally satisfied by showing that the employee is on call for the business of the employer.

B. **Statutory fringe benefits—§132:** The value of any fringe benefit that qualifies as any of the following eight fringe benefits is excluded from the gross income of the employee. In some cases, the provision of the benefit must meet antidiscrimination rules.

1. **No additional cost service—§132(b):** If the employer regularly provides the service to the public and provides it to the employee without incurring any significant additional cost, it will be excluded from the gross income of the employee who receives the service.

2. **Qualified employee discounts—§132(c):** If employees enjoy a discount on property or services provided to the public by the employer, and the discount does not exceed a certain percentage, the value of the discount will be excluded from the gross income of the employees taking advantage of the discount.

3. **Working condition fringe—§132(d):** An employee receiving a benefit that would have generated a deduction as a trade or business expense or as depreciation to the employee had he or she purchased the benefit individually may exclude the benefit from gross income.

4. **De minimis fringe—§132(e):** If the benefit provided to the employees is so small that accounting for it would be unreasonable or administratively impractical, it will be excluded from the gross income of the employees receiving it.

5. **Qualified transportation fringe—§132(f):** An employee who receives transit passes, van transportation, or parking may exclude the benefit from gross income, within specified dollar limitations.

6. **Qualified moving expense reimbursement—§132(g):** If an employee receives reimbursement for amounts that would be deductible as moving expenses under §217, he or she may exclude these amounts from gross income.

7. **Athletic facility—§132(j):** The value of an on-premises athletic facility may be excluded from the gross income of an employee if it is operated by the employer and is used mostly by employees.

8. **Qualified retirement planning services—§132(m):** An employer may provide financial planning services if certain conditions are met.

C. Insurance premiums and payments—§§79, 105, 106: The cost of employer-provided health insurance premiums is excluded from the gross income of the employee. When an employee receives benefits, these are excluded from gross income up to the amount of the employee's medical expenses. The employee may also exclude the cost of employer-provided term life insurance attributable to coverage up to $50,000; premiums attributable to excess coverage are includable in the employee's gross income.

D. Dependent care assistance—§129: The employee may exclude up to $5,000 of employer-provided dependent care assistance in the form of actual care provided or as reimbursement. The exclusion and the dependent care credit may not be claimed for the same expenditure.

E. Educational assistance—§127: The employee may exclude up to $5,250 of qualifying educational assistance provided by the employer.

F. Adoption expenses—§137: An employer may provide up to $12,650 (in 2012) of adoption assistance to employees, which may be excluded from their gross incomes, subject to certain income limitations.

G. Group legal services—§120: An employer may provide up to $70 per year to provide group legal services plans to employees.

X. EDUCATION PROVISIONS

A. Qualified scholarships—§117: Amounts received as a "qualified scholarship," which generally means amounts received by degree candidates at regularly operated educational institutions for tuition, books, fees, and supplies, are excluded from gross income. A qualified scholarship does not include room and board or amounts paid for services.

B. Interest on certain U.S. savings bonds—§135: To the extent the redemption proceeds of certain U.S. savings bonds are used for qualified education expenses, the income element of such redemption is excluded from gross income. Income level restrictions apply.

C. Section 529 plans—§529: Distributions from §529 plans, which are state-sponsored plans for education savings, are excluded from gross income to the extent they are used for qualified education expenses. Unlike many education incentives, these funds can be used for K–12 as well as postsecondary education.

D. Education savings accounts—§530: Distributions from education savings accounts are excluded from gross income to the extent they are used for qualified education expenses. Unlike many education incentives, these funds can be used for K–12 as well as postsecondary education.

XI. PAYMENTS FOR SUPPORT OF FAMILY

A. Child support: A custodial parent may exclude child support received from his or her gross income. Remember, too, that gifts are not included in gross income, so the amounts a family pays to support a family member in college, for example, are not included in the recipient's gross income—they are considered gifts.

B. Foster care payments: Qualified foster care payments are excluded from gross income.

CHAPTER 5

DEDUCTIONS—IN GENERAL

I. DEFINITION OF "DEDUCTION"

A deduction is a subtraction from income in computing AGI or taxable income.

A. Compare exclusion: By contrast, an exclusion causes an item of income not to be included in gross income. An exclusion and a deduction will have the same tax effect for taxpayers but will reach this result by very different paths.

B. Compare tax credit: A tax credit is a dollar-for-dollar reduction in the amount of tax due.

II. ROLE OF DEDUCTIONS

Deductions figure prominently in two phases of computation of taxable income. One group of deductions is subtracted from gross income in computing AGI. Another group is subtracted from AGI in computing taxable income. The benefit of many deductions is limited for higher-income taxpayers through the mechanism of phaseouts based, directly or indirectly, on AGI.

III. COMMON THEMES OF DEDUCTION CONTROVERSIES

Three common themes arise in deduction controversies. Always construe narrowly; each and every requirement of a deduction statute must be met in order for a taxpayer to qualify for a deduction.

A. An event: A taxpayer must experience an outlay, an outflow, or a loss in which there is no realistic possibility of recovery of the item.

B. Personal versus business expenses: A common theme in the analysis of deductions is the question whether an expense is "personal" or "business." This distinction is important because, as a general rule, personal expenses are not deductible unless a specific statute provides otherwise. Business expenses are generally deductible. Taxpayers seek to characterize deductions as business related, rather than personal, in order to deduct them.

C. Expense or capital expenditure? An expense may be deducted currently, but if an expenditure is for a capital item (a capital expenditure), its cost must be added to basis and be recovered in accordance with the statutory scheme governing capital recovery. Taxpayers prefer to characterize expenditures as expenses rather than capital expenditures in order to accelerate capital recovery.

CHAPTER 6

PERSONAL DEDUCTIONS

I. IN GENERAL—§262

While personal expenditures are not generally deductible, specific Code provisions allow a taxpayer to deduct certain personal expenses if statutory requirements are met. See Figure 3. Many personal deductions, like some exclusions, are subject to phaseouts based on some measure of income. For current phaseout amounts, see www.aspenlawschool.com/books/tax_outline.

II. TWO KINDS OF PERSONAL DEDUCTIONS

A. **"Above-the-line" deductions:** This group of deductions is subtracted from gross income in computing AGI. Taxpayers seek to increase "above-the-line" deductions because AGI serves as a measure for certain itemized deductions, and lowering AGI will potentially increase the deductible portion of these itemized deductions.

B. **"Below-the-line" deductions:** This group of deductions is subtracted from AGI in computing taxable income and includes the personal exemption and either the standard or the itemized deduction. The itemized deduction is the sum of a number of deductions, including home mortgage interest, taxes, casualty losses, medical expenses, charitable contributions, bad debts, and miscellaneous expenses.

III. "ABOVE-THE-LINE" PERSONAL DEDUCTIONS

A. **Alimony—§215:** A taxpayer may deduct the amount of alimony or separate maintenance paid during the year. Alimony has a special definition under federal tax law.

B. **Moving expenses—§217:** A taxpayer may deduct qualifying moving expenses associated with a move to a new place of employment that is 50 or more miles from the taxpayer's former employment.

C. **Contributions to regular IRAs—§219:** A taxpayer may claim a deduction for certain retirement savings. In general, an individual may deduct the lesser of $5,000 of his or her earned income to an individual retirement account (IRA). Taxpayers 50 years of age and older can make an additional contribution. If the taxpayer participates in a qualified plan and has income in excess of a certain amount, the contribution may be made, but no deduction is allowable.

D. **Losses—§165:** A taxpayer may deduct losses incurred during a taxable year that are not compensated for by insurance or otherwise. However, an individual taxpayer may deduct only three types of loss. See Figures 6-9.

1. **Trade or business losses—§165(c)(1):** A taxpayer may deduct losses incurred in a trade or business. Neither the Code nor the regulations include a definition of a "trade or business," but a good working definition is "engaged in regular and continuous activity for the purpose of profit." See Figure 7.

2. **Investment losses—§165(c)(2):** A taxpayer may deduct losses incurred in an activity engaged in for profit, which does not constitute a trade or business. For example, losses on the sale of stock would be investment losses, but losses on the sale of a principal residence would not be, as a principal residence is held for personal, rather than investment, purposes. See Figure 8.

3. **Casualty losses—§165(c)(3):** A taxpayer may deduct certain casualty losses, such as losses from theft, fire, storm, and flood. Casualty losses up to the amount of casualty gains are deducted from gross income when computing AGI. The remaining deductible losses constitute an itemized deduction to the extent that they exceed 10% of the taxpayer's AGI. See Figure 9.

E. **Interest on education loans—§221:** Up to $2,500 of the interest paid on certain student loans is potentially deductible, as an above-the-line deduction, depending on income limitations.

F. **Medical savings accounts—§223:** A taxpayer subject to a high-deductible health plan can deduct certain contributions to a Health Savings Account (HSA).

G. **Costs incurred in civil rights or whistleblower actions:** A taxpayer who incurs attorneys' fees or other costs in certain civil rights actions may deduct such expenses. There are only a limited number of actions that qualify, and otherwise, the taxpayer would probably be required to deduct these amounts as miscellaneous itemized deductions.

IV. THE CHOICE: STANDARD OR ITEMIZED DEDUCTION

A taxpayer may deduct either the standard or the itemized deduction, but not both. The rational taxpayer will choose the larger of the two. The standard deduction is a specified amount based on filing status, and the itemized deduction is the sum of the taxpayer's itemized deductions.

V. ITEMIZED DEDUCTIONS   *can deduct immediately.*

A number of deductions are available to the taxpayer only if he or she claims the itemized deductions. The principal itemized deductions are discussed below.

A. **Interest—§163:** Personal interest is not deductible. Personal interest is interest other than (1) trade or business interest, (2) qualified residence interest, or (3) investment interest.

1. **Qualified residence interest—§163(h):** Qualified residence interest is deductible by individuals. There are two types of qualified residence interest attributable to loans on the taxpayer's principal residence and one other

qualifying residence (which the taxpayer uses at least 14 days per year for personal purposes).

    a. Acquisition indebtedness: Interest is deductible on loans up to $1,000,000, the proceeds of which are used to acquire or construct a qualifying residence, and that are secured by that residence.

    b. Home equity indebtedness: Interest is deductible on loans up to $100,000, which are secured by a principal residence and do not exceed the taxpayer's "equity" in the residence; i.e., the difference between the fair market value and any indebtedness secured by that residence.

  2. Investment interest—§163(d): A taxpayer may deduct interest to finance the purchase of investments, but only to the extent of net income from those investments.

B. Taxes—§164: A taxpayer may deduct state, local, and foreign real property, personal property, and income taxes.

C. Casualty losses—§165(c)(3), (h): A casualty loss is a loss through complete or partial destruction of property from a sudden, unexpected, and unusual cause such as fire or storm. A taxpayer may deduct casualty losses to the extent that they exceed (1) $100 per event and (2) 10% of the taxpayer's AGI. See Figures 6 and 9.

D. Medical expenses—§213: A taxpayer may deduct medical expenses, but only to the extent that they exceed 7.5% of his or her AGI. Medical expenses are expenses for the cure, treatment, or management of a disease or accident, and include health insurance premiums paid by the taxpayer but do not include certain other items such as non-prescription drugs and certain elective cosmetic surgery.

E. Charitable contributions—§170: A taxpayer may deduct contributions to qualifying charitable organizations. The amount of the deduction is the amount of cash or the fair market value of any property contributed. Limitations based on a taxpayer's AGI are imposed; usually, this is 50% of AGI. The taxpayer must not receive a personal benefit as a result of the contribution.

F. Miscellaneous expenses—§67: A number of expenses are deductible only to the extent that they, in the aggregate, exceed 2% of the taxpayer's AGI. These include employee's unreimbursed business expenses and certain investment expenses.

VI. PERSONAL EXEMPTION—§151

A taxpayer is entitled to deduct a personal exemption for himself or herself and for any dependent of the taxpayer. Only certain individuals, known as qualifying children and qualifying relatives, may be claimed as dependents.

CHAPTER 7

9/28/2015

BUSINESS AND INVESTMENT DEDUCTIONS

I. IN GENERAL

Net business income is included in a taxpayer's gross income, and net loss from a trade or business constitutes a deduction subject to certain limitations. To compute net income or loss from business, a taxpayer begins with gross income from the business and subtracts available deductions. A taxpayer doing business as a sole proprietor reports this income and the available deductions on Schedule C, and the net result (income or loss) is then reported on his or her own tax return, subject to certain limits on losses. See Figure 4. A taxpayer who owns rental or royalty property will compute the income and deductions associated with this activity on Schedule E and report the net result (profit or loss) on his or her own tax return, subject to certain limitations. See Figure 5. In both situations, it is critical to identify available deductions.

II. ORDINARY AND NECESSARY BUSINESS EXPENSES—§162

A taxpayer may claim a deduction for all the ordinary and necessary expenses paid or incurred in carrying on a trade or business, or while away from home, and rental payments for business property.

A. **Five requirements:** There are five distinct requirements for deduction of an expenditure under §162.

1. **Ordinary:** Ordinary means "usual in the course of general and accepted business practice," arising from a transaction commonly encountered in the type of business in question, even if the expenditure is unique for the particular taxpayers. See *Deputy v. DuPont,* 308 U.S. 488 (1940). In addition, the expenditure must be reasonable in amount. This particular issue often arises in the area of compensation.

2. **Necessary:** There must be a reasonable connection between the expense and the furtherance of the business. Necessary means "appropriate and helpful" to the business, but the courts are reluctant to second-guess the judgment of business people, except in extreme cases.

3. **Expense:** The expense requirement distinguishes between expenses (which may be deductible) and capital expenditures (which must be capitalized).

4. **Trade or business:** To be deductible, the expense must be incurred in connection with a taxpayer's trade or business. The principal function of the trade or business requirement is to distinguish between personal activities and business activities.

   a. **Definition:** To be engaged in a trade or business, a taxpayer must be involved in an activity with continuity and regularity and must have the primary purpose of creating income or profit rather than merely engaging in a hobby. See *Commissioner v. Groetzinger,* 480 U.S. 23 (1987).

   b. Hobbies: A trade or business requires a profit motive, which is not characteristic of hobbies. Hobbies may generate income, however, and certain deductions may be available under §183.

5. **Carrying on:** The expense must be incurred during the time the taxpayer is actually engaged in carrying on a trade or business.

   a. Going concern: A taxpayer is carrying on a trade or business from the date that it is a going concern; i.e., has regular activity in the areas in which the business is organized.

   b. Pre-opening expenses—§195: Expenses incurred prior to opening must be capitalized. Up to $5,000 of expenses that would have been deductible if the taxpayer had been engaged in a trade or business when they were incurred may be deducted in the year of opening, but this amount is reduced by the amount by which pre-opening expenses exceed $50,000. Any remaining amount is amortized over 15 years.

B. **Limits on deduction:** Section 162 is riddled with exceptions and special rules; only the principal exceptions are discussed here.

1. **Public policy:** No deduction is allowed for illegal bribes and kickbacks, for fines or similar penalties paid to the government, or for the two-thirds portion of the treble damages of antitrust damages.

2. **Excessive CEO compensation:** There is no deduction for compensation of a chief executive officer (CEO) of a publicly traded company in excess of $1,000,000 unless it is performance based.

III. OTHER DEDUCTIONS FOR A TRADE OR BUSINESS

A taxpayer engaged in business may deduct other expenses of doing business, including certain charitable contributions, bad debts, interest on debt incurred in connection with the trade or business, taxes, and losses incurred in the business.

IV. DEDUCTIONS FOR CAPITAL RECOVERY

A. **In general—§263:** A taxpayer may not claim a current deduction for capital expenditures, generally defined as "permanent improvements or betterments made to increase the value of any property or estate." See Figure 11.

1. **Capital recovery:** When a capital expenditure is made, the cost is said to be "capitalized." The taxpayer will be entitled to recover that capitalized amount at some point during his or her ownership of the asset (capital recovery). "Recovery" means that the taxpayer's economic investment in the asset will constitute a tax benefit, either as a deduction during the ownership of the asset, or at sale when the taxpayer reports as gain the amount received in excess of his or her investment in the property.

2. **Timing:** The timing of capital recovery is completely within the discretion of Congress. Taxpayers prefer to recover capital as soon as possible, preferring accelerated depreciation systems to systems that defer capital recovery until sale or other disposition of the asset.

B. Definition of capital expenditure: Neither the Code nor the regulations offer a precise definition of a capital expenditure.

1. **Separate asset test:** If an expenditure creates a separate, identifiable asset with a useful life that will extend substantially beyond the taxable year, the expenditure is probably a capital expenditure. See *Commissioner v. Lincoln Savings & Loan Assn.,* 403 U.S. 345 (1971), and Treas. Reg. §1.263-2(a).

2. **Future benefits test:** Even if a separate asset is not created, if an expenditure creates more than an insignificant future benefit, it is a capital expenditure. See *Indopco, Inc. v. Commissioner,* 503 U.S. 79 (1992).

C. Section 179 deduction: Section 179 allows a taxpayer to deduct up to a specified amount attributable to capital expenditures for equipment and tools purchased for the business. This deduction also reduces the basis of the asset(s) by the amount of the deduction claimed. In 2012, the §179 amount is $500,000, reduced by the cost of §179 property the taxpayer places in service that exceeds $2,000,000. The §179 deduction cannot exceed the taxable income of the taxpayer computed without regard to this deduction.

D. Modified accelerated cost recovery system (MACRS) deduction for tangible business assets—§§167, 168: MACRS is the method by which taxpayers claim capital recovery for tangible business assets.

1. **Dual function of deduction:** The MACRS deduction is a deduction from gross income in computing net business income or loss. Each time the taxpayer claims a MACRS deduction, the basis of the asset is reduced by the same amount (producing the "adjusted basis" of the asset).

2. **Calculation of MACRS deduction:** The MACRS deduction is computed by applying the "applicable recovery method" to the "basis" of the asset over the "applicable recovery period," taking into account "applicable conventions."

   a. **Applicable recovery method:** Three different recovery methods are available under MACRS: straight-line and two accelerated methods.

   b. **Basis:** The basis of an asset is generally its cost, unless it is acquired by some other means.

   c. **Applicable recovery period:** The recovery period for an asset is the period of years over which the taxpayer claims capital recovery for the item. The recovery period for assets is defined by statute or by the IRS.

   i. **Real property:** Residential real property has a recovery period of 27.5 years. Nonresidential real property has a recovery period of 39 years.

   ii. **Personal property:** Personal property can be 3-, 5-, 7-, 10-, 15-, or 20-year property. For example, office furniture is 10-year property.

   d. **Applicable conventions:** The applicable convention expresses the beginning date of capital recovery. Recovery generally begins when property is placed in service, and the conventions provide that regardless of when the property is actually placed in service, it will be deemed placed in service on a particular

date. Real property uses a midmonth convention, and personal property a
midyear convention.

E. Section 197 intangibles: Section 197 allows a taxpayer to amortize the cost of
"§197 intangibles" ratably over 15 years. A §197 intangible includes purchased
goodwill, going-concern value, covenants not to compete, patents, copyrights, secret
formulas or processes, and various other intangibles.

V. ACTIVITIES ENGAGED IN FOR PROFIT THAT ARE NOT TRADES OR BUSINESSES

A taxpayer who owns rental property, or property that generates royalties, probably is not
engaged in a trade or business. Nevertheless, the taxpayer may deduct the ordinary and
necessary expenses incurred to generate this income and may depreciate or amortize
assets that are subject to periodic capital recovery.

A. Investment activities: The expenses of carrying on investment activities are
deductible unless the expense must be capitalized (such as commissions on the
purchase of stock). The 2% floor of §67 may restrict the availability of these
deductions.

B. Rental real estate: A taxpayer that holds real or personal property for rental is
entitled to deduct the expenses of that property, including interest, taxes, repairs, and
the usual deductions for capital recovery.

VI. SUBSTANTIATION

A taxpayer must be able to substantiate his or her deductions.

CHAPTER 8

MIXED BUSINESS AND PERSONAL EXPENSES

I. IN GENERAL

Business expenses are usually deductible, while personal expenses are not. Some expenses,
however, have a mixed character. They are connected to the taxpayer's business but also
have a connection to his or her personal life. This mixed character raises questions about
their deductibility. The Code takes a variety of approaches to these types of expenses.

II. ORIGIN TEST

For an expense to be deductible as a business expense, it must have its origin in the
taxpayer's business, not his or her personal life. In making this determination, the courts
will inquire into the so-called origin of the expense—the reason the expense was incurred—
considering all the facts and circumstances of the situation. See *United States v. Gilmore*,
372 U.S. 39 (1963).

III. TRAVEL

A taxpayer's expenses while traveling away from the taxpayer's tax home primarily for business are deductible. Commuting expenses are not deductible. A taxpayer's tax home is the taxpayer's principal place of business or, if the taxpayer doesn't have one, the taxpayer's primary abode in a real sense.

IV. CLOTHING

A taxpayer may deduct the cost of special clothing, such as a uniform, that is required for his or her job or business. But the cost of clothing that can be worn for regular purposes is not deductible.

V. EDUCATION EXPENSES

A taxpayer may deduct the cost of education that improves his or her skills in the taxpayer's current trade or business, or is required as a condition of remaining licensed in that business. Education that prepares a taxpayer for a new trade or business is not deductible.

VI. MEALS AND ENTERTAINMENT

Meals and entertainment expenses are subject to the especially stringent rules of §274. First, the meals and entertainment must be sufficiently connected with the trade or business of the taxpayer. Even then, only 50% of the cost of such items is deductible.

VII. HOME OFFICES AND VACATION HOMES—§280A

When a taxpayer uses a portion of his or her residence as an office or rents out a vacation home while still using it for part of the year for personal purposes, an allocation must be made between deductible (business) and nondeductible (personal) expenses associated with use of the residence.

A. **Home offices:** In order to deduct any expenses attributable to a home office, the taxpayer must use the office as the principal place of business, or as a place where the taxpayer regularly meets with patients, clients, or customers.

1. **Restriction on deductions:** If the taxpayer meets this test, a portion of the expenses allocable to the business activity may be deducted, but not in excess of the gross income from the business minus the sum of the nonbusiness deductions plus business deductions not related to the use of the property.

2. **Remember §121:** Section 121 allows a taxpayer to exclude from gross income some or all of the gain on the sale of a principal residence. This exclusion does not apply to deductions previously claimed for depreciation on a home. Thus, taxpayers must carefully consider whether it is worthwhile to claim such a deduction.

B. **Vacation homes:** Deductions attributable to rental use of a home cannot exceed the percentage of those expenses equal to the total expenses multiplied by a fraction. The numerator of the fraction is the total number of days the unit is rented at fair rental value, and the denominator is the total number of days during the year in which the unit is used. This limitation does not apply to deductions that are allowable regardless of rental use, such as qualified residence interest.

VIII. "LUXURY" AUTOMOBILES AND LISTED PROPERTY—§280F

A. **Automobiles:** Section 280F limits the amount of MACRS deductions that may be claimed each year for passenger automobiles, which limits the amount of depreciation each year for "luxury" automobiles. "Luxury" doesn't come close to being an accurate description of the effect of this Code section, however, as most passenger vehicles (except SUVs) will fall within these limits.

B. **Listed property:** For certain types of property, the taxpayer will be required to use the straight-line method of depreciation unless the predominant use of the property is for business.

IX. HOBBY LOSSES—§183

A taxpayer who has no profit motive for an activity may deduct only the expenses associated with the activity to the extent that such expenses are deductible under Code sections that do not require a profit motive (nonbusiness expenses) plus expenses in the amount equal to the gross income from the activity minus the nonbusiness expenses.

A. **Existence of profit motive—Treas. Reg. §1.183-2:** Whether a taxpayer has engaged in an activity for profit is to be determined from all of the facts and circumstances of the situation. The regulations offer nine factors indicative of a profit motive.

B. **Exception—§183(d):** If an activity produces income in three out of the five consecutive years ending in the year in question, it is rebuttably presumed to be engaged in for profit.

X. GAMBLING LOSSES

Gambling losses are deductible only to the extent of gains from gambling.

CHAPTER 9

TRANSACTIONS IN PROPERTY

I. SECTION 1001—IN GENERAL

Section 1001 defines realized gain or loss as the difference between the amount realized (what the taxpayer receives in the transaction) and the taxpayer's adjusted basis in the property transferred. See Figures 10-12.

II. TRANSACTIONS IN PROPERTY

While most transactions in property are easy to identify—sales or trades of real estate, personal property, or stocks—in some situations, it can be difficult to distinguish between sales of property and acceleration of streams of ordinary income. Only the former potentially generates capital gain.

III. REALIZATION EVENT—§1001

A realization event occurs when a taxpayer exchanges property, receiving some materially different item. A "materially different" item of property is one that bestows on a taxpayer a different legal interest than what he or she had before. See *Cottage Savings Association v. Commissioner*, 499 U.S. 554 (1991). Thus, all sales and most exchanges will be realization events. A gift is not a realization event because there is no quid pro quo; compare a bargain sale, which is treated as part gift and part sale.

IV. REALIZED GAIN OR LOSS—§1001(a)

Realized gain or loss is equal to the difference between the amount realized on a sale or other disposition of property and the adjusted basis of the property transferred.

A. **Amount realized—§1001(b):** A taxpayer's amount realized on the sale or other disposition of property is equal to the sum of the cash and fair market value of property or services received, plus the amount of liabilities assumed by the other party to the transaction. TUFTS.

B. **Adjusted basis:** The adjusted basis of property is equal to its initial basis adjusted upward for improvements and downward for capital recovery (depreciation) deductions. See Figure 10.

   1. **Basis—purchases—§1012:** The basis of property is usually equal to its cost. If a taxpayer performs services and receives property in payment, the amount the taxpayer includes in gross income as payment will constitute the basis of the property.

   2. **Basis—other transactions:** The basis of property received other than by purchase is determined under specific Code sections.

      a. **Property received from a decedent—§1014:** Property received from a decedent takes a basis equal to its fair market value on the date of death.

      b. **Property received by gift—§1015:** If property is received by gift, the donee generally takes the property with the same basis as the donor had in the property, increased by a portion of any gift tax paid. If, at the time of the gift, the adjusted basis of the property in the donor's hands is greater than its fair market value, for purposes of determining loss on sale or other disposition by the donee, the donee's basis is the fair market value of the property on the date of the gift. *So, there is a lower loss that will be taken from gross income.*

      c. **Property received in divorce—§1041(d):** Property received incident to a divorce has the same basis that it had immediately prior to the transfer.

V. RECOGNIZED GAIN OR LOSS—§1001(c)

Realized gain is recognized unless a specific Code section prohibits or limits recognition. Realized loss is recognized if allowed by the Code. See, e.g., §165.

VI. TRANSFERS OF ENCUMBERED PROPERTY

A. **Amount realized includes liabilities assumed:** A taxpayer's amount realized includes the face amount of the liabilities that another party assumes as part of the transaction, regardless of the fair market value of the property.

B. **Recourse vs. nonrecourse loans:** In the sale of property subject to a nonrecourse loan, the greater of the fair market value of the property or the face amount of the loan minus the taxpayer's adjusted basis in the property produces the realized gain or loss on the transaction. If the loan is recourse, however, the transaction is bifurcated: (1) gain or loss equal to the difference between the fair market value of the property and the adjusted basis, and (2) discharge of debt equal to the difference (if any) between the debt discharged and the fair market value of the property.

C. **Distressed real estate:** Distressed real estate can produce several different kinds of transactions: sale, foreclosure, "short sales," and renegotiation with the lender. These can produce very different tax consequences.

VII. BASIS OF PROPERTY RECEIVED IN THE SALE OR DISPOSITION

If the taxpayer sells property for cash, there is no need to determine the basis of the property received (because cash neither appreciates nor depreciates in value, there is no need to assign cash a basis for tax purposes). If, however, the taxpayer receives property in an exchange, the basis of that property must be determined, for later the taxpayer may sell or otherwise dispose of the property.

A. **Full-recognition transactions:** In a transaction in which the selling taxpayer recognizes all realized gain or loss, the property received will have a basis equal to its fair market value.

B. **Nonrecognition transactions:** In transactions in which the selling taxpayer does not recognize all or part of the realized gain or loss, the property received will have a basis different than its fair market value, determined under specific Code sections.

VIII. CHARACTER

The character of the gain or loss recognized will depend on the nature of the asset in the hands of the transferor.

CHAPTER 10

NONRECOGNITION TRANSACTIONS

I. IN GENERAL

In some property transactions, realized gain or loss is not recognized in whole or in part at the time of the transaction. These transactions are called "nonrecognition transactions" and include like-kind exchanges, involuntary conversions, divorce transactions, and other transactions. When realized gain or loss is deferred rather than recognized, the property received in the transaction takes a basis that preserves that realized gain or loss for later recognition.

II. LIKE-KIND EXCHANGES—§1031. See Figure 14

A. Requirements: There are five requirements for a qualifying like-kind exchange.

1. **Exchange of property:** The taxpayer must exchange property for property, rather than selling property or engaging in some other transaction. See *Jordan Marsh Co. v. Commissioner,* 269 F.2d 453 (2d Cir. 1959).

2. **Nature of property—§1031(a)(2):** The property must not be inventory, stocks, bonds, notes, other evidences of indebtedness, interests in a partnership, certificates of trust or beneficial interest, or choses in action.

3. **Property transferred—use:** The taxpayer must have held the relinquished property for use in a trade or business, or for investment. The IRS has recently issued guidance on the application of §1031 to vacation or second homes rented for part of the year.

4. **Property received—use:** The taxpayer must intend to hold the replacement property for use in a trade or business, or for investment. The IRS has recently issued guidance on the application of §1031 to vacation or second homes rented for part of the year.

5. **Like kind:** The replacement property received must be like kind to the relinquished property. "Like kind" refers to the nature and character of the property rather than to its grade or quality.

    a. **Real property:** An exchange of real property for real property is a like-kind exchange regardless of the development status of the two properties. *Koch v. Commissioner,* 71 T.C. 54 (1978).

    b. **Depreciable personal property—Treas. Reg. §1.1031(a)-1(b):** The regulations offer a safe harbor for determining whether depreciable personal properties are like kind, in which properties of the same "class" are considered like kind. Properties outside the same class must be examined under the general like-kind test.

    c. Other personal property: Intangible and nondepreciable personal property and personal property held for investment must be examined under the general like-kind test.

B. Effect of qualifying like-kind exchange: If a taxpayer engages in a qualifying like-kind exchange of property for property, he or she will not recognize any of the realized gain or loss on the transaction.

    1. Effect of boot—§1031(b): If the taxpayer receives boot (nonlike-kind property), the taxpayer will recognize gain, but not loss, in the amount of the lesser of the fair market value of the boot or the realized gain.

    2. Basis of property received—§1031(d): The basis of like-kind property received in a like-kind exchange is equal to the basis of the property transferred, plus the gain recognized, minus the fair market value of the boot received, minus any loss recognized, plus any boot paid (additional investment in the property). The basis of any boot (nonlike-kind property) received is its fair market value.

C. Deferred and three-party exchanges—§1031(a)(3): A potential problem arises when the taxpayer wishes to transfer property in a like-kind exchange, but the potential buyer who wants the taxpayer's property does not have suitable property to exchange. This problem can be overcome by creating a deferred exchange, but the property to be received by the taxpayer must be identified within 45 days after the taxpayer relinquishes his or her property and must be received before the earlier of the 180th day after the date the taxpayer relinquishes his or her property or the due date of the taxpayer's return for the year of transfer of the relinquished property. Any intermediary used must meet specific identity requirements to avoid agent status.

D. Effect of mortgages in like-kind exchanges

    1. One mortgage: If the property transferred in a like-kind exchange is subject to a mortgage, the transferee's assumption of that mortgage as a part of the transaction is treated as boot to the transferor. The mortgage assumption is also treated as boot for purposes of computing the taxpayer's basis in the property received.

    2. Two mortgages: If both the property transferred and the property received are subject to mortgages assumed in the like-kind exchange, the regulations allow the "netting" of the mortgages. The party with the net relief from liabilities (i.e., whose property was subject to the higher mortgage at the outset) is treated as having received boot in the amount of the net relief from liability. The mortgage netting rule applies only to the computation of gain recognition; the full amounts of the mortgages are considered in the computation of basis of the properties received by each party.

    3. Two mortgages plus boot: The mortgage netting rule allows the party with net assumption of debt to avoid recognition of gain. But this applies only to the mortgage portion of the transaction. If the person with net assumption of debt receives boot, the usual recognition rules will apply so that realized gain will be recognized to the extent of the fair market value of the boot received.

III. INVOLUNTARY CONVERSIONS—§1033. See Figure 13

A taxpayer may be able to defer, in whole or in part, recognition of gain on the "involuntary conversion" of property.

A. Conversion into similar property: If a taxpayer's property is involuntarily converted into property that is similar or related in service or use, the taxpayer will not recognize any of the realized gain on the conversion.

B. Conversion into money: If the taxpayer's property is involuntarily converted into money, the taxpayer may elect to recognize gain in the amount of proceeds that are not reinvested in property similar or related in service or use to the converted property.

C. Similar property: Real property used in a trade or business or held for investment must be like kind to the property converted, invoking the same standard as in §1031. All other property must meet the "similar" standard, which is a stricter standard than "like kind." The similar standard requires that the properties have the same physical characteristics and that the taxpayer use the properties in the same way.

D. Statutory replacement period: The taxpayer must reinvest within two years after the close of the taxable year in which the taxpayer realizes any portion of the gain on conversion.

E. Basis of replacement property: The basis of the replacement property will be the basis of the property converted, plus the gain recognized, minus the unreinvested proceeds of conversion, minus any loss recognized on the conversion.

F. Inapplicable to loss: Section 1033 does not apply to loss realized on the involuntary conversion of property; those losses would be casualty losses, potentially deductible under §165(c).

IV. SPOUSAL AND DIVORCE TRANSFERS—§1041

A. Nonrecognition: Section 1041 provides that no gain or loss will be recognized on transfers of property between spouses or on transfers incident to a divorce.

1. Incident to a divorce: A transfer of property is incident to a divorce if it occurs within one year of the date the marriage is terminated, or if it is contemplated by the divorce decree and occurs within six years of the date of termination of the marriage (or later if there is a good reason for the delay).

2. Indirect transfers: A transfer usually occurs directly from one spouse to the other. However, a qualifying transfer also can be made to a third person if made by direction or ratification of the other spouse or provided for in the divorce decree.

B. Effect of qualifying transfer to spouse or former spouse: The transferor in a §1041 transfer will not recognize gain or loss on the transfer. In addition, the recipient of property will not include any amount in gross income and will take the property with the same basis as the property had immediately prior to the transfer.

C. Related material: Consider in connection with §1041 the rules relating to alimony and child support.

CHAPTER 11

TIMING OF INCOME AND EXPENSES

I. THE ANNUAL ACCOUNTING CONCEPT

Federal income tax returns are filed on an annual basis, in which taxpayers tote up their income, deductions, and allowable credits for their taxable year and apply the tax rates for that year to their taxable income.

A. Calendar and fiscal years: A taxpayer may use a calendar year or a fiscal year (which is a year other than a calendar year). Most individuals use a calendar year.

B. Problems with annual accounting: While annual accounting is administratively easy, it can measure a taxpayer's ability to pay inaccurately, particularly for transactions that span more than one taxable year. Several Code sections have evolved to address these difficulties.

    1. The net operating loss deduction—§172: A taxpayer's excess of deductions over expenses constitutes a net operating loss that the taxpayer may carry back 2 years and forward 20 years. This allows the taxpayer to reflect income over a period of years more accurately.

    2. Claim of right doctrine and §1341: A taxpayer must include amounts in gross income over which he or she has a claim of right and unfettered use, even if the taxpayer may be required to return all or a portion of the amount to another person. Section 1341 calculates the tax due, if the taxpayer is required to return items previously included in gross income, in a taxpayer-friendly way.

    3. Tax benefit rule—§111: The recovery of an item that constituted a deduction or credit in a prior year will be income to the taxpayer to the extent of the prior tax benefit. A "recovery" is an event that is fundamentally inconsistent with the previous deduction or credit.

II. METHODS OF ACCOUNTING

A. Cash method of accounting: A taxpayer using the cash method of accounting will report income when it is received, actually or constructively, and will claim deductions when amounts are actually paid (regardless of when they are due).

    1. Constructive receipt: A taxpayer will be considered to have received items to which he or she had a right and had the ability to claim but did not do so.

    2. Restrictions on use of the cash method: Some taxpayers may not use the cash method of accounting, as Congress has determined that it would unreasonably accelerate deductions for these taxpayers.

B. Accrual method of accounting: A taxpayer using the accrual method of accounting will report income when all events that fix the taxpayer's right to the income have occurred, and the amount thereof can be determined with reasonable accuracy. Accrual-method taxpayers will deduct expenses when all events that fix the liability have occurred and its amount can be determined with reasonable accuracy, subject to special rules that defer deductions until "economic performance."

III. ACCOUNTING FOR INVENTORIES

Taxpayers engaged in manufacturing and retail activities are required to account for inventories. Under an inventory approach, the taxpayer deducts from gross sales the cost of goods sold to determine the profit from sales for the year. Included in inventory are amounts attributable to the cost of manufacturing or purchasing the product, and certain taxpayers also must include in inventory an amount attributable to indirect costs (administrative costs, for example) under the uniform capitalization (UNICAP) rules.

IV. INSTALLMENT METHOD OF REPORTING INCOME—§453

When a taxpayer sells property other than inventory in a sale in which at least one payment will be received after the close of the taxable year, the taxpayer may report the gain realized on the sale over the period of time payments are received by using the installment method, unless the taxpayer elects out.

A. Applicable to gain: The installment method is applicable to gain, not loss. It is also not applicable to the interest portion of the transaction; interest is determined and accounted for separately.

B. Amount includable in gross income: The amount of gain to be reported each year is the payment for the year multiplied by the gross profit ratio, which is a fraction, the numerator of which is the gross profit (sales price minus adjusted basis) and the denominator of which is the total contract price (amount to be received under the contract). The remaining amount of any payment is excluded from gross income as capital recovery.

V. RESTRICTED PROPERTY—§83

In many deferred compensation situations, the taxpayer receives property in exchange for the performance of services that is restricted in some fashion as to transfer or enjoyment. Section 83 defines (1) whether the taxpayer has income, (2) when the taxpayer has income, and (3) how much income the taxpayer has in these situations.

A. Income? A taxpayer potentially has income if there is a "transfer" of property to the taxpayer. An employer's setting aside of funds or property for the taxpayer's benefit is not income if the property can be reached by the employer's general creditors. But if the taxpayer has rights in the property that are not subject to the employer's creditors' claims, the taxpayer may have income.

B. When? A taxpayer must include the value of the property in gross income in the earlier of the first year in which the taxpayer owns the property without a requirement that he or she perform significant future services (i.e., the property is not subject to a "substantial risk of forfeiture") or the first year in which the property is transferable.

C. How much? The taxpayer includes in gross income the value of the property minus the amount the taxpayer paid for it. A taxpayer who receives restricted property may make what is known as a §83(b) election, in which the taxpayer includes in gross income the value of the property (minus amounts paid for it) within 30 days of receiving it, even though it is restricted. This would be appropriate for restricted property that is expected to increase greatly in value.

VI. SPECIAL LIMITATIONS ON LOSS DEDUCTIONS

In addition to the restrictions on deductible losses of §165(c), discussed above, the Code imposes specific loss restrictions on certain types of losses. These are properly viewed as timing rules because they potentially cause losses incurred in a particular taxable year to be deferred to future taxable years.

A. Passive losses—§469: Passive losses are losses from passive activities, i.e., activities that qualify as trades or businesses but in which the taxpayer does not materially participate. Passive losses incurred during a taxable year may be deducted only to the extent of the taxpayer's passive income for that year, and losses that are disallowed under this rule carry forward to future years when the taxpayer has passive income or disposes of the investment generating the passive loss.

B. Amounts at risk—§465: A taxpayer's losses from certain activities are limited to a taxpayer's amount "at risk," i.e., the amount by which the taxpayer can be held liable to third parties upon failure of the venture. Losses disallowed by the at-risk rules carry forward to future years in which the taxpayer has amounts at risk.

CHAPTER 12

CHARACTER OF INCOME AND LOSS

I. IN GENERAL

When a taxpayer sells or exchanges property and recognizes gain or loss, the character of that gain or loss—as capital or ordinary—must be determined. See Figures 15-17.

II. CAPITAL/ORDINARY DISTINCTION

The capital/ordinary distinction has implications for both income and loss.

A. Income—§1(h): Tax is imposed on an individual's ordinary income at rates up to 35%. However, the maximum rate on "net capital gain" is potentially much lower, ranging generally from 15% to 28%, with some capital gain escaping tax entirely for taxpayers with relatively small amounts of other kinds of income. Thus, taxpayers prefer to characterize income as capital gain subject to the preferential rate.

B. Loss—§1211: Section 1211 imposes a significant restriction on the deductibility of capital losses. Corporations may deduct capital losses only to the extent of their capital gains. §1211(a). Individuals may deduct capital losses to the extent of their capital gain income, plus $3,000 of ordinary income. §1211(b). Unused capital losses carry forward (and, for corporations, carry back) to other taxable years.

C. **Taxpayer preference:** Taxpayers prefer capital gain and ordinary loss.

D. **Policy:** Several rationales are suggested for the preference for capital gain, including the general incentive toward savings and investment, preventing lock-in, avoiding bunching of income, and countering the effect of inflation.

III. AN APPROACH TO CHARACTERIZING GAIN OR LOSS

A. **An approach to characterization problems:** Figure 15 offers an approach to characterizing gain or loss as capital or ordinary, which requires analysis of the following issues, discussed in the sections that follow.

1. **Did the taxpayer experience a realization event with respect to which gains or losses are recognized?**

2. **Did that event constitute a "sale or exchange" of "property"?**

3. **Was the property a "capital asset"?**

4. **Was the property a §1231 asset?**

5. **Do any special recharacterization rules apply?**

B. **Did the taxpayer experience a realization event with respect to which gains or losses are recognized?** For a taxpayer to have a capital gain or loss, there must be a realization event, and any gains or losses from that event must be recognized.

C. **Did that event constitute a "sale or exchange" of "property"?** For the taxpayer to have a capital gain or loss, the recognized gain or loss must arise from the "sale or exchange" of "property." This generally requires a "giving, a receipt, and a causal connection between the two." See *Yarbro v. Commissioner,* 737 F.2d 479 (5th Cir. 1984). Some events that might not otherwise meet this standard are deemed to be sales or exchanges by statute, such as losses from the worthlessness of stock or securities. Moreover, the item in question must constitute a sale or exchange of property, not the prepayment of income. See *Hort v. Commissioner,* 313 U.S. 28 (1941) (lease cancellation payment).

D. **Was the property a "capital asset"?** For the taxpayer to have a capital gain or loss, the recognized gain or loss must be from sale or exchange of a property that qualifies as a "capital asset."

1. **Excluded categories:** Section 1221 defines a capital asset as "property held by the taxpayer (whether or not in connection with his trade or business)" except for eight enumerated categories of property, of which only five are usually important in the basic tax class. Thus, an item is a capital asset *unless* it falls within any of these five categories.

a. **Inventory/stock in trade—§1221(a)(1):** A taxpayer's stock in trade or inventory held primarily for sale to customers in the ordinary course of business is not a capital asset.

      i. Definition: "Primarily" means "of first importance" or "principal."

      ii. Dealers: To have inventory, the taxpayer must hold the property primarily for sale to customers in the ordinary course of business. It is the relationship of the taxpayer to the assets, not the taxpayer's status generally, that determines whether assets constitute inventory. See *Van Suetendael v. Commissioner,* 3 T.C.M. 987 (1944), aff'd, 152 F.2d 654 (2d Cir. 1945).

      iii. Real estate: Whether a taxpayer holds real estate as an investor or as a dealer depends on the analysis of seven factors discussed in *United States v. Winthrop,* 417 F.2d 905 (5th Cir. 1969).

    b. Real and depreciable property—§1221(a)(2): Real property used in a trade or business or property used in a trade or business that is subject to depreciation under §167 is not a capital asset. This type of property is §1231 property, discussed below.

    c. Creative works—§1221(a)(3): Creative works generated by the taxpayer, such as material subject to copyright, letters, and memoranda, are not capital assets. There is an exception for certain musical works, for which the taxpayer may elect capital asset treatment.

    d. Accounts/notes receivable—§1221(a)(4): A taxpayer's accounts or notes receivable from the sale of inventory are not capital assets.

    e. Supplies—§1221(a)(8): Supplies and similar items used in a taxpayer's business are not capital assets.

  2. "Related to" the trade or business: Relying on the case of *Corn Products Refining Co. v. Commissioner,* 350 U.S. 46 (1955), taxpayers asserted that items that were integrally connected with their trade or business should be treated as noncapital assets. In *Arkansas Best Corp. v. Commissioner,* 485 U.S. 212 (1988), the U.S. Supreme Court reexamined *Corn Products,* concluding that the relation of an asset to a taxpayer's business was irrelevant in determining its status as a capital or noncapital asset. In determining whether an item was included in the noncapital category of inventory, certain "inventory substitutes" could be included in that category. The Court limited the holding of *Corn Products* to an application of the inventory substitute idea.

E. Was the property a §1231 asset? Section 1221(a)(2) excludes from the definition of a capital asset real and depreciable property used in a trade or business or held for investment. But all is not lost. Section 1231 may apply to treat net gains from this kind of property as capital.

  1. An approach to §1231: Figure 16 offers an approach to characterizing gain or loss arising from §1231 property. The first question is whether the property sold is §1231 property. If the property is not §1231 property, its character is determined under the usual rules set forth in Figure 15. If the property is §1231 property, the next question is whether the recapture rules of §§1245 or 1250 apply, because recapture income cannot be classified as §1231 gain. Then, the taxpayer determines all of the recognized gains and losses from §1231 assets involving casualties, and if such losses exceed such gains, all are removed from the calculation.

If such losses do not exceed gains, all are included, along with all other §1231 gains and losses, and the losses and gains are netted against one another. If the final result is a net loss, all §1231 gains and losses are ordinary. If the final result is a net gain, all gains and losses are capital, except to the extent of unrecaptured §1231 losses during the previous five years.

2. **Section 1231 property:** Section 1231 gains and losses arise from the sale of property used in the trade or business of the taxpayer, or from the involuntary or compulsory conversion of property used in the trade or business, or any capital asset held for more than a year and held in connection with the taxpayer's trade or business.

3. **Recapture rule:** The recapture rule may limit the recharacterization of gains as capital under §1231. If the taxpayer has had, within the previous five years, §1231 losses that were characterized as ordinary, the current year's gain must be characterized as ordinary to the extent of the previous loss.

F. **Do any special recharacterization rules apply?** Recognized gain or loss on the sale or exchange of a capital asset will usually be capital. However, the Code may, in certain circumstances, require all or a part of the gain or loss to be characterized as ordinary.

1. **Recapture for personal and real property:** The recapture provisions require that upon sale or exchange of property that would otherwise generate capital gain, a portion of the recognized gain be characterized as ordinary. Recapture thus seeks to account for the previous benefit of depreciation deductions taken with respect to the property.

   a. **Personal tangible property—§1245:** On the sale or exchange of depreciable personal property that otherwise qualifies as a capital asset or a §1231 asset generating capital gain, the portion of the gain equal to the lower of the realized gain or depreciation previously claimed with respect to the property will be characterized as ordinary. Any remaining balance will be capital.

   b. **Real property—§1250:** Section 1250 requires recapture of the accelerated portion of depreciation taken with respect to real property to be recaptured upon sale. However, since real property acquired since 1987 has been depreciated using the straight-line method, the practical impact of this provision is minimal today.

2. **Small business stock—§1244:** Individual taxpayers and partnerships may claim a portion of the loss on the sale or worthlessness of small business stock as ordinary rather than capital. The maximum amount considered ordinary is $50,000 for a single taxpayer or $100,000 for a married couple filing a joint return. A small business corporation is a corporation that issues the stock to the taxpayer in exchange for property and must have derived more than 50% of its income from active business sources during the five-year period ending on the date of the loss.

3. **Sales and exchanges between related parties—§1239:** If the property is depreciable in the hands of the transferee, the transferor's gain or loss will be ordinary rather than capital.

IV. CALCULATING CAPITAL GAIN AND LOSS

The final step in addressing character issues is determining the taxpayer's net capital gain (which is included in the taxpayer's gross income and is taxed at preferential rates) or deductible capital loss, and the net capital loss carryforward.

A. **Definitions:** Section 1222 sets forth a number of definitions relating to capital gains and losses that are relevant in calculating capital gain and loss. There are three baskets of capital gain/loss: the 28% group (collectibles), the 25% group (unrecaptured §1250 gain), and the 15%/0% group (everything else). If a taxpayer is in the 10% or 15% bracket for ordinary income, he or she will enjoy the 0% rate on capital gains, but only to the extent theses gains exceed his or her ordinary income.

B. **Holding period:** Capital gains and losses must be characterized as long-term or short-term. Long-term gain or loss is gain or loss from the sale of an asset held for more than one year. Short-term gain or loss is gain or loss from the sale of an asset held for one year or less. The period of time during which a taxpayer owns (or is deemed to own) an asset is his or her holding period for the asset. The calculation of a taxpayer's capital gain and loss depends on the taxpayer's holding period of the assets generating capital gain and loss. The holding period usually begins with the taxpayer's acquisition of the asset, but in some cases, the taxpayer's holding period will include another person's holding period for the asset or the taxpayer's holding period for another asset.

   1. **Exchanged basis property—§1223(1):** For exchange transactions involving the transfer of capital or §1231 assets in which a taxpayer's gain is deferred in whole or in part, the taxpayer's holding period for the property received in the transaction will include the period the taxpayer held the property he or she transferred in the transaction. An example of this is the holding period for property received in a qualifying like-kind exchange.

   2. **Transferred basis property—§1223(2):** If a taxpayer receives property in a transaction in which the taxpayer's basis is determined by reference to another person's basis in the same property, the taxpayer's holding period includes the period of time that other person held the property. An example of this is the holding period for a gift.

C. **An approach to calculating net capital gain and net capital loss:** A systematic approach for calculating net capital gain and net capital loss is helpful in solving problems in which the taxpayer disposes of varying kinds of assets. See Figure 17. First, the taxpayer's long- and short-term capital gains and losses are categorized into each group (28%, 25%, and 15%/0%). Then, the gains and losses in each group are netted against one another to produce gain or loss in each category. Then, any losses in the short-term, 28%, or 15%/0% group are applied to reduce gains in the other categories. This produces a net gain or a net loss in each category. The maximum rate of tax is the tax rate applicable to the group (such as 28%), but if the taxpayer's regular rate is lower, that rate will apply.

CHAPTER 13

TAX RATES AND CREDITS

I. IN GENERAL

The applicable tax rate is applied to taxable income to produce the tentative tax. Available tax credits are subtracted from the tentative tax to produce the actual tax due.

II. TAX RATES

The current tax rate on ordinary income is progressive within a limited range, with tax rates for individuals ranging from 10% to 35% (in 2012). The specific rate applicable to an individual depends on his or her taxable income and filing status.

    A. Sunset 2012: The current tax rates are scheduled to expire on December 31, 2012, unless Congress acts to extend them or amends the Code. If not, the pre-2001 rates will apply, which are significantly higher (i.e., more progressive) and, for capital gains, are calculated differently.

    B. Children: Children with sufficient income to owe tax file their own tax returns reporting their gross income and available deductions and credits. In some circumstances a child's parents may claim the child's investment income on the parents' return pursuant to the kiddie tax.

    C. Preferential rates on capital gains: Net capital gain is taxed at a maximum rate of 28% (collectibles), 25% (unrecaptured §1250 gain), or 15% or 0% (everything else). If the taxpayer's rate on ordinary income is lower, the taxpayer gets the benefit of that rate.

    D. Qualified dividend income: Qualified dividend income is subject to the 15%/0% tax rate regime applicable to capital gains in the 15%/0% category, removing the distinction between capital gain and ordinary income for many corporate distributions. This is scheduled to sunset on December 31, 2012, unless Congress acts. If it does not, qualified dividend income will be taxed at the rates applicable to ordinary income.

III. THE ALTERNATIVE MINIMUM TAX

    A. In general: The alternative minimum tax (AMT) is a surtax imposed on taxpayers with certain kinds of income or deductions. The purpose of the AMT is to ensure that taxpayers with the kinds of activities that reduce tax through tax-exempt income or significant deductions pay at least some amount of tax.

    B. AMTI: The AMT is imposed on "alternative minimum taxable income" (AMTI). AMTI is computed by taking regular taxable income and adding back in certain items that were excluded and certain items that were deducted in the computation of regular taxable income. Important adjustments include the deduction for state taxes, the deduction for personal exemptions, the inclusion of certain tax-exempt interest, miscellaneous expenses, and a longer, slower depreciation period for certain assets.

C. Exemption/tax rates: The AMT is imposed on AMTI in excess of an exemption amount, which changes frequently. The first $175,000 of AMTI is taxed at 26% and the remaining AMTI is taxed at 28%. The AMT often applies to relatively low income taxpayers, and Congress fiddles with the exemption amounts from time to time to reduce the reach of this tax.

D. *Banks v. Commissioner,* 543 U.S. 426 (2005): Contingent fee attorney engagements result in the attorney being paid a percentage of the total award. In *Banks*, the U.S. Supreme Court confirmed that for awards that are not within the purview of §§104 and 62(a)(19), the amount of the attorneys' fees are gross income to the client, who then is entitled to a miscellaneous itemized deduction for the amount payable to the attorney. However, for AMT purposes, the client would not be entitled to this deduction. This can result in an unexpected AMT liability.

IV. TAX CREDITS

A tax credit is a dollar-for-dollar reduction in the amount of tax due. A refundable credit can reduce tax below zero, generating a refund. A nonrefundable credit can only reduce tax to zero and will not generate a refund.

A. Contrast deductions and exclusions: While a tax credit is a dollar-for-dollar reduction in the amount of tax due, a deduction is a subtraction from either gross income or AGI in computing taxable income. Moreover, if an amount is excluded from gross income, it is never included in the computation of gross income.

B. Credit for tax withheld—§31: Perhaps the most familiar tax credit is the credit for the amount of tax withheld from wages, salaries, bonuses, and similar payments.

C. Dependent care credit—§21: Expenses for care of a dependent are not deductible because they are personal expenses. Section 21 allows a taxpayer who maintains a household with at least one qualifying individual to claim a nonrefundable tax credit for certain expenses, equal to the taxpayer's "applicable percentage" multiplied by the "employment-related expenses."

    1. Qualifying individual: A qualifying individual is a dependent under the age of 13 for whom the taxpayer is entitled to a deduction as a dependent, or any other dependent or a spouse of a taxpayer who is physically or mentally unable to care for himself or herself.

    2. Applicable percentage: The taxpayer's applicable percentage ranges from 35% for taxpayers with AGI of $15,000 or less, to 20% for taxpayers with AGI above $43,000.

    3. Employment-related expenses: Employment-related expenses are those incurred for care of a qualifying individual while the taxpayer works, subject to two limitations.

        a. Dollar limitation: Employment-related expenses are limited to $3,000 for one qualifying individual and $6,000 for two or more qualifying individuals.

    b. Earned income limitation: Employment-related expenses are limited to the earned income of a single taxpayer, or if a married couple files a joint return, to the earned income of the lesser-earning spouse. Special rules impute an amount of income to students and disabled taxpayers for purposes of this limitation.

   4. Coordination with §129: Section 129 allows a taxpayer to exclude from gross income up to $5,000 of dependent care assistance provided by an employer. A taxpayer may not claim both the exclusion and the tax credit for the same dollar of dependent care assistance.

D. Earned income tax credit—§32: A low-income, eligible individual may claim a refundable tax credit. To compute the amount of the credit, the credit percentage is multiplied by the taxpayer's earned income, up to a certain amount known as the "earned income amount." Then, from that figure is subtracted the taxpayer's phaseout percentage, multiplied by the taxpayer's AGI, reduced (but not below zero) by the phaseout amount. These percentages and amounts vary depending on the income and family status of the taxpayer. For current credit percentages, earned income amounts, and phaseout amounts, see www.aspenlawschool.com/books/tax_outline.

   1. Eligible individual: An eligible individual is an individual with a dependent child under the age of 19 or a taxpayer who is a U.S. resident between the ages of 25 and 65 and who cannot be claimed as a dependent on another person's tax return.

   2. Earned income amount: Earned income includes wages, salary, and self-employment income.

E. Education credits: Section 25A allows taxpayers to claim tax credits for certain education expenses. The HOPE scholarship credit is a credit of up to $1,500 of qualified education expenses, and the lifetime learning credit is a credit equal to 20% of certain expenses. Income level restrictions apply. The American Opportunity Credit is a $2,500 credit available for certain qualified educational expenses.

F. Other tax credits: The Code contains a variety of other tax credits usually given less attention in the basic federal income tax course.

   1. Child tax credit—§24: A taxpayer may claim a credit for $1,000 per child, with income limitations starting at $75,000 for single taxpayers, and $110,000 for married taxpayers. This is a partially refundable credit.

   2. Blind/elderly/disabled tax credit—§22: A taxpayer who qualifies as blind, elderly, or disabled is entitled to an additional tax credit.

   3. Adoption expense credit—§23: A taxpayer who incurs certain qualifying adoption expenses may claim a credit for up to $12,650 of these expenses, but this credit is phased out as AGI rises.

CHAPTER **14**

IDENTIFYING THE TAXPAYER

I. IN GENERAL

The identification of the proper taxpayer to report income and claim deductions is crucial in maintaining a tax system that fairly allocates income tax among various taxpayers. This question is inherent in all tax questions. See Figures 1 and 18.

II. "PERSONS" SUBJECT TO TAX

Both natural persons and legal entities may be subject to tax.

A. Individuals—§1: Single individuals, including children, file a tax return reporting only their income. Married couples can, and usually do, file a joint return reporting their combined income and deductions. Married couples have the option of filing separately but usually do not, as this can produce a higher joint tax liability.

   1. Child's services income—§73: Income from a child's services is reported on the child's tax return, even if the parent is entitled to the income under state law.

   2. The kiddie tax—§1(g): A child's investment income may be subject to tax at the parental rate, and parents may elect to report a child's investment income on the parents' tax return. A "child" is a person under age 19, or under age 24 if a full-time student.

B. Legal entities: A legal entity—such as a corporation, partnership, estate, or trust—may be required to file a tax return reporting its items of income, deduction, and credit. These are usually beyond the scope of the basic tax class.

III. ASSIGNMENT OF INCOME

In a progressive tax system, an incentive exists for those in high tax brackets to direct income to related persons in lower tax brackets in order to reduce the overall tax imposed on the group. This strategy is known as "assignment of income." Because assignment of income threatens to undermine the integrity of the progressive tax structure, a variety of judicial and legislative responses have arisen over the years to combat it.

A. Judicial views on services income: A common scenario involves the taxpayer who performs services for compensation but attempts to direct the compensation to another person (usually a relative in a lower tax bracket) prior to receiving it.

   1. Diversion by private agreement: If a taxpayer who performs services attempts to direct the compensation to another person by private agreement, the taxpayer (not the transferee) will be required to include the amount in gross income. See *Lucas v. Earl,* 281 U.S. 111 (1930).

   2. Diversion by operation of law: By contrast, if the law governing the legal relationships provides that both the taxpayer and another person have legal rights to the income, the tax consequences will follow from these legal relationships. As a result, the taxpayer and the other party will include their proportionate shares of the income in gross income. See *Poe v. Seaborn,* 282 U.S. 101 (1930).

B. Judicial views on income from property: If an owner of income-producing property gives some interest in the property to another person, the issue arises of which person (the donor or donee) should be taxable on the income from the property.

    1. Transfers of property: If the donor transfers the property itself, the donee will properly report the income from the property.

    2. Transfers of income only: The general rule is that attempts to transfer only the income from the property to another, without a transfer of the property itself, will be respected only if the income interest is transferred for its entire duration. Otherwise, the donor will be taxed on the income and will be deemed to have made a gift of the income to the donee. See *Blair v. Commissioner,* 300 U.S. 5 (1937); *Helvering v. Horst,* 311 U.S. 112 (1940).

C. Statutory responses to assignment of income and related problems

    1. The kiddie tax—§1(g): Certain investment income of a child under the age of 14 must be taxed at his or her parents' tax rate. The special tax rate applies only to "unearned income" in excess of $1,900. The parents have the option of including the child's investment income on their own returns.

    2. Reallocation of income and deductions—§482: Under the broad statutory authority granted in §482, the IRS may reallocate among related entities items of gross income, deduction, and credit if necessary to prevent the evasion of tax or clearly to reflect income. This statute goes far beyond assignment of income principles, giving the IRS a powerful tool with which to combat the misallocation of tax items among related entities.

CHAPTER 15

TIME VALUE OF MONEY: PRINCIPLES AND APPLICATIONS

I. IN GENERAL

While the concept of the time value of money is not specifically invoked in any tax statute, its principles permeate much tax-planning activity. Taxpayers invoke basic time value of money concepts when they attempt to defer income and accelerate deductions. The IRS, and ultimately Congress, may seek to block these strategies by accelerating income and precluding the early deduction of expenses.

II. INTEREST

Interest is the cost of using money. A lender charges the borrower interest for the privilege of using the lender's funds during the period of the loan, and thus the lender is said to "earn interest" on the loan. Interest is what creates the concept of the "time value of money." A specified sum of money will earn interest at the market rate over a period of time; thus, the value of that sum a year in the future will be the sum plus the interest earned during the year.

A. Simple interest: Simple interest is calculated as a percentage of the principal sum only.

B. Compound interest: Compound interest is computed by applying the interest rate to both the principal sum and the accrued but unpaid interest. Compounding generally occurs daily, monthly, semi-annually, or annually.

III. VALUING AMOUNTS

A. Future value: Future value is the value of a sum of money invested for a specified period at a specified interest rate. The future value of a sum will be the amount that an investor will have at the maturity of the investment, given the number of years to maturity and the rate of return (i.e., the interest rate) of the investment. Future value can be calculated using present and future value tables, or by using the following formula:

$$FV = PV(1 + i)^n$$

B. Present value: Present value is the current value, given an assumed interest rate, of the right to a stated amount in the future. Another way to express this is that present value is the sum that must be invested today at a given interest rate to produce a stated sum in the future. Present value can be calculated using present and future value tables, or by using the following formula:

$$PV = \frac{FV}{(1 + i)^n}$$

IV. SPECIFIC TIME VALUE OF MONEY APPLICATIONS

The Code recognizes time value of money principles in specific applications, even though it does not import the concept on a global basis.

A. Applicable federal rates: The IRS publishes interest rates monthly for calculations under various Code provisions, such as imputed interest and interest on tax overpayments and underpayments. These are known as the "applicable federal rates" or "AFR."

B. Tax underpayments and overpayments—§6621: The U.S. government pays interest on tax overpayments, and taxpayers must pay interest on tax underpayments. The interest rate is published from time to time by the IRS.

C. Original issue discount (OID): While most debt instruments provide for a market rate of interest payable currently or otherwise, some debt instruments may not specifically provide for market interest. Yet these instruments do pay interest in an economic sense, for no creditor would lend money without compensation. Without the OID rules, such instruments might create two misstatements of tax reality. First, repayment of the principal plus an additional sum might be considered a return of capital and capital gain rather than interest, which is ordinary income. Second, the creditor might defer the inclusion of any income until maturity, even though presumably the interest is accruing during the entire outstanding period of the loan. The OID rules, while complicated in the extreme, seek to address these character and timing issues.

D. **Imputed interest—§483:** Section 483 imputes to the creditor interest on certain loans made in connection with sales or exchanges of property to which the OID rules do not apply.

1. **General approach:** The creditor must include in gross income the total unstated interest ratably over the term of the contract. §483(a).

   a. **Which loans?** Section 483 applies to contracts for the sale or exchange of property for which at least one payment is due more than one year after the date of the contract. §483(c).

   b. **Total unstated interest:** Total unstated interest is the excess of the total payments due under the contract, over the sum of the present values of those payments and the present value of any payment provided for in the contract, using a discount rate equal to the applicable federal rate. §483(b).

2. **Correlative effects of imputed interest:** The imputation of interest under §483 reduces the amount characterized as the amount realized (principal) by the parties to the transaction. This reduces the gain (usually capital) reported by the seller of the property and, in turn, reduces the basis of the purchaser in the property. Moreover, the purchaser of the property, who is deemed to pay interest, may be able to deduct that interest if the deduction requirements of §163 are met.

3. **Exceptions to §483:** Section 483 does not apply to sales not exceeding $3,000 and to any debt instrument to which the OID rules apply.

E. **Below-market loans—§7872:** If a taxpayer makes a loan to another that does not provide for market interest, the transaction may be recharacterized to ensure that the creditor includes market interest in his or her gross income and that any other aspects of the transaction (such as compensation or gifts, for example) are properly taken into account. §7872(a).

1. **General approach:** Below-market "demand," "term," and "gift" loans are recharacterized so that the creditor includes the appropriate amount of interest in gross income. §7872(a)(1).

   a. **Demand and gift loans:** For demand and gift loans, the forgone interest is treated as transferred from the lender to the borrower and retransferred from the borrower to the lender on the last day of the taxable year. §7872(a)(1). Each leg of the transaction is characterized in accordance with its substance. For a gift loan, for example, the first leg (lender to borrower) is treated as a gift, and the second leg (borrower to lender) is treated as interest.

b. **Other types of loans:** For other types of loans, first compute the excess of the amount loaned over the present value of all payments to be received under the loan. The lender is deemed to have transferred this amount to the borrower on the date the loan is made, and the below-market loan is treated as having OID in that same amount. The transfer from the lender to the borrower is characterized in accordance with its substance (e.g., compensation), and the characterization of the loan as having OID means that the lender must include the OID in gross income over the period of the loan.

   i. **Demand loan:** A demand loan is a loan payable on demand of the creditor.

   ii. **Term loan:** A term loan is a loan payable on a certain date that is fixed or determinable. §7872(f)(6).

   iii. **Gift loan:** A gift loan is a loan in the context of which the creditor's forbearance of interest is most appropriately viewed as a gift. §7872(f)(3).

   iv. **Below-market loan:** A demand loan is below market if its stated interest rate is less than the applicable federal rate at the time the loan is made. §7872(e)(1)(A). A term loan is below market if the amount loaned is greater than the present value of the payments due under the loan, using the applicable federal rate as the discount rate. §7872(e)(1)(B).

2. **Exceptions to §7872:** Section 7872 doesn't apply to gift loans between individuals, to compensation-related loans, and to shareholder loans if the total outstanding principal amount of such loans does not exceed $10,000. §7872(c)(2), (3). Section 7872 also does not apply to any loan to which either the OID rules or §483 applies. §7872(f)(8).

V. BASIC TAX STRATEGIES: INCOME DEFERRAL, ACCELERATION OF DEDUCTIONS, AND CLAIMING TAX CREDITS

Time value of money principles inspire the most basic tax strategies. The best of all tax strategies from the taxpayer's point of view is the exclusion of amounts from gross income entirely (so that tax will never be due on these amounts) or a deduction for the full amount of an expenditure (that shelters the same amount of income from tax). However, exclusions are relatively rare in the Code, and deductions are limited. Most strategies rely on a delay in tax; the taxpayer invests the amount that would otherwise be paid in tax and earns interest on that amount. The tax ultimately will be due, but the taxpayer who has invested the saved tax will usually come out ahead.

A. **Income deferral:** A taxpayer may seek to defer the inclusion of an amount of gross income to a future year. This requires that the taxpayer have a sufficient ownership interest in the funds so that they are invested for his or her benefit but have an interest that will not require the taxpayer to include the amounts in gross income currently. Many income deferral strategies also assume that the taxpayer will be in a lower tax bracket when amounts will be included in his or her gross income (e.g., at retirement). Examples of income deferral strategies include the following:

1. **Method of accounting:** A taxpayer may attempt to take advantage of the rules of his or her particular method of accounting to defer income to future years. Consider in this context the limitations on the use of the cash method of accounting and the doctrine of constructive receipt as limitations on the cash method taxpayer's ability to defer items of gross income.

2. **Realization principle:** Because income from the sale or exchange of property must be realized before it can be recognized, taxpayers may invest in property to defer the recognition of income until sale. Also consider in this context the effect of §1014, which, by giving an heir a fair market value basis in property received from a decedent, encourages taxpayers to hold property until death and thus to exclude from the income tax the appreciation in the property prior to death.

3. **Nonrecognition provisions:** Certain nonrecognition provisions may allow the taxpayer to defer the recognition of gain on the disposition of property. These include like-kind exchanges, spousal and divorce transactions, and involuntary conversions.

4. **Retirement planning:** Most of retirement planning is based on the income deferral strategy. Employers' contributions to retirement plans are not included in the gross income of the employee until retirement, and the fund earns interest for the benefit of the employee during the employee's working years.

5. **Education savings incentives:** Section 529 plans and education savings accounts allow taxpayers to invest money but not be taxed on the earnings until distribution, and then only if the distributions are not used for qualified education expenses.

B. **Deduction acceleration strategies:** Taxpayers prefer to accelerate and maximize deductions because a deduction "shelters" an amount of income from tax. The tax benefit from a deduction is equal to the amount of the deduction multiplied by the taxpayer's tax rate. Examples of deduction strategies include the following:

1. **Method of accounting:** A taxpayer may attempt to take advantage of the particular rules of his or her method of accounting to accelerate deductions. Consider in this context the limitations placed on deductions of prepayments for cash-method taxpayers and the economic performance rules for accrual-method taxpayers.

2. **Capital recovery:** A taxpayer prefers accelerated capital recovery for investment in assets. For example, a taxpayer usually will claim double-declining balance depreciation rather than straight-line depreciation for an asset for which the double-declining balance method is available. Consider in this context §179 deductions, the MACRS method of capital recovery, §195 (amortization of pre-opening expenses), and §197 (amortization of intangibles). But consider the effect of recapture on the claiming of capital recovery deductions.

3. **Loss limitations:** Various loss limitations restrict taxpayers' ability to claim a deduction for certain losses. Consider in this context the capital loss restrictions

(§1211), the passive loss restrictions (§469), the at-risk limitations (§465), and the rules against the recognition of losses in certain transactions (§165 and various nonrecognition rules).

CHAPTER 16

PUTTING IT ALL TOGETHER: RECOGNIZING AND ANALYZING COMMON TAX PROBLEMS

I. A SYSTEMATIC APPROACH TO TAX PROBLEMS

One approach to ensuring a complete analysis of a tax question is to take a systematic approach to the question. See Figure 18.

A. Understand the events: The very first step in any tax problem is to study the facts of a transaction carefully. Be sure you understand who did what with whom, when, why, and how. It may be helpful to draw the transaction to ensure that you understand its various components.

B. What is the call of the question? A specific tax question may accompany a set of facts. More commonly, however, the facts end with a general question such as "What are the tax consequences of these transactions?" or "Advise the taxpayer." These raise two different kinds of tax problems.

    1. Reactive problem: In a reactive problem, events have occurred already, and the problem is to determine their tax consequences. Consider the alternative characterizations of the transaction, and conclude which one is most appropriate.

    2. Proactive (planning) problem: In a proactive problem, the taxpayer is typically considering a transaction and seeks advice on how best to structure it. Consider alternative means to achieve the taxpayer's goals, and choose the one that produces the best overall tax and nontax consequences.

C. Recognize the transaction: What *is* it for tax purposes? The transaction must be characterized and is usually one of several frequently encountered transactions, such as a compensation or property transaction.

D. Ask the seven fundamental tax questions: There are seven fundamental issues in tax, all or some of which may be relevant to a particular transaction.

    1. Who is the relevant taxpayer?

    2. Does the taxpayer have income?

    3. What deductions may the taxpayer claim?

    4. What is the character of income or loss?

    5. When must a taxpayer include an item in gross income, and when may a taxpayer claim a deduction?

6. **What is the taxpayer's rate of tax?**

7. **Is the taxpayer entitled to any credits?**

E. **Identify and apply the applicable Code sections:** The characterization of the transaction as a type is very helpful in identifying potentially applicable statutes and concepts. Once potentially applicable rules are identified, requirements of each statute are examined with the facts in mind to determine if the concept or statute actually applies.

F. **Give advice:** In the final step, recall that the point of the exercise is tax advice. Whether advising the taxpayer or the government, the tax problem posed must be addressed. Consider in this context what would be an appropriate return position or structure for a transaction, advice with respect to a tax controversy, or an appropriate government position. Basic tax strategies such as income deferral, deduction acceleration, and the claiming of credits should be considered, along with congressional and judicial responses to these techniques.

II. COMMONLY ENCOUNTERED TRANSACTIONS

Commonly encountered transactions can be analyzed using the systematic approach.

A. **Compensation transactions**

1. **Recognizing this transaction:** To recognize the basic transaction, look for a person performing services in exchange for value or a promise to transfer value.

2. **Tax analysis:** For the payor, the essential question is whether a deduction is available for amounts paid for services. For the service provider, the essential question is whether he or she has income, and if so, how much and when it will be included in gross income. The expenses of performing services may be deductible, and compensation income will be ordinary income, potentially taxable at the highest tax rate. Advice to taxpayers in compensation transactions generally focuses on strategies to accelerate the deduction to the payor and defer the inclusion of income to the service provider.

B. **Transactions in property:** A second major category of commonly encountered transactions is the sale or other disposition of property, including sales and various types of exchanges. (Gifts are treated as intrafamilial transfers, discussed below.)

1. **Recognizing this transaction:** Transactions in property involve a taxpayer transferring an item of property that he or she owns, usually in exchange for value. In a gift transaction, the donor will not receive value for the property, but in nongift contexts, we assume that the seller will dispose of the property at fair market value.

2. **Tax analysis:** The tax problem may be posed for the buyer, the seller, or both. For the seller, the essential questions are the amount of gain or loss to be recognized on the transaction and the character of that gain or loss. Sales or exchanges of property may generate capital gain or loss, subject to the preferential rate for net capital gain and the capital loss restrictions of §1211. If the seller has received something other than cash in the transactions, the basis of that property must be computed. For the buyer, the essential question is the basis of the property acquired. Advice to

taxpayers in this situation centers on the computation of realized and recognized gain or loss and strategies to exclude or defer income and accelerate loss.

C. Personal expenditure transactions

1. **Recognizing this transaction:** In a personal expenditure transaction, the taxpayer is making expenditures for essentially personal items that would not be deductible but for specific Code sections that allow deduction.

2. **Tax analysis:** The crucial questions for the taxpayer are whether he or she is entitled to claim a deduction for these amounts, and when. Income issues may arise if the taxpayer has been compensated for personal losses or physical injuries. Advice to taxpayers in personal expenditure transactions involves identification of allowable deductions and acceleration of these deductions to the earliest possible year.

D. Business transactions

1. **Recognizing this transaction:** Business transactions generally involve a taxpayer's sale of inventory or services for profit. Look for a taxpayer potentially engaged in business—the regular undertaking of an activity for profit.

2. **Tax analysis:** For the business taxpayer, the essential question is the net income from the business, which requires a determination of the taxpayer's gross business income and available deductions. Timing issues (including inventory issues) generally figure prominently in the computation of income and deductions. The character of the business income generally will be ordinary, potentially subject to the highest rate of tax. Advice in business transactions involves calculation of gross income from business and identification of available deductions and credits.

E. Intrafamilial transfers

1. **Recognizing this transaction:** In this type of transaction, members of a family are transferring money or property among themselves, and the typical transactions include gifts, divorce transfers, and inheritances.

2. **Tax analysis:** The tax consequences to the transferor and transferee of any intrafamilial transfer must be considered.

   a. **Gifts—§§102, 1015:** The making of a gift is not a taxable event to the transferor, and thus the transferor realizes and recognizes no gain or loss on the transfer (unless it is a partial sale, which is properly treated as a sale transaction). The transferee generally receives property tax-free, i.e., without being required to include its value in gross income. The recipient of a gift takes the property with the same basis that the property had in the hands of the donor, unless the property's fair market value was less than its basis at the time of the gift. In that situation, for purposes of determining loss only, the donee takes the fair market value of the property on the date of the gift as his or her basis.

   b. **Inheritances—§§102, 1014:** The recipient of property by bequest or inheritance need not include its value in gross income and takes the property with a basis equal to fair market value on the date of death or at the alternate valuation date six months later, if elected.

c. **Divorce transfers—§§71, 215, 1041:** The payment of alimony (federally defined) constitutes a deduction to the payor and is includable in the gross income of the recipient. The payment of child support, by contrast, generates no deduction to the payor and no income to the recipient. The transferor of property "incident to a divorce" recognizes no gain or loss on the transfer, and the recipient of the property need not include its value in gross income. The recipient takes the property with the same basis that it had immediately before the transfer.

d. **Assignment of income and the "kiddie tax"—§1(g):** Taxpayers in high tax brackets may attempt to allocate income from services or property to related taxpayers in lower tax brackets. Attempted assignments of services income or income from property that constitutes a "carved-out interest" will not be respected by the IRS or courts, and the transferor will be taxed on the income purportedly assigned. Taxpayers may, however, transfer property to another so that the income from that property is properly taxed to the transferee. The "kiddie tax," however, serves as a check on this strategy by requiring certain unearned income of children to be taxed at their parents' tax rate rather than their lower individual rates.

e. **Advice:** Advice in intrafamilial transfers centers around ensuring that the transfer is tax-free to both the transferor and transferee, computing the basis of the property transferred, and identifying proper (and improper) assignments of income.

EXAM TIPS

SUMMARY OF CONTENTS

Exam Tips on *GETTING STARTED IN FEDERAL INCOME TAX*

☞ Make sure you understand the "big picture" of how the federal tax is imposed:

Gross Income
− Certain Deductions
_____
= Adjusted Gross Income (AGI)
− Either Standard or Itemized Deduction
− Personal Exemptions
_____
= Taxable Income
× Tax Rate
_____
= Tentative Tax
− Tax Credits
_____
= **Tax Due or Refund Owed**

☞ The most valuable thing you can do at the beginning of the course is to become comfortable reading the Code and applying it.

☞ The first step is finding Code sections. Become facile in finding Code and regulations sections in your statute book *before* you need to do this in class—or on an exam. Can you find IRC §102(b)(2)? Or §117(b)(2)(A)? Or §108(f)(2)(C)(iii)? How about Treas. Reg. §1.61-2? Or Treas. Reg. §1.132-5?

☞ Give parsing a try, as described in this chapter. Doesn't work for you? Find some other *systematic* way to approach Code sections.

☞ When you read a tax case, read the statute on which the case is based. Analyze how the taxpayer interpreted the statute, how the IRS interpreted it, and the differences between them. Of course, you will want to know how the court ultimately interpreted it.

☞ Tax professors almost universally allow students to take the Code book into the exam. By that time, you will have "parsed" the important statutes for later reference. When discussing a tax problem on an exam, it never hurts to cite the statutes involved, but if pressed for time, don't cite particular subsections, paragraphs, etc.

☞ On a test, an ingenious tax professor often will offer an imaginary tax statute that you've never seen before, and then pose problems from it. This tests your ability to read statutes. Use the parsing approach, and you'll be fine. (The good news: It's usually a relatively simple statute.) Some professors will ask you to evaluate this statute from a policy point of view as well.

☞ Given the recent important changes in the standards of tax practice, be ready to discuss the propriety of various return positions, and the different standards involved in penalty assessment, tax preparer assessment, and—most important—lawyers' ethical duties in giving tax advice.

☞ Tax procedure, including how cases get to court, is usually tested *indirectly* on tax exams. If a question is about a position that is being challenged by the IRS, it may be helpful to consider what the taxpayer's choices are for appealing an adverse determination by the IRS.

☞ *Look for:* A taxpayer who has filed a return with a problematic return position.

☞ *Analyze:* The likelihood of success if challenged on the merits, and the taxpayer's options for resolving this controversy.

☞ Many tax professors are more interested in tax policy than in technical questions of tax law. If you are using this book at the end of the course, you already know the emphasis your professor places on policy. If you are using it as you go, pay attention to the emphasis that the professor puts on policy versus technical tax issues.

☞ Policy questions place you in the position of a legislator, an aide, or even an advocate faced with changing some aspect of the tax code.

☞ There is no "right" answer to these questions; you're being tested on your understanding of tax fairness, how tax statutes are administered, and your ability to see expected and unexpected consequences of tax statutes. These questions can easily be paired with the "new statute" described above.

☞ Even if you are an advocate for a particular approach, be sure to present both sides of the argument.

☞ Given recent discussions about the federal budget, you should expect a policy question about tax expenditures. Such a question might involve asking you to evaluate one of the "big six" tax expenditures from a policy point of view: exclusion for health insurance; retirement accounts contributions and deferrals; home mortgage interest; child tax credit; deductions of state and local taxes; exclusion of gain on sale of principal residence.

Exam Tips *on* IDENTIFYING GROSS INCOME

☞ If a tax exam question stumps you, simply return to that linchpin of the income tax: §61. Is the taxpayer somehow "better off" because of an event of an economic nature? If so, is this event captured by §61? This will get you started.

☞ If the question is whether the taxpayer has "income," determine what theory is being used to define gross income. Is this a theoretical question based on comparing a broad tax base (Haig-Simons) with the more practical statutory scheme? Or is this a question based solely on a single theory, or on the statutory system of the Code, i.e., §61?

☞ Questions requiring identification of gross income focus on a taxpayer receiving "stuff" of value. Ask yourself whether there has been an "inflow" to the taxpayer, even if the taxpayer had to do something in return, such as perform services. Look for "inflows" such as

☞ Cash

☞ Property

☞ Services

☞ The use of the taxpayer's own property, or the value of the taxpayer's own services (imputed income)

☞ Discharge of debt

☛ Questions requiring identification of gross income also focus on the few things that are *not* income in our system:

☞ Loan proceeds are not income because of the offsetting obligation to repay.

☞ Capital recovery is not income; a taxpayer is entitled to recover his or her invested capital without tax.

☞ Imputed income is not income in the U.S. tax system, but it is income under other theories.

☞ Some payments made for the general welfare of the taxpayer are not income, but the parameters of this exclusion are not exact.

☞ Noneconomic benefits, such as living in a beautiful place or the enjoyment of one's job, are not income.

☛ Some questions combine a nontaxable receipt and a later development that might change the result.

☞ Example: In Year 1, Kelly borrows $45,000 from Alex. That isn't income because Kelly is required to pay Alex back. But later, Alex forgives the debt. This is income to Kelly in the year of forgiveness because she has been discharged of the obligation. (It might, however, be excludable under a specific statutory rule, but that's for Chapter 4.)

☛ Exam questions involving barter are common. A barter transaction involves the exchange of goods or services and is distinguishable from imputed income, which involves the use of property or services for oneself.

Exam Tips on
SPECIFIC INCLUSIONS IN GROSS INCOME

☛ If a tax question stumps you, consider the list of types of income that are contained in §61, such as compensation, investment income, or discharge of debt. Have any of these events occurred? This will get you started.

☛ Tax questions typically involve transactions between two or more people. *Which person's* tax consequences are you asked to address in the question?

☞ Recall one of the principles of Chapter 2: Some receipts aren't income, by definition. If these rules apply, you do not reach the specific statutory inclusions in gross income. These excluded amounts are

  ☞ Loan proceeds

  ☞ Capital recovery

  ☞ Imputed income

  ☞ Some general welfare payments

☞ Questions about income inclusion involve the taxpayer's receipt of something of value. Identify the transfer of things of value, such as

  ☞ Cash or checks

  ☞ Services

  ☞ Property

  ☞ Discharge of debt

☞ Section 61 is the cornerstone of basic income tax. Expect a question about whether a type of income is included in gross income.

☞ Compensation for services is a common transaction.

  ☞ *Look for:* Someone providing services to another in exchange for something of value.

  ☞ *Analyze:* Focus on the service provider—what he or she did and what was received. The fair market value of services or property received is gross income to the service provider.

☞ Most, if not all, kinds of investment income are includable in gross income. Dividends, rents, royalties, and interest are all includable.

☞ Annuities are a corner of the tax law that some professors find interesting because they illustrate the concept of recovery of basis (investment in the contract). You probably won't be required to know the details, but you should know how each annuity payment is treated for income tax purposes: partial return of investment and income.

☞ In a divorce setting, one party may pay alimony to the other. Be sure to analyze the transaction from both sides and include any alimony in the gross income of the recipient.

  ☞ *Look for:* The payment of cash from one party to the other in a divorce setting.

  ☞ *Analyze:* Are the requirements for alimony met? Are the payments front end loaded?

☞ Understand loan transactions. A loan isn't a taxable event, nor is the repayment of the loan principal. When a taxpayer takes out a loan, what he or she does with the proceeds (buying a house, for example) is an independent transaction, even if the seller of the property is the one making the loan (seller financing).

☞ Be able to identify discharge of debt situations.

☞ *Look for:* A loan from one party to the other, and then the lender doing something that reduces or eliminates the debt, or a discharge by operation of law. The payment of a debt, whether by the debtor or someone else, is not discharge of indebtedness income.

☞ *Analyze:* How much discharge income does the taxpayer have? In later chapters, we will consider possible exclusions.

☛ Some payments are partially includable in gross income, such as

☞ Some annuity payments

☞ Some Social Security payments

☛ Most receipts are includable in gross income. If in doubt, include an item in gross income because gross income is a broad category that involves much more than what is specifically enumerated.

☛ *Don't forget timing issues*: If an item is includible in gross income, is there an issue regarding the year in which it is properly included? If in doubt, include it in the earliest possible year.

☛ *Don't forget character issues:* If the taxpayer has an item of gross income, is it ordinary income or capital gain?

Exam Tips *on*
SPECIFIC EXCLUSIONS FROM GROSS INCOME

☛ An exclusion from gross income means that an item of income is never included in the tax base at all.

☛ Be ready to discuss the policy implications of each major exclusion statute, such as the exclusion for life insurance. Does it make the system more "fair"? Is it administratively practical? Does it lead to the intended (or unintended) economic effects?

☞ Be ready to discuss phaseouts—how they work (in general) and the tax policy implications of them.

☞ Be ready to discuss the pros and cons of a tax benefit being framed as an exclusion or a deduction. Which is "better"? This is a tax policy question, and you should discuss in particular administrative practicality and the "upside-down subsidy" of deductions.

☛ Questions about exclusions focus on the taxpayer's receipt of something of value that would otherwise be included in the taxpayer's gross income.

☞ *Look for:* Receipt of property, money, or some other benefit to the taxpayer that would be considered gross income under §61. Especially consider the employment context.

☞ *Analyze:* Is there a specific statutory exclusion that exempts it from gross income?

☛ Some exclusions are subject to phaseouts and restrictions that can change each year with inflation adjustments. Few professors care about your knowledge of these details. Faced with a phaseout question? Show that you know the policy behind phaseouts, show that you know how they work, and, if necessary, assume a reasonable phaseout amount for illustration purposes.

☛ Interpret exclusions narrowly.

☞ Make sure the purported exclusions precisely fit within the requirements of the statute. If in doubt, don't exclude an item; include it in gross income.

☞ Many exclusions (and deductions) have complex limitations based on income. In a test situation, the limitation phaseout figures would usually be given to you, and the goal would be to demonstrate your ability to understand how these limitations work and to show that you comprehend the structure of the statute. Many professors simply don't care about these technical issues; they want you to know in general how phaseouts work and the reasons for them.

☛ Understand the difference between the exclusion for gifts for income tax purposes and the so-called annual exclusion for gift tax purposes.

☞ A person can receive an unlimited amount of gifts, in terms of value, without including them in gross income for income tax purposes.

☞ The gift tax exclusion is limited to a dollar amount ($13,000 in 2012); this is the amount any person may give to another person without counting against the donor's lifetime exclusion amount for gift tax purposes.

☛ **Remember:** Damages for nonphysical injuries are includable in gross income; damages for physical injuries are excludable; punitive and delay damages are included in the gross income.

☛ Section 108 provides a number of potential exclusions from gross income for discharge of indebtedness income.

☞ *Look for:* A discharge of debt situation that generates gross income to the taxpayer, but surrounding circumstances that make it seem somewhat "unfair" to tax the income.

☞ *Analyze:* Does some subsection of §108 apply? If so, are there corresponding reductions in tax benefits? Or is there a gift that would protect otherwise-includable discharge of indebtedness income from being taxed? Recent economic conditions make it likely that a professor will test on qualified principal residence indebtedness through questions involving adjustment of mortgages or foreclosures. Be sure to understand how §108 interacts with §1001, which addresses gain and loss on the sale of property.

☛ Consider the employment situation carefully.

☞ *Look for:* Compensation income in the form of noncash items, such as medical insurance, fringe benefits, dependent care assistance, or other benefits.

☞ *Analyze:* Does the taxpayer meet the requirements of the statute? Consider in particular whether the person is an "employee" (if required by the statute) or whether the benefit can extend to spouses, partners, or dependents. Also, consider whether any nondiscrimination rules apply.

☛ Timing issues usually do not figure prominently in exclusion settings, but when an inflow of income occurs over a couple of years, it is necessary to ask whether the requirements of the statute are met in one year but not in another (e.g., employment).

Exam Tips on
DEUCTIONS—IN GENERAL

☛ Deduction questions involve either an outflow of value from the taxpayer in question to another person or a loss in which the taxpayer experiences a casualty or reduction in value.

☞ *Look for:* The taxpayer paying someone else for something, in cash or property, or experiencing some other outflow, as in a loss.

☞ *Analyze:* Is this item deductible? If so, how much is deductible? When is it deductible?

☛ If an expenditure is deductible, is it a deduction from gross income in computing AGI (an above-the-line deduction)? Or is it deductible from AGI in computing taxable income (a below-the-line deduction)? Make sure you understand why the distinction is important. Deductions are construed narrowly. If in doubt, deny the deduction. The allowance of a deduction is not the whole story. *When* will it be deductible? Some outlays involve either deductions or credits—or both.

☞ Be ready to explain which is more valuable to the taxpayer. A credit is a dollar-for-dollar reduction in tax, so it is usually more valuable, while a deduction is potentially worth the marginal tax rate of the taxpayer multiplied by the amount of the deduction.

☞ *Remember:* A taxpayer cannot claim a credit and a deduction for the same dollar of outlay.

☛ Some deductions are subject to phaseouts and restrictions that can change each year with inflation adjustments. Few professors care about your knowledge of these details. Faced with a phaseout question? Show that you know the policy behind phaseouts, show that you know how they work, and, if necessary, assume a reasonable phaseout amount for illustration purposes.

☛ Be ready to discuss the policy implications of any particular deduction or a newly proposed deduction. Does it make the system more or less fair? Is it administratively practical? Does it lead to the intended economic effects, or does it lead to unintended economic effects? Congress is increasingly using tax credits instead of deductions to achieve nontax goals. Why?

Exam Tips on
PERSONAL DEDUCTIONS

☛ ***Remember:*** Always construe deductions narrowly. If in doubt, discuss but deny the deduction.

☛ Questions involving personal deductions deal with expenditures associated with a taxpayer's personal life. Address these separately from business deductions.

   ☞ *Look for:* Outlays by taxpayers for charity, health, etc.

   ☞ *Analyze:* The default rule is that a personal expense is not deductible—unless there is a specific statute that allows it. Analyze questions by going through each expenditure: Is each particular expense a deductible expense, and if so, how much is deductible?

☛ Know which deductions belong where: "above the line" or "below the line," i.e., deductible from gross income in computing AGI (above the line) or deductible from AGI in computing taxable income (below the line).

☛ Many deductions are subject to phaseouts based on income. Most professors are not overly interested in the technical aspects of phaseouts but want you to know that they exist, how (in general) they work, and the policy reasons for them.

☛ Most taxpayers described on law exams are "itemizers," i.e., they do not take the standard deduction but instead take the deductions listed on Schedule A as itemized deductions.

☛ Many deductions have specific limitations tied to AGI.

   ☞ *Look for:* Charitable donations, medical expenses, casualty losses, educational loans, miscellaneous expenses, retirement savings, etc.

   ☞ *Analyze:* Determine if the outlay is deductible at all; if it is, apply the limitations to determine the deductible percentage.

☛ *Don't* allow a taxpayer to claim *both* the standard and itemized deduction.

☛ Personal deductions are usually deductible in the year the outlay is made, if at all—not later. Timing issues are usually not a large feature of these questions. Nevertheless, as a precaution, think about *when* an amount is deductible.

☞ Given recent events, a professor may be interested in testing your knowledge of the tax policy implications of major tax expenditures, particularly the deduction for home mortgage interest. Be ready to discuss the rationales for the deduction for home acquisition indebtedness, for home equity indebtedness, and for mortgage insurance premiums and how they may have contributed to recent economic woes, particularly the foreclosure crisis.

Exam Tips on
BUSINESS AND INVESTMENT DEDUCTIONS

☞ Questions dealing with pure business deductions involve a taxpayer's activities with respect to trade or business.

   ☞ *Look for:* Regular, continuous activity with a profit motive. In the basic tax course, a sole proprietorship usually is selected to test for these issues, but a trade or business can also be carried on by a corporation or partnership.

   ☞ *Analyze:* Identify the particular outlays. Analyze them, expenditure by expenditure. Is an expenditure deductible, and if so, how much is deductible?

☞ Work through the five requirements to test deductibility: ordinary, necessary, incurred in carrying on (not pre-opening) a trade or business, and being an expense (not a capital expenditure). If an expense flunks any of these requirements, it is not currently deductible under §162.

☞ A person can have more than one trade or business, and remember that an employee is in the trade or business of providing services to an employer. For example, an employee might moonlight as a consultant. Be sure to assign expenses to the correct trade or business.

☞ Timing questions often arise in these questions.

   ☞ *Look for:* The taxpayer's method of accounting—cash or accrual.

   ☞ *Analyze:* If an expenditure is deductible, *when* is it deductible?

☞ Watch for expenses that have benefits for a longer period than the taxable year. Usually, these must be capitalized. If so, when will the taxpayer be allowed to recover the invested capital? Over time (as in MACRS), or upon disposition of the investment?

☞ Each professor seems to require a different level of understanding with regard to depreciation and amortization. Check with your professor as to the level of understanding required about the different MACRS methods.

☞ MACRS questions involve some arithmetic skills. Intimidated about math, or pressed for time? Explain how MACRS would be applied to the particular situation, and come back later to do the math if you have time.

☛ Some expenditures have both personal and business connections. In that case, usually some or all of the expenditures will be nondeductible. See "Exam Tips on Mixed Business and Personal Expenses," which follows.

Exam Tips on MIXED BUSINESS AND PERSONAL EXPENSES

☛ **Remember:** Personal expenses are nondeductible unless a specific statute allows them. But many expenses have a connection with both a taxpayer's personal and business life. Mixed business and personal expenses are often a major focus of deduction questions because they offer ample opportunities to test your statutory skills.

☞ *Look for:* A taxpayer making an expenditure that benefits his or her business, yet also is integrally tied to personal enjoyment or lifestyle (food, entertainment, vacations, equipment used for business and personal use, etc.).

☞ *Analyze:* Find the applicable statute (e.g., §§183, 280A). Which approach does the statute take: nondeductible, partially deductible, or deductible in full if requirements are met? Make sure the taxpayer's situation meets the applicable requirements in order to qualify for a deduction.

☛ **Remember:** It is not enough to have expended funds and to have met the statutory requirements for a deduction. The taxpayer has the duty of substantiating the deduction with adequate records.

☛ Many professors are not interested in the mechanics of the home office/vacation home rules. They just want you to know that these activities cannot generate a deductible loss for a taxpayer. Find out the level of interest your professor has in §280A.

☛ Similarly, professors who don't require a deep understanding of the mechanics of MACRS are also not interested in the mechanics of depreciating listed property. However, the policy behind §280F offers ample opportunity for questions:

☞ Do the limitations make sense in an era of big SUVs?

☞ Do you think this section is effective in achieving its goals? How do taxpayers likely change their behavior in response to the limitations on listed property, for example? Or are gas prices more effective in changing behavior?

☛ Most of the statutes contain objective tests. But §183 is an "intent" test.

☞ *Look for:* Facts relevant to the nine factors evidencing profit motive.

☞ *Analyze:* Analyze each factor as to its particular impact on the taxpayer. Does the question ask you to be an advocate? Or an advisor?

☞ Use the origin of the expense test when there is no statute on point.

☞ *Remember:* Construe deductions narrowly. If in doubt, deny the deduction.

🎯 *Exam Tips on*
TRANSACTIONS IN PROPERTY

☞ Questions involving transactions in property involve gifts, sales, exchanges, trades, and other dispositions of property.

   ☞ *Look for:* First, identify the "property." The usual suspects that pop up on tax exams are real estate, equipment, and personal property. Then, look for a taxpayer giving up property in exchange for something else—cash, other property, promises, services, or the assumption of liabilities.

   ☞ *Analyze:* Which taxpayer's tax consequences are you asked to analyze? Both, or just one of them? If both taxpayers are at issue, analyze them separately.

   ☞ *Tip:* It can help to diagram the transaction. Who had which property, and what happened to that property? Who exchanged what, with whom, and for how much (or what other property, services, or assumption of liabilities)? You don't want to get deep into the question and discover that you have misunderstood the transaction.

☞ *Careful:* Don't jump right to the question of gain included in income, or loss deductible from income. Make sure there is a realization event, and that there is realized gain or loss, before asking what gain or loss is recognized.

   ☞ If in doubt, consider a transaction a realization event. Most transactions (except gifts) are realization events.

   ☞ Compute realized gain by subtracting the adjusted basis of the property given up from the value of what the taxpayer receives. If the property received is difficult to value, refer to the value of the property given up.

☞ *Remember:* Rational, unrelated taxpayers will trade value-for-value and will adjust differences in value by paying or receiving additional property. If taxpayers are related, there may be a gift involved.

☞ Most realized gain is recognized. If in doubt, include it in income.

☞ Realized loss is recognizable only if there is a statute that allows it. Deductions are a matter of legislative grace and are interpreted narrowly. If in doubt, deny the deduction of the loss.

☞ When will the taxpayer recognize income or loss? Unless a nonrecognition rule applies, the taxpayer will recognize the gain or loss (if allowed) in the year of the sale or exchange.

☞ Given recent economic events, tax professors may be interested in testing on fore-closures and related transactions involving distressed properties, particularly principal residences. Be ready to analyze these transactions and, in particular, the situation in which the taxpayer's mortgage (or mortgages) on the property exceed the fair market value of the property.

 Exam Tips on
NONRECOGNITION TRANSACTIONS

☞ Nonrecognition provisions (§§1031, 1033, and 1041) are commonly tested areas of tax law.

☞ Can you articulate Congress's reasons for nonrecognition treatment for some—but not all—transactions? These are ripe policy questions.

☞ The nonrecognition statutes are relevant only if there is realized gain or loss on the disposition of property.

☞ *Look for:* An exchange of one property for another, in which the taxpayer realizes gain or loss—usually in a situation in which the taxpayer hasn't fundamentally changed the nature of the investment.

☞ *Analyze:* Which taxpayer's tax consequences are relevant? One or both? Compute the realized gain or loss, and then ask if the requirements of a nonrecognition statute are met.

☞ Section 1031 is probably the most popular statute for testing, not only because it is important in tax law in general, but because it offers fertile ground for testing the student's knowledge of the requirements and consequences of the statute.

☞ *Look for:* Situations that raise questions about the taxpayer's use of the properties or the like-kind nature of the properties.

☞ *Analyze:* Each requirement; make sure you analyze realized gain or loss, recognized gain or loss, and adjusted basis in the property received in the exchange. If you are in doubt (at all) about whether a particular requirement is met, analyze the transaction in the alternative—the results if it qualifies under §1031, and the results if it does not.

☞ ***Remember:*** Section 1031 is not optional. A taxpayer may not recognize loss on a transaction that qualifies as a §1031 exchange. A better way to recognize loss: Sell the old property and buy the new property with cash.

☞ Involuntary conversions can generate realized gain or loss. Section 1033 applies only to realized gain.

☞ *Look for:* A disaster, or some event outside the control of the taxpayer that leads to the loss of property.

☞ *Analyze:* In the case of realized gain (receipt of insurance proceeds or exchange of properties), are the requirements of §1033 met? If in doubt about the taxpayer meeting specific requirements, analyze the transaction in the alternative—the tax consequences if it qualifies, and the tax consequences if it does not.

☞ If loss is realized, §1033 doesn't apply to that loss. Does §165 allow a deduction for a casualty loss? Are there both casualty losses and recognized casualty gains? Offset them.

☞ Divorces also offer fertile ground for testing because they involve not only a nonrecognition provision, but also issues of income and deduction.

　☞ *Look for:* Divorce or separation and the transfer of money or property pursuant to the divorce.

　☞ *Analyze:* Is this a transfer of property, or is it alimony or child support? If a transfer of property, the nonrecognition rules of §1041 will usually apply, but watch for special circumstances that would disqualify the transaction. Be sure to determine the basis of property received in the divorce. Is there alimony or child support? If so, who gets the deduction, and who must include payments in gross income?

☞ One of the fundamental principles of the nonrecognition provisions (and one they all have in common) is the use of a substituted basis to preserve the inherent gain or loss that goes unrecognized in the transaction. Make sure you understand this and can explain the function of substituted basis.

☞ Another fundamental principle of all of the nonrecognition provisions is that the receipt of boot results in gain recognition. Make sure you can explain why this is, and how this affects the substituted basis computation.

Exam Tips *on*
TIMING OF INCOME AND EXPENSES

☞ Questions of timing arise only *after* you have determined that there is an item of income or an expense that may be deducted. Unless the exam question directs you to timing issues specifically, don't get ahead of yourself by jumping ahead to timing before analyzing income and deduction issues.

　☞ *Look for:* Is there an item of income, and if so, how much? Is there an expense or loss that is deductible, and if so, how much?

　☞ *Analyze:* Then, and only then, ask *when* is the income includable in the taxpayer's gross income, and when is the expense or loss deductible?

☞ When the facts describe a transaction occurring over two or more years, timing issues are likely to be important. If a result seems "unfair" to a taxpayer because of multiple-year transactions, timing issues are likely to be a big issue. Or, if the taxpayer seems to be claiming a result that is too good to be true, timing issues are likely to be a culprit.

☞ *Look for:* Income in one year, and deductions in another; profit in one year, and losses in another; recovery of previous deductions; repayment of amounts received in previous years.

☞ *Analyze:* Chronologically—address the first year first, then later years, in order. Explain how the years affect each other, if they do. Think about claim of right, tax benefit, and NOL issues.

☛ Know what taxpayers are trying to do: defer income and accelerate deductions. What's the IRS trying to do? (Accelerate income and defer deductions, when taxpayers try to play games!)

☞ *Look for:* Taxpayers playing games by accelerating deductions and postponing income. Look for situations in which taxpayers have access to income but don't report it or haven't yet made an economic outlay of some sort but still claim deductions.

☞ *Analyze:* Statutory and regulatory responses to those games.

☛ Some kinds of property transactions raise important timing issues.

☞ *Look for:* Sales of property with deferred payment, or stock or other property given to employees or others for services.

☞ *Analyze:* Over what period of time will income be recognized, or in what year will there be a sudden influx of income from property received in exchange for services? Be sure you understand how the installment method works—it is a commonly tested area in basic income tax.

☛ If a question describes the taxpayer's method of accounting, it may have important timing issues. Taxpayers on basic income tax exams use the cash method—but not always.

☞ *Look for:* When is an amount paid or received? When is the obligation due? Is there uncertainty about the amount?

☞ *If in doubt:* Include an amount in income and defer the expense, particularly for accrual-method taxpayers.

☞ *Tip:* Before diving into the details of a question, scan for the words "cash method" or "accrual method."

☛ If a question describes the taxpayer's accounting year, it may have important timing issues. Scan for the words "calendar year" or "fiscal year."

☞ *Look for:* Transactions occurring at the end of one year and carrying over to the beginning of the next year, or multiyear cycles of performance of services and payments.

☞ *Analyze:* Chronologically—analyze the first year first, then move to the next year. Explain how the two years affect each other, if they do.

Exam Tips *on*
CHARACTER OF INCOME AND LOSS

☛ *Warning:* Different professors have varying degrees of interest in the technical aspects of calculating net capital gain or loss. Some are happy if you know the different categories of capital gain and are content to leave the rest to a computer program. Others insist that you know the exact process—and can explain it as well as apply it. *Ask your professor about his or her approach.*

☛ Professors who are not interested in the technical details of calculating capital gain and loss may be interested in the policy issues implicit in a capital gains preference and restrictions on capital losses.

☞ Make sure you can articulate the various rationales for the special tax rates for capital gains (and that you can comment on them from a tax policy point of view).

☞ Make sure you can articulate the rationale for the restrictions on capital losses.

☛ Many professors are not interested in the technical details of §1231 gains and losses. Many professors simply want you to know that "net losses are ordinary; net gains are capital." Others require more detail. *Ask.* Make sure you know the historical context of the taxpayer-friendly §1231 rules.

☛ Questions of character arise only after there is a determination that gain or loss has been recognized. If there is no recognized income or loss, there is no question of character.

☛ Be able to recognize when a taxpayer is trying to characterize income as capital or a loss as ordinary—and know why. Make sure the requirements for capital gain or loss are met (see Figure 15).

☛ If there is a sale or exchange of an asset, determine what kind of asset it is: capital, noncapital, or §1231 asset.

☞ *Look for:* Is the taxpayer engaged in a trade or business?

☞ *Analyze:* Business assets are likely to be inventory (noncapital) and §1231 assets. Nonbusiness assets are likely to be capital assets. But the connection with the business isn't the determinative factor. (See *Arkansas Best*.) Study §1221 carefully for the definition of capital assets.

☛ Is there a "deemed" sale or exchange? Even if there is no direct sale, there still may be a sale or exchange leading to capital gain/loss.

☛ Get to know the different kinds of capital gain: 28%, 25%, and 15%/0%.

☛ To get ready for any capital gain/loss calculation problem, have your friends pose various scenarios to you (and you to them). Don't stop until the process of categorizing and netting capital gains and losses is second nature to you.

Exam Tips on
TAX RATES AND CREDITS

☛ The computation of tax is the *last* step in analyzing a taxpayer's tax consequences. It is not usually the case that law students are asked to actually compute the tax; instead, they are asked to understand the concepts involved in tax computation.

☛ Tax rates vary from year to year, so make sure you have checked the latest incarnation of the income tax rates. *Remember:* You can't rely on the income bracket numbers stated in §1, as these are adjusted for inflation.

☛ Know the differential in tax rates on ordinary income and capital gain and qualified dividend income.

　☞ *Look for:* A taxpayer with gain from dealings in property (not inventory) and other kinds of income, such as salary income.

　☞ *Analyze:* Differentiate between the types of income and note the different tax rates that apply.

　☞ *Note:* Most taxpayers one meets on exams have relatively high ordinary income levels, so that the preferential rates for capital gains will make a difference. However, when a taxpayer has low levels of ordinary income and significant amounts of net capital gain in the 28% or 25% categories, the regular rates of tax will usually produce a lower rate than the capital gains rates. The capital gains rates are maximum rates; if the tax produced by the regular tax rates is lower, those rates will apply.

☛ Be able to explain the rationale for the AMT and to comment on its effectiveness.

　☞ Different professors have different levels of interest in the actual computation of AMT. If your professor is interested in this, be ready to compute AMTI using taxable income as the starting place. Know the adjustments to taxable income. Look for taxpayers who have relatively high itemized deductions or tax-exempt income or can take advantage of significant income deferrals.

☛ The *Banks* case is good fodder for testing, not only because it is a relatively recent Supreme Court tax case, but also because it combines issues of gross income, deductions, and the AMT. Make sure you understand *Banks* and the stakes of the controversy.

☛ Understand the difference between a credit, a deduction, and an exclusion, and the impact of each on a taxpayer.

☛ Some credits are subject to phaseouts and restrictions that can change each year with inflation adjustments. Few professors care about your knowledge of these details. Faced with a phaseout question? Show that you know the policy behind phaseouts, show that you know how they work, and, if necessary, assume a reasonable phaseout amount for illustration purposes.

☛ Be familiar with the numerous credits available to taxpayers.

    ☞ *Look for:* Adoptions, day care, and low-income taxpayers.

    ☞ *Analyze:* Have the taxpayers met the specific requirements for claiming the credit? If so, is it limited by the taxpayer's income level?

    ☞ *Look for:* A taxpayer paying for higher education expenses—for the taxpayer or a spouse or child.

    ☞ *Analyze:* What incentives are available: exclusions, deductions, credits, or deferral devices? Are the specific requirements of the statutes met? What limitations apply, particularly with respect to income levels? Don't let the taxpayer "double dip," i.e., claim two benefits for the same dollars.

Exam Tips on
IDENTIFYING THE TAXPAYER

☛ Even though the discussion of the assignment of income doctrine comes close to the end of this book, it is conceptually one of the first questions you should ask yourself in analyzing tax questions. The basic question is this: *Which* taxpayer should be taxed on income or entitled to claim a deduction?

    ☞ *Look for:* Intrafamily transfers, usually from a senior generation to a younger generation, with the opportunity to lower taxes on the overall economic unit.

    ☞ *Analyze:* Has there been an impermissible assignment of income from one person to another? What is the result of this assignment? Is there a judicial doctrine or statutory "fix" that prevents this assignment?

☛ The progressive rates of the income tax system inspire assignment of income strategies. The more progressive the rates, the greater the incentive to assign income to persons in lower brackets. *Be ready* for a policy question involving a change in tax rates to make them more progressive. What would be the advantages of such a change? Be aware of a potential unintended economic effect: an increase in administrative burden, as the IRS would be required to use more resources to police the inappropriate assignment of income strategies. Or, the Code could become more complex if statutory means are used to police these strategies.

☛ Does it seem that income has been earned by one person but received by another? If so, you probably have an assignment of income problem.

☛ The assignment of income doctrine applies most often to services income.

    ☞ *Look for:* One person performing services but another person receiving the compensation, in money or other property. That other person just happens to be in a lower tax bracket.

☞ *Analyze:* Compensation income is taxed to the person who performs services. Then, that person is considered to have made a gift to the person who ended up with the income. However, if state, federal, or foreign law divides the income between two people, that will usually be respected.

☛ The assignment of income doctrine also applies to income arising from property.

☞ *Look for:* Assignments of dividends, interest, rent, royalties, etc.

☞ *Analyze:* Did the assignor transfer the underlying property or just the income stream? If only the income stream, it is likely to be an impermissible assignment of income.

☛ Remember two fundamental principles:

☞ Familial transfers are subject to particular scrutiny.

☞ The substance of a transaction governs its federal income tax consequences—not its form. If a result seems too good to be true, it probably is.

Exam Tips *on* TIME VALUE OF MONEY

☛ Most law exams do not ask pure time value of money questions like Questions 171 through 174 in "Quiz Yourself" in this book. Time value of money principles are embedded in other kinds of questions.

☞ *Look for:* A taxpayer's choice between two alternative receipts, or an opportunity to defer income or accelerate deductions.

☞ *Analyze:* Discuss time value of money principles to explain why a taxpayer would choose one alternative or plan over another.

☛ In the low-interest-rate environment that exists today, time value of money strategies do not produce the valuable results that they can when interest rates are high. Some professors may choose not to focus on these issues for that reason. Pay attention, however, to how much emphasis the professor has placed on time value of money issues during the course.

☛ The statutory rules (OID, §483, §7872) are all based on making a loan transaction reflect economic reality: Interest would be charged and must be imputed if it is not stated.

☞ *Look for:* Loans, sales of property, etc., without an adequate stated interest rate.

☞ *Analyze:* Which section applies; what exactly does it impute; what are the results to the taxpayers? Analyze each side of the transaction separately.

☞ Education Savings Accounts and §529 plans are just two of many education incentives, but they are the only two available to relatively higher income taxpayers. Consider these two benefits in connection with education deductions, the HOPE credit, and the Lifelong Learning Credit.

☞ *Math anxiety?* Forget running the numbers. Discuss the theory of the time value of money and what it causes taxpayers (and Congress) to do in a particular situation.

SHORT-ANSWER QUESTIONS
AND ANSWERS

SHORT-ANSWER QUESTIONS

Note: These questions are from the "Quiz Yourself" section of the full-length *Emanuel Law Outlines: Basic Federal Income Tax.*

CHAPTER 1

GETTING STARTED IN FEDERAL INCOME TAX

1. Why would a taxpayer disclose the details of a particular return position even though not required to do so by the usual tax return reporting rules? _____

2. The IRS is assessing additional taxes, interest, and penalties against Leona. She is outraged because in her opinion, "Only the little people pay taxes!" She is further outraged because she relied on an article in *Time* magazine and followed that advice in taking one of her return positions and disclosed that on the return. After calming her down, you must explain which authorities do and do not have "precedential value." How do you do that? _____

3. Willie received a Statutory Notice of Deficiency assessing $13,000,000 in back taxes, interest, and penalties. He hasn't a cent to his name—only a guitar, a collection of records, and an old pickup truck. If Willie wants to contest this assessment, how should he do so? _____

4. Why might a taxpayer prefer to litigate in a U.S. District Court rather than the U.S. Tax Court? _____

5. What is the difference between a Revenue Ruling and a private letter ruling? _____

6. Carla was surprised to hear from her tax preparer that a position she and her tax preparer had taken for years in the past needs to be disclosed on the return, or else the preparer can't sign the return. What is motivating this change in approach? _____

7. Why would taxpayers be subject only to the "not frivolous position" standard on their own tax returns, while tax preparers are subject to a higher standard? _____

8. Your congressman proposes a new Code provision that allows a person getting a divorce to deduct $5,000 in the year the divorce is final. His rationale is that taxpayers have additional expenses in that year, and their taxable income should reflect that reality. You're his aide and his official tax guru. What do you tell him as to the advisability of this? (Disregard budget and budget process implications.) _____

CHAPTER 2

IDENTIFYING GROSS INCOME

9. Why wouldn't a tax system based on the Haig-Simons approach to measuring income be a good idea? Or would it? _____

10. What is the difference between "income" and "gross income"? _____

11. This year, Bev earned $100,000 in salary as a lawyer. She spent $40,000 on housing, $10,000 on clothing, and $5,000 on food. She spent $25,000 on other items. The rest she invested in a Certificate of Deposit (CD) earning 5%. Using the Haig-Simons definition of income, what is Bev's income? _____

12. Assume that Bev (from the previous question) liquidated the CD in the next year and invested the proceeds ($10,500) in stock in EndRun Co. During that year, the value of the stock plummeted to $1,000. What effect does this have on Bev's income in the later year, using the Haig-Simons definition of income? _____

13. Nick's grandparents pay off his student loans for him as a graduation present. Does this result in income to Nick under the economic benefit theory of income? _____

14. After graduation, Nick had identical job offers in Utah and Texas. He chooses to work in Utah rather than Texas because he loves to ski. Does Nick have income as a result of this choice? _____

15. Ken borrowed $15,000 from his credit union to buy a car. Does he have income when he receives the loan proceeds, under the economic benefit theory of income? Why or why not? _____

16. Martha is the ultimate stay-at-home mother. She raises the children and, in her spare time, she decorates the home she and her husband own, repairs their appliances if they break, creates fabulous meals on a shoestring, and gives advice on cooking, cleaning, and crafts to her many friends, neighbors, and acquaintances. What is her "income" from these activities? _____

17. Don purchased a parcel of unimproved real estate for $500,000. His plans for building an office complex on the property never matured, and several years later, he sold the parcel for $750,000. What is Don's "income" from the sale of the parcel, and why? _____

18. Donna provides legal services to Mandy in exchange for Mandy's boarding Donna's dogs while she travels. Does Donna or Mandy have income from this exchange? _____

19. Lana has saved $10,000. She purchases 100 shares of ABC stock with this money. Does she have income as a result of this transaction? _____

20. Heidi purchased an insurance policy. Her broker gave her a check to reimburse her for the first year's premium. Heidi later discovered that this was an illegal practice called "rebating." What are the tax consequences to Heidi of this event? _____

CHAPTER **3**

SPECIFIC INCLUSIONS IN GROSS INCOME

21. Diane's employer falls on hard times. Instead of giving her a paycheck, the employer gives her a used car worth $3,500. Will Diane have gross income as a result of this transaction? _____

22. Michael, a noted basketball player, realizes that he needs a plan for his retirement. He pays a $500,000 one-time premium for an annuity, which will pay him $40,000 per year for the rest of his life. At the time of the purchase, Michael's life expectancy is 20 years. When Michael receives his first year's payment of $40,000, must he include it in his gross income? _____

23. Assume Michael, from the previous question, died on January 30 of the third year in which he received a payment, i.e., he died after receiving $120,000. The terms of the annuity provided that if the annuitant died before the end of his life expectancy, the remaining amounts that would have been received, based on his life expectancy at the time the annuity began paying, would be paid to his estate or beneficiary. What are the tax consequences if $680,000 is paid to the estate or beneficiary in that year? _____

24. Cindy and Bill are getting a divorce. The divorce decree says that Cindy must pay Bill $100,000 within 30 days of the entering of the decree, $50,000 on the first anniversary of the divorce, and $25,000 on the second anniversary of the divorce, unless Bill dies during this period. They have no children. Will these payments be includable in Bill's income? _____

25. Bruce and Debi are divorced. Under the divorce decree, Bruce is obligated to pay Debi $24,000 per year for ten years. Is this alimony, under the federal definition? _____

26. Aging film star Greta's mansion in Bel Air is virtually falling apart. She leaves for a trip around the world and rents it to carpenter-turned-starving-actor Harrison for $200 per month and Harrison's agreement to spend 20 hours a week repairing it. What are the tax consequences to Greta of this arrangement? _____

27. Marc borrowed $1,000,000 from the bank. He absconded to Europe and never paid it back. The bank determined that the amount was uncollectible and wrote it off. The time period for collection expired. What are the tax consequences of this transaction to Marc? _____

28. Assume the same facts as in the previous question, except that Marc's mother is mortified at her son's behavior, and she repays the loan. What are the tax consequences of the loan and its repayment to Marc? _____

29. Frieda owed $40,000 on her credit card. She convinced the credit card company to accept a reduced amount of $25,000 in full satisfaction of the debt. What are the tax consequences of this transaction to Frieda? What if Frieda had been disputing some of the charges with the credit card company at the time of the discharge? _____

30. Rookie pitcher Greg listened to his parents' advice and purchased disability income insurance. It's a good thing he did, because in his very first major league game, he injured his shoulder and was released from the team. He receives payments from the insurance company. What is the tax treatment of these payments to Greg? _____

31. Bea was selected to win the Nobel Prize for her work in chemistry. She immediately donated the monetary prize to the Red Cross. Will she be taxed on this award? _____

32. Carlotta was a bookkeeper for ABC Corp., and she felt she was underpaid. She took matters into her own hands and embezzled $50,000 from the company before being discovered. She promises to repay the money as soon as possible. What are the tax consequences to Carlotta? _____

33. Of the following, which is *not* includable in an individual taxpayer's gross income? _____

    (a) Dividends received from corporations
    (b) Royalties received from the licensing of patents
    (c) Unemployment compensation received from the government
    (d) Interest on a loan made to a relative
    (e) Loan proceeds received from a credit union

CHAPTER **4**

SPECIFIC EXCLUSIONS FROM GROSS INCOME

34. Upon settlement of her grandfather's estate, Rikki received a pair of antique carved mongooses worth $50,000. Her grandfather had won these in a poker game in India many years before. What are the tax consequences of this receipt to Rikki? _____

35. XYZ Corp. falsely filed a criminal complaint against Brenda for passing a bad check. Before the charges were dropped and she was released, she was arrested, handcuffed, searched via pat-down, forced to undress and put on an orange jumpsuit, photographed, and confined to a holding area. Brenda sued XYZ Corp. for false imprisonment, claiming that while she did not suffer any physical injury from her arrest and detention as a result of the incident, she suffered significant emotional injuries: emotional distress, humiliation, mental anguish, and damage to her reputation. To treat these, she visited a psychologist for about eight sessions. Brenda won and was awarded damages of $100,000. May Brenda exclude the $100,000 from gross income? _____

36. DotComInc has debts of $1,000,000, property with a fair market value of about $50,000 (with a basis of zero), and a net operating loss of $400,000. Negotiating with creditors, DotComInc obtains cancellation of $700,000 worth of debt. What are the tax consequences to the company of this cancellation? _____

37. On each annual Administrative Assistant's Day, ABC Law Firm gives each member of its non-lawyer staff a gift certificate for a spa day. Is the value of the gift certificate includable in the gross incomes of the recipients? _____

38. Sheri is a flight attendant whose employer provides certain fringe benefits, including medical insurance for herself and her husband and the opportunity to fly free on a standby (seats available) basis for her and her family. What are the tax consequences of these fringe benefits to her? _____

39. Not to be outdone by ABC Law Firm in Question 37, FEG Law Firm provides to staff and lawyer associates free breakfasts and lunches, as well as a "personal concierge service," which runs personal errands for them (such as picking up dry cleaning, standing in line for tickets, etc.). The firm explains these benefits as a way to improve morale and help associates and staff balance work and home life expectations. What are the tax consequences of these benefits to the staff and associates? _____

40. Travis bought a home in Year 1. He used it as his principal residence in Year 1 and Year 2. He then decided to change his life: He abandoned his career as a tax lawyer, got his private detective's license, and moved onto a houseboat in Florida. The house sat empty for a couple of years, but he sold it in Year 5 at a gain of $75,000. What are the tax consequences of this sale to Travis? Assume all transactions occur on the first day of each year. _____

41. Bob purchased Blackacre for $200,000. A friend loaned him $180,000, secured by the residence, and he paid the rest of the purchase price in cash. Bob used Blackacre as his principal residence for several years. Real estate prices plummeted, and Bob fell on hard times. At a time when Bob was insolvent, and the outstanding principal balance of the mortgage was $140,000, Bob negotiated with his friend that he would repay only $100,000 of the loan. What are the tax consequences to Bob? _____

42. Lisa's employer provides her and her family with health insurance and also provides disability insurance for Lisa. In Years 1 through 5, the employer spent $10,000 on these premiums for Lisa. In Year 4, Lisa became very ill. She incurred $25,000 of medical expenses, of which the insurance company reimbursed her for $20,000. Eventually, she was determined to be disabled, and now she receives $2,000 per month under the disability policy. What are the tax consequences of these events to Lisa? _____

43. In Hamm and Brenda's divorce decree, Hamm was to pay Brenda the sum of $1,000 per month until their only child reached age 18, at which time the amount was to be reduced to $250 per month. Hamm has paid $1,000 per month for each of the last five years, and Brenda has not included any amount in her gross income. Is this the correct reporting position? _____

44. Of the following, which are excluded from a taxpayer's gross income?

   (a) A $2,000 prize awarded by a taxpayer's employer for "the best idea of the year"
   (b) A scholarship for tuition for one year of undergraduate education
   (c) A $300 rebate from the local utility company for purchase of an energy-efficient appliance
   (d) (a) and (b)
   (e) (b) and (c)

CHAPTER 5

DEDUCTIONS—IN GENERAL

45. Lee owns a small business, which he runs as a sole proprietorship. His view is: "What's the point of owning a business unless you can run all your expenses through it?" Therefore, he deducts all his living expenses (food, rent, vacations, etc.), in addition to his business expenses, on his Schedule C. What's wrong with that, if anything? _____

46. On his federal income tax return, Double Dip Dan deducted both the standard deduction and his itemized deduction, which exceeded the standard deduction. The IRS assessed additional tax. Why? _____

47. T. C. "Cat" Adorre is a congressman. He is considering proposing a tax code change that would benefit taxpayers who incur expenses in adopting animals from shelters. You are his aide and his official tax guru. He asks, "Would it be more beneficial for taxpayers to allow a tax deduction or a tax credit for these expenses? What's the difference, anyway?" _____

48. Jodi runs her hair salon as a sole proprietorship. This year, she invested $50,000 in new styling equipment, an upgrade to her facilities, and a car to be used for business purposes. She intends to deduct all of these costs. Is she correct? (Assume §179 does not apply.) _____

49. What is the rationale for the standard deduction? _____

50. What is the difference between adjusted gross income (AGI) and taxable income? Why do taxpayers try to minimize AGI? _____

51. Of the following, which are deductible from gross income in computing AGI, and which are deductible from AGI in computing taxable income? Medical expenses, personal exemption, standard deduction, moving expenses, retirement savings, capital losses, net personal casualty losses, charitable contributions, alimony. _____

CHAPTER 6

PERSONAL DEDUCTIONS

52. Under the terms of their divorce decree, Tom will pay Nicole $10,000 per month as alimony that qualifies under the federal definition, and $1,200 per month as child support. Assume that the alimony meets the federal definition of alimony. May Tom deduct these payments? _____

53. Dorothy has AGI (without considering the following described events) of $200,000 for last year. During the year, her home in Kansas was destroyed by a tornado. The basis of the home was $250,000, and its fair market value was $500,000. Dorothy had no insurance on the home. What are the tax consequences of this event to Dorothy? _____

54. Assume the same facts as in the previous question, except that Dorothy also received $100,000 from an insurance company attributable to the theft of a very valuable pair of shoes. She had a basis of $20,000 in the shoes. What are the tax consequences to Dorothy, considering *both* events? _____

55. Avid whale watcher Molly decides to move to Seattle. She purchases a new principal residence on the ocean there for $1,500,000. She takes out a mortgage of $1,200,000 from Friendly Bank and pays for the balance in cash. She owns no other properties. May she deduct the interest on the debt? _____

56. Sam owns a parcel of property on which he has built a new home. During construction, he lived in a dilapidated home on the property. Under applicable land use regulations, only one home suitable for occupancy may exist on this parcel. Now that the new home is ready for its occupancy permit, Sam wants to donate the older home to the local fire department (a governmental unit) for a training exercise in which the old home will be burned to the ground. By removing the old residence, the burning exercise will allow him to move into the new home. He intends to claim a deduction equal to the fair market value of the older home. May he do so? _____

57. Of the following, which is not deductible for federal income tax purposes?

    (a) Federal income taxes
    (b) State income taxes
    (c) State property taxes
    (d) State sales and use taxes
    (e) None of the above is deductible.

58. Pete's hobby is auto racing. This year, he was in a car wreck and incurred $100,000 in medical expenses. His medical insurance company reimbursed $75,000 of these expenses this year, and he paid for the balance with a $10,000 distribution from a qualifying health savings account (HSA) and the rest with savings. His AGI is $250,000. May Pete deduct any of these medical expenses? _____

59. Tom is an outside sales representative for Oldies But Goodies, Inc. (OBG). Under the terms of their agreement, OBG will reimburse Tom for up to $2,500 of travel expenses associated with his sales activities. This year, Tom incurred $30,000 of such expenses, of which $2,500 were reimbursed by OBG. He also had $500 in other qualifying miscellaneous expenses. His AGI is $140,000. How should Tom treat these expenses?
    _____

60. Janet, a single taxpayer, has a complicated household. The following people live with her. Assume that none of these individuals plan to claim an exemption for themselves on their own tax return. For whom may she be able to claim a personal exemption on her income tax return? _____

    Her daughter, age 16;

    Her son, age 23, a full-time college student who lives at college nine months of the year;

    Her stepdaughter from a prior marriage, age 18;

    Her mother, age 86, who has Social Security benefits of $1,000 per month;

Her brother, who is currently unemployed;

A foster child, age 12;

Her single niece, age 30, who is visiting the United States for an extended period from her home in Mexico; and

An unrelated boarder, who pays Janet $500 per month for room and board.

61. The parents of a dyslexic child send him to a boarding school where part of the program of the school is devoted to overcoming reading disabilities. May the parents deduct the tuition, room, and board they pay to the school as a medical expense? _____

62. Catherine is employed as a nurse by DocInaBox, Inc., an outpatient clinic. DocInaBox maintains a qualified retirement plan in which Catherine participates. Catherine would like to establish an IRA. May she do so, and if so, how much can she contribute? _____

63. Assume the same facts as in the previous question and that in the next year, Catherine could not make a deductible contribution to a regular IRA, and that she is not able to qualify for a Roth IRA. Why might she still want to make a contribution to a regular IRA, even though the contribution is not deductible? _____

64. Donald tells Maurice, "You're fired!" Maurice then incurs the following expenses: $10,000 in attorneys' fees in an unsuccessful attempt to sue his employer for breach of contract; $1,500 in job search expenses to obtain a similar position; $500 to a moving company to move his things out of his office at Donald's building; and $5,000 in psychological counseling to help him recover from this harrowing experience. Of these, which are deductible—and in what manner? What if Maurice says, "I've had it with this business! I'm only going to take a job in a completely different profession."? _____

CHAPTER 7

BUSINESS AND INVESTMENT DEDUCTIONS

65. Chris's job with Ad-Men, Inc., requires him to develop advertising campaigns for outdoor sports clothing manufacturers. Each year, Chris goes on a lengthy adventure trip, and he always takes along a few of the newest items to test and discuss with fellow travelers. He says it gives him all his ideas for ad campaigns. Chris's employer doesn't reimburse him for these trips. This year, Chris spent $20,000 on a trip to Antarctica, and he wants to deduct this expense. May he do so? _____

66. Clean Machine is a sole proprietorship operating a mobile car-detailing service. This year, the owner, Win, made a number of expenditures, as follows:

Wages to employees	$25,000
Waxes, soaps, etc.	$6,000

Licenses	$500
Parking fines	$600
Advertising	$10,000
Séance to get business advice from deceased father	$3,000
Legal fees to settle dispute with car owner	$5,000
Legal fees to quiet title to parking lot	$15,000
New van	$35,000

Which of these expenditures are deductible to Win? If not deductible, how should they be treated? _____

67. Jody purchased a rental house on July 1 of Year 1 for $55,000. She rented it for $3,000 in Year 1, and $6,000 in each of Years 2 and 3. She sold it on January 15, Year 4, for $80,000. Assuming no improvements to the home, what is her gain or loss on the sale? _____

68. Grant purchased a bagpipe store from Adam. He purchased the entire bagpipe inventory and a list of all the customers who love bagpipe music, and he obtained a promise from Adam not to engage in the retail bagpipe business for five years from the date of sale. He paid Adam $30,000 for the promise. How should Grant treat the $30,000 for tax purposes? _____

69. Kaitlin is the latest teen idol. She embarked upon a concert tour arranged by Carefree Promoters. At just the fourth event, Kaitlin fell off the stage when it suddenly broke into pieces. Kaitlin sued Carefree for negligence resulting in both physical injuries and the humiliation she suffered as a result of the fall. She ultimately settled for a $200,000 payment, which was allocated as follows in the settlement agreement: 75% to physical injuries and 25% to emotional injuries. Kaitlin has to pay her lawyer $60,000 in legal fees, and she incurred $40,000 in costs. Assume she had $50,000 of income from her teen idol career in that year. May Kaitlin deduct these costs? _____

70. Baxter is a large animal veterinarian. This year, he returned to his hometown to open a practice. He spent $50,000 on equipment, and on June 1 he hired an assistant, Penny, to whom he paid $2,500 per month. He spent $10,000 on fixing up his leased premises and another $5,000 on various miscellaneous expenses associated with opening his business. He was finally ready to open on August 1. His expenses after that date were $35,000. Which expenses are deductible, if any? How should nondeductible expenses be treated? _____

71. Under what circumstances would a taxpayer purchasing eligible property not elect to take the §179 deduction? _____

72. Lenore purchases the Wallflower Hotel on January 1, Year 1. She expects to be able to claim 12 months of depreciation for the hotel during Year 1. Is she able to do so? Why or why not? _____

73. Xavier makes a loan of $25,000 to Zena. Eventually, it becomes clear that Zena will never repay the loan. What is the proper tax treatment of the loan to Xavier if:

- Xavier is Zena's father? _____
- Xavier is Zena's employer? _____
- Xavier is in the business of making loans to individuals? _____

74. Of the following, which is *not* a capital expenditure?

   (a) Commissions paid on the purchase of stock
   (b) Purchase price of raw land
   (c) The cost of designing and implementing a website
   (d) Expenses for advertising designed to restore customer confidence after a major corporate mistake
   (e) None of the above; they are all capital expenditures

75. Wendy is a lawyer in solo practice. Well aware of how the Internet can be used to destroy reputations, Wendy hires Repu.com, a company that constantly monitors what people are saying about her on the Internet and seeks to remove damaging content. May Wendy deduct the cost of this service? _____

76. Richard is a law librarian. He decides to go to law school. He wants to deduct the costs of his education. May he do so? _____

77. After graduating from law school, Sara pays $2,000 for a bar review course, and a $500 application fee to the state bar of Missouri. May she deduct these expenses in the year she incurs them?

   (a) No, they are personal expenses.
   (b) Yes, because they are related to her trade or business of being a lawyer.
   (c) Yes, but they are subject to the 2% floor of §67.
   (d) No, but some or all of these expenses may be capitalized and amortized over Sara's lifetime.
   (e) The application fee will be deductible, but not the expenses of the bar review course.

78. Bonbon owns a rental house. She was paid rental income of $10,000. Her expenses were repairs ($1,500), property management ($3,000), and taxes ($2,500). She also spent $15,000 adding another bedroom to the home. How should Bonbon report these items? _____

79. What is the rationale for allowing depreciation or amortization deductions? _____

80. Felicia is an employee and minority shareholder in Z Corporation. When the corporation falls on bad times, she makes a $15,000 loan to the company to try to keep it afloat. When the company is unable to repay this debt, Felicia claims this as a deduction as a business bad debt. Is she correct in doing so? _____

CHAPTER **8**

MIXED BUSINESS AND PERSONAL EXPENSES

81. Marco is a state Assistant Attorney General who practices litigation. Recognizing the increasing importance of negotiation and mediation in his practice, he takes two psychology courses at the local college—PSYCH 4840 (Goals, Needs, and Desires) and PSYCH

4300 (Moral Reasoning)—and pays for the books and tuition personally (his employer does not reimburse him). May Marco deduct these expenses? What if Marco decides, after taking these courses, to earn a degree in clinical psychology? May he deduct the books and tuition for all of the required courses? _____

82. What is the rationale for the disallowance of 50% of the cost of meals as a deduction under §274(n)? _____

83. Tom is a lawyer in a highly successful private practice. He receives a letter from the IRS questioning his deductions for the following expenses on his tax return:

    - Lunches and dinners with other attorneys who refer cases to him: $2,500
    - Skybox at local basketball arena where he invites his referral sources to attend the game: $10,000
    - Potential expert witnesses: $50,000
    - Attendance at a conference on Trial Techniques at a fishing lodge in Alaska: $6,000

    What are the IRS's likely arguments with respect to these expenses, and what should Tom's response be? _____

84. Billie, a cardiovascular surgeon, is considering buying a horse farm and several horses. She's allergic to hay, but her teenage daughters are avid riders, and she currently has to pay an expensive riding academy for her daughters to ride. Billie is a city gal but longs for the country life. She understands that, at least in the first few years, farms are "losing propositions," but she thinks she can eventually turn a profit by having her daughters board and train other people's horses. In the meantime, she's looking forward to deducting the losses from the farm. You're her tax advisor. What do you tell her? _____

85. Rudy's principal residence is in New York City, but he has a second home in the Adirondacks. Each year, he spends four weeks in his second home and then rents it to vacationers for the rest of the year. In the past, Rudy has reported all of the rent received from the property in his gross income each year and has deducted 100% of the expenses, including taxes, insurance, and repairs. He also has been depreciating the property on a straight-line basis over 27.5 years. Has Rudy's reporting position been correct? Why or why not? _____

86. Susan is a clinical psychologist in Boston. She sees patients as does any psychologist, and she also acts as an expert witness in various trials. Susan owns a townhouse: The bottom floor is her office, and the top floor is her home. In her office, she sees patients, talks with lawyers in person and on the telephone, keeps records, bills insurance companies and lawyers, and does her research. She uses the office exclusively for work. May she deduct expenses associated with the home office? Why or why not? If she can deduct expenses, which ones are deductible? _____

87. Jeff spends most of his time playing poker, entering poker tournaments, and studying poker. This year, he earned $120,000 in winnings and had $300,000 in losses. Last year, the reverse was true: He had much more winnings than losses. Will Jeff be able to deduct his losses from gambling from this year? If so, how? If not, why not? _____

88. Gerry's business has two locations: manufacturing in City A and retail sales in City B. The two cities are 100 miles apart. Gerry lives in City A, and he goes to the plant there every workday. About three days a week, he travels to City B and back. He travels by car and has

traditionally deducted the travel expense using the standard mileage allowance. Gerry has decided to purchase a small airplane, as he recently earned his pilot's license. Use of the airplane would significantly reduce his travel time between City A and City B—and it would be, as Gerry says, "a lot more fun!" Plus, he says, "I can use it to fly to City C to see my grandchildren—and I can finally travel to see the Ducks play football, wherever they are!" Gerry is looking forward to a "big tax deduction" resulting from his purchase. As Gerry's new tax adviser, what is your advice to him? Will he get "the big deduction"? _____

89. Steve owns a home in Oregon, and Mike owns a home in Florida. They agree to "swap" houses for three months: Steve lives in Mike's house, and Mike lives in Steve's house, from July through September. No cash changes hands. Steve wants to deduct one-fourth (three months' worth) of repairs, utilities, depreciation, and other expenses associated with his home. Will he be successful? _____

90. Roma is a celebrity whose occupation is simply "being famous." Frankly, it's hard work. Roma is always on the go, being seen everywhere that matters, and playing cat-and-mouse with the paparazzi. Perfect strangers bombard her with so-called gifts and beg her to tout their products and services. Other jet-setters pay for her travel and meals, send her tickets to major events, and host her for month-long skiing vacations in the Alps. Roma keeps meticulous records of all of her activities and includes all of these items in her gross income (this year: $1,000,000). In addition to being hard work, fame is expensive. Left to her own devices, Roma says, she would wear ratty sweatpants and T-shirts all the time, but she is forced to wear the latest (and weirdest) fashions to maintain her image—after all, image is what makes her profession of being famous possible. This year, her clothing costs were $350,000. May Roma deduct her clothing expenses? _____

Chapter 9

TRANSACTIONS IN PROPERTY

91. As a favor to an old friend, Carolyn invested $1,000 in shares of WikiLearn, a web-based company that matches tutors with students needing help. She put the shares in a desk drawer and promptly forgot about them until yesterday, when she learned from her old friend that her shares were now worth $1,000,000. Panicked that she will owe taxes on $999,000 of income, she consults you. What is your advice? _____

92. What is the difference between "realized" gain and "recognized" gain? _____

93. Al and Sal are avid sports memorabilia collectors. Al owns a baseball signed by Mickey Mantle. Sal owns a football signed by Joe Montana. Both purchased these items years ago, and the items have appreciated in value. They trade items. What are the tax consequences to them of this trade? (Disregard any nonrecognition provisions of the Code.) _____

94. Taylor owns a collectible sports car, which she purchased many years ago for $10,000. It has appreciated significantly in value. Taylor gives it to Melique in satisfaction of a

debt she owes him. What are the tax consequences to Taylor of this payment? _____

95. What is the function of "basis"? Of "adjusted basis"? _____

96. Jessica buys Blackacre, an office building on two acres of land, for $395,000. She claims $10,000 of depreciation on Blackacre in Year 2. Is she correct? _____

97. Dick owns Bleak House, a bed-and-breakfast inn for literary types. He had an initial basis of $140,000 in this property and has claimed $40,000 of depreciation deductions over the years. He agrees to sell the property to Tom for $300,000 cash. What are the tax consequences of this sale to Dick? _____

98. Assume the same facts as in the preceding question, except that Dick has a mortgage on Bleak House in the amount of $100,000. He agrees to sell Bleak House to Jerry. Jerry will pay Dick cash of $200,000 and, in addition, Jerry will assume the debt on Bleak House. What are the tax consequences of this transaction to Dick? What is Jerry's basis in Bleak House? _____

99. Courtney purchased the Emerald Apartment Building for $1,000,000. She financed 100% of the purchase price through Very Friendly Bank, which loaned her the money on a nonrecourse basis. Over the years, she properly claimed $250,000 of MACRS deductions with respect to the property. Unfortunately, the value of the property declined and became a stone around her neck. One day she simply marched into the bank, gave them the deed to the property, and walked away. She had paid off only $50,000 of the debt, and so her mortgage balance was $950,000 at that time. The bank ultimately sold the property for $600,000. Courtney reported a $150,000 loss on this transaction on her tax return. Was she correct? _____

100. Linda purchased the Bates Motel for $500,000, the entire amount of which she financed with a recourse mortgage from a bank. Over the years, she claimed $100,000 in depreciation deductions. Some spooky things happened at the motel, and it declined in value because few visitors wanted to stay there. Linda was unable to repay the debt. Last year, when Linda had a mortgage balance of $450,000, the bank foreclosed on the property. The property was sold for $200,000, all of which was applied to Linda's loan. The bank tried to collect the remaining $250,000 but ultimately decided it was uncollectible because Linda's debts were well in excess of her assets. The bank wrote off the debt. What are the tax consequences of this transaction to Linda? _____

101. Would the result in the previous question be any different if the bank and Linda had simply agreed that she would transfer the motel to the bank in full satisfaction of the debt? _____

102. Would the result in Question 100 be any different if the property had been Linda's principal residence, not the Bates Motel? _____

103. Craig purchased a home, which he used as his principal residence, for $475,000. To purchase the home, Craig paid $75,000 in cash and borrowed $400,000 from the bank on a recourse basis. Later, the property increased in value, and the bank loaned him an additional $120,000 as a home equity line of credit (HELOC) (also recourse). The value of Craig's home has fallen to $400,000, and he still owes $500,000 to the bank ($380,000 on his original mortgage and $120,000 on the HELOC). What are the tax consequences if Craig:

(a) Negotiates a reduction in the HELOC to $20,000 and leaves the primary mortgage intact at $380,000? _____

(b) Negotiates a reduction in the primary mortgage to $280,000 and leaves the HELOC in place at $120,000? _____

104. Fred purchased an airplane, which he used for business 60% of the time and used for personal purposes 40% of the time. His original cost was $1,000,000. At the time that he sold the airplane for $500,000, he had taken $350,000 of depreciation deductions associated with it. Fred plans to report a $200,000 loss on this sale. Is he correct? _____

105. What is "tax cost" basis? Can you offer an example? _____

106. Darcy inherited a painting from her grandmother, who had purchased it for $100 from a starving artist in Paris. At her grandmother's death, the painting was worth $1,000,000. The grandmother's estate paid $350,000 of estate tax attributable to the painting. What is Darcy's basis in this painting?

(a) $100
(b) $1,000,000
(c) $1,350,000
(d) $350,100
(e) $0, because Darcy detests all Impressionist art

CHAPTER **10**

NONRECOGNITION TRANSACTIONS

107. Al and Sal are avid sports memorabilia collectors. Al owns a baseball signed by Mickey Mantle. Sal owns a football signed by Joe Montana. Both purchased these items years ago, and the items have appreciated in value. They trade items. What are the tax consequences to them of this trade? _____

108. What are the rationales for the nonrecognition sections of the Code? _____.

109. Katherine owns Blackacre, in which she has a basis of $40,000. It has a fair market value of $100,000. Spencer owns Blueacre, in which he has an adjusted basis of $30,000. It has a fair market value of $90,000. Both Blueacre and Blackacre are parcels of land held for investment by their owners. Both parties intend to hold the property received for investment. Katherine and Spencer trade their properties, and as part of the trade, Spencer transfers a sports car to Katherine. What are the tax consequences of this trade to Spencer and Katherine? _____

110. Assume the same facts as in the previous question, except that Spencer did not hold Blueacre for investment, although he intends to hold Blackacre for investment. _____

111. Assume the same facts again as in Question 109, except that Katherine and Spencer are married at the time of the transaction. What are the tax consequences to Katherine in this situation? _____

112. Jim owns Wineacre, a parcel of land on which he has unsuccessfully tried to grow grapes for years. The land has fallen in value, so now his basis is $200,000 and the fair market value of Wineacre is $150,000. Jim is giving up the wine business. A friend of his is in the squash-growing business and offers to trade Squashacre for Wineacre. Jim agrees. How should he go about this transaction from a tax point of view? _____

113. Tony owns Rome Tower and Cleo owns Egypt Tower. Both are commercial office buildings. The properties have the following characteristics:

	Tony—Rome Tower	**Cleo—Egypt Tower**
Fair market value	$300,000	$180,000
Adjusted basis	$160,000	$200,000
Mortgage	$150,000	$0

Cleo transfers Egypt Tower to Tony. Tony transfers Rome Tower to Cleo, subject to its mortgage. Tony also transfers $30,000 to Cleo as part of this transaction. Both Tony and Cleo intend to hold their new properties for investment. What are the tax consequences of this exchange to Tony and Cleo? _____

114. Let's take another look at Tony and Cleo from the previous question. Assume the following alternative facts:

	Tony—Rome Tower	**Cleo—Egypt Tower**
Fair market value	$300,000	$180,000
Adjusted basis	$160,000	$100,000
Mortgage	$180,000	$60,000

They exchange properties, each assuming the other's mortgage, with the lenders' approval. What are their tax consequences? _____

115. Harry and Sally are getting a divorce. Under the terms of their divorce decree, Sally will be deeded the marital home, which has a fair market value of $200,000 and an adjusted basis of $150,000. She will also receive stock in ABC Corporation, with a fair market value of $100,000 and an adjusted basis of $175,000. Harry will receive the rest of the assets. What are the tax consequences to Harry and Sally of these transactions? _____

116. Ivanna and Steve are getting a divorce. In the divorce decree, the marital home is given to Ivanna in her sole name, with the proviso that it must be sold within eight years and the proceeds split 50/50. In the meantime, Steve must continue to pay the mortgage, taxes, insurance, and repairs. The home is sold eight years after the divorce and the proceeds are split between Steve and Ivanna. Steve insists that he has no gross income to report on the sale transaction. Is he correct? _____

117. Don owned a commercial fishing boat in Miami in which he had an adjusted basis of $200,000. It had a fair market value of $600,000. The fishing boat was destroyed by a hurricane in December of Year 1. In January of Year 2, Don received insurance proceeds of $600,000 from the insurance company. He spent the rest of Year 2 looking for a suitable replacement. In December of Year 2, he purchased a new fishing boat for $500,000. What are the tax consequences of these events to Don? What if he decided that the commercial fishing business was an industry of the past and the new boat was designed to take tourists on deep sea fishing trips? _____

CHAPTER **11**

TIMING OF INCOME AND EXPENSES

118. Why does the U.S. income tax system use an annual accounting system? _____

119. Jerry is a talk show host on a local radio station. He produces the show himself and had income from advertising of $25,000 in each of Years 1, 2, and 3 from this activity. In Year 4, he experienced a loss of $30,000. In Year 5, the business had taxable income of $20,000. Can Jerry average these years' income to reflect his overall taxable income of $65,000? If so, how can this be done? _____

120. Sandy entered into a consulting contract for services with Rocky Corp. The contract said that Sandy was to be paid $100,000, but if its consulting services did not increase Rocky's sales of gravel and sand by 35 percent by the end of the next year, the consulting contract price would be reduced based on a formula. Sandy received $100,000 in Year 1, but she had to repay $15,000 in Year 2. How should Sandy treat the receipt of income in Year 1? _____

121. Tom is a lawyer using the calendar year and the cash method of accounting. Tom performed work in December and gave the client his bill, but the customer didn't pay until January. When will Tom properly include this payment in his gross income? _____

122. Consider Tom from the previous problem. What if Tom's client had showed up at his office on December 31 with a check, but Tom refused to let him in? _____

123. Pam, a calendar-year, cash method taxpayer, wants to claim a Year 1 deduction for the following payments. Which of the following, if any, will be deductible in Year 1?

   (a) Her check written and mailed on December 29, Year 1, for payment of state personal income taxes.
   (b) Her check written and mailed December 29, Year 1, but postdated January 1, Year 2, for a charitable contribution.
   (c) Her check written and mailed December 29, Year 1, for otherwise deductible trade or business expenses on an account for which she is aware there are insufficient funds to honor the check.
   (d) Same as (c), except that because of a levy against her account of which she had no knowledge, there are insufficient funds in the account to honor the check.

(e) Her check written December 29, Year 1, for alimony that will be due January 31, Year 2.

124. Opie is a motivational speaker who uses the calendar year and the cash method of accounting. He paid otherwise deductible expenses of $5,000 this year, by paying $2,000 by check and $3,000 by credit card. He also owed the local office supply store $4,500 as of year-end. When will Opie properly deduct these amounts?

_____

125. Oils R Us, an aromatherapy store, opened the year with $10,000 of inventory on hand. It purchased another $25,000 of products from suppliers, and its year-end accounting shows $12,000 of inventory on hand. It had gross sales of $50,000. What is its net income considering only inventory expenses? _____

126. Adam works for BigCo. On each anniversary of his commencement of employment with BigCo, Adam receives 500 shares of BigCo stock from BigCo. However, Adam cannot sell the stock, and if he leaves BigCo prior to the fifth anniversary of receiving the stock, he must forfeit all his rights to such stock. What are the tax consequences of Adam's receipt of the stock? _____

127. GoTown Recording Studios uses the calendar year and the accrual method of accounting. It engages Soundbites Corp. to provide mixing services in Year 2 for a stated amount. GoTown will pay Soundbites in two payments, one at the end of Year 1 and the second six months later in Year 2. When will GoTown properly deduct the payments to Soundbites? _____

128. Samantha owned Hideaway Hills, a ranch in California. Samantha is not a dealer in such property, and the ranch is not her personal residence. She has a basis of $300,000 in the ranch. She sold Hideaway Hills to Darin for $1,000,000. Darin will pay her $200,000 per year, plus interest at market rates, for the next five years. When will Samantha report the gain on the sale of the ranch? Is there any other income to report? _____

129. Sara paid $5,000 of state income taxes and deducted this amount on her federal tax return for Year 1. This entire amount reduced her tax. In Year 2, she received a refund of $2,000 of those state income taxes. What are the tax consequences to Sara of receipt of the refund in Year 2? _____

130. Bev, a college basketball coach, inherited an apartment building from her mother. This year, it produced a net loss for tax purposes of $40,000. Bev wants to deduct this amount on her income tax return. May she do so? _____

131. Harry purchased 100 shares of XYZ Co. from his father for $10,000. His father's basis in the shares was $60,000. What is Harry's recognized gain or loss if he later sells the shares for:

(a) $150,000
(b) $60,000
(c) $40,000
(d) $10,000
(e) $5,000

CHAPTER 12

CHARACTER OF INCOME AND LOSS

132. Your best friend is applying to be an IRS auditor. She's been studying for weeks and is very nervous about the upcoming test. She calls you and asks: "Why is it, exactly, that taxpayers seek to characterize income as ordinary and loss as capital?" Please answer her. _____

133. Wally is a sole proprietor engaged in the business of selling hand-carved duck decoys. Which of the following is *not* a capital asset in his hands: (1) his residence, (2) his supply of wood, (3) his stamp collection, (4) his antique tractor? _____

134. Laura won the lottery and is entitled to receive $100,000 a year for 25 years. She did not want to wait for her money. So, just one year after the date she won, she sold her rights to Mr. X for $1,400,000 in order to receive the cash. She claimed that the gain on sale (her lottery ticket cost $5, so her gain is $1,399,995) is capital and she is entitled to be taxed at 15% on the gain. Is she correct? _____

135. Lee sold stock in ABC Company for $10,000. He had a basis of $2,000 in the stock. He had a *capital* gain, right? If he had held the stock, he would have received dividends from ABC Company, which would be ordinary income. In fact, some people value stock by simply taking the present value of the future right to income from the stock. Under the rationale of *United States v. Maginnis,* 356 F.3d 1179 (9th Cir. 2004), why isn't Lee's gain ordinary income? _____

136. Wally (from Question 133) also owns a van in which he travels to country fairs to display his ducks. He has an adjusted basis of $35,000 in the van. He sells it for $25,000. What is the character of his loss on the sale, and how will he be taxed on it? Alternatively, what if in the same year he sold his display cabinets at a gain of $35,000? _____

137. John is a singer and songwriter. He has a collection of guitars and other musical instruments that he acquired from a famous singer many years ago. He purchased them for $50,000 and has taken $30,000 of depreciation on them. The instruments have appreciated in value, and when his wife insists he get a "real job," John sells all of them for $100,000. What are the tax consequences to him of this sale? _____

138. Why are there two rates for the 15%/0% category of net capital gain? _____

139. Michael purchased a parcel of land in Hawaii for $2,000,000. He held it for several years, while he proceeded to get the proper zoning for homes of five acres or less, and put in streets and essential services, such as water and sewer lines. He then sold the entire parcel to Gwyneth for $5,000,000. Is he entitled to capital gains treatment? Why or why not? What if, instead of selling the entire parcel, he sold ten lots to people who proceeded to build vacation homes on the property? _____

140. Tillie has decided to become an investor in real estate. She plans to purchase a couple of rental homes, fix them up, and rent them. When she retires, she plans to sell them. Tillie tells you that one reason this is a great plan is that she will be taxed at the very lowest rates on the appreciation in the homes on sale. Is she correct? _____

141. Andrea had the following transactions during the year:

(a) Sale of land held for investment and held more than one year: $5,000 loss

(b) Sale of ABC stock held for more than one year: $15,000 gain

(c) Sale of NOP stock held for less than one year: $25,000 loss

(d) Sale of stamp collection held for more than one year: $20,000 gain

Andrea is not a dealer in any of these assets. What are the tax consequences of these transactions to Andrea? _____

142. Bev is in the business of manufacturing basketballs. This year, the following events occurred with respect to equipment used in the trade or business:

- Property A was destroyed by fire. Loss = $30,000.
- Property B was sold. She recognized a gain of $45,000, of which $10,000 was §1245 recapture income.
- Property C was sold. She recognized a $15,000 loss on that sale.

What are the tax consequences of these transactions to Bev? _____

143. In the previous question, what if Bev had experienced a net $5,000 §1231 loss in the previous year? _____

144. What are the principal arguments *for* having a tax preference for capital gain income? Against? Why are there substantial restrictions on the deduction of capital losses? _____

145. Brian, strapped for cash, sells his blood plasma. He makes two claims to reduce his taxes. First, he argues that he has no income at all from the sale because he is worse off—he feels terrible for days afterward. Second, even if he has income, it is capital gain, not ordinary income. Is Brian correct? _____

146. Why do the ordering rules for applying capital losses to reduce capital gains exist? Do they make a difference in actual tax due for taxpayers? _____

Cʜᴀᴘᴛᴇʀ **13**

TAX RATES AND CREDITS

147. How does a tax credit differ from a tax deduction? How does it differ from an exclusion from gross income? _____

148. What is the rationale for the AMT? Give two examples of AMT adjustments that support this rationale. _____

149. Of the following deductions, which are treated differently for AMT and regular tax purposes in computing the tax base for these taxes?

(a) State real property taxes and alimony

(b) Charitable contributions and MACRS

(c) State income taxes and miscellaneous expenses

(d) Personal exemption and charitable contributions

(e) None of the above

150. Catherine, a single taxpayer, had the following items of income and deduction this year:

Salary income:	$97,200
Taxable interest income:	$3,000
Alimony payments:	$12,000
Interest on private activity, tax-exempt bonds:	$2,000
Home mortgage interest on condo:	$5,000
State income tax:	$9,000
Medical expenses in excess of 7.5% of adjusted gross income	$1,000
Charitable deductions:	$2,000
Miscellaneous itemized deductions in excess of 2% floor:	$3,000

Assume the following:
Personal exemption amount: $4,000
AMT exemption amount: $50,000
Tax Rates (excerpt)— if Taxable Income is:

- More than $35,000 but not over $85,000: $5,000, plus 25% of amount > $85,000
- More than $85,000, but not over $180,000: $17,000 plus 25% of amount > $180,000

Will Catherine pay AMT? Why or why not? _____

151. Catherine, from the previous example, tells you that her obligation to make alimony payments will terminate at the end of 2015. Assuming that all of Catherine's other items remain the same, and the exemption amounts also remain unchanged, will Catherine's glee in having the alimony payments terminate be dampened by having to pay AMT? _____

152. A reckless newspaper reporter wrote a story about Becky, saying that she was negligent in her duties as an employee of a child care facility. Becky sued the reporter and the newspaper for libel, and was awarded $300,000 in damages. Under Becky's agreement with her attorney, the attorney was entitled to one-third of this amount, or $100,000. What are the tax consequences of this transaction to Becky? _____

153. Candace is a single mother of two children, ages six and eight. Her AGI is $38,000. She spends $3,000 per year on child care while she works, and another $500 for their care while she travels as a volunteer for the American Cancer Society. What are the tax consequences to Candace of these expenditures? _____

154. Jordan has earned income of $10,000 and is a single father of one child, age ten. To what earned income credit, if any, is he entitled? Assume the 2012 earned income tax credit amounts. _____

155. Kara and Jim are married, filing jointly. They have three children. Their earned income is $43,000. Are they entitled to an earned income credit and if so, what is the amount of the credit? Assume the same earned income tax credit amounts as in the previous question. _____

156. In what significant way does the earned income credit, the paid-taxes credit, and, to some extent, the child credit differ from the dependent care credit? _____

157. David and Li have a child who is a sophomore in college, and they have spent $10,000 this year on tuition and other qualifying expenses. "Well," says David, "at least we're going to get a tax credit of $4,500, as well as an above-the-line deduction for $10,000." Is David correct? _____

CHAPTER **14**

IDENTIFYING THE TAXPAYER

158. What is the tax incentive for a taxpayer to assign income? If tax rates become more progressive, is there a greater or lesser incentive to engage in assignment of income strategies? _____

159. Danielle writes romantic novels. Her daughter Tiffany is 12 years old. Danielle requests that her publisher (the owner of the copyright to Danielle's works) pay all the royalties on the book to be published this year to Tiffany so that Tiffany can begin saving money for college. Her publisher does so, and reports Tiffany as the taxpayer on the required Form 1099. Is this correct? _____

160. Assuming the same facts as in the previous question, will Danielle be successful in having the royalties taxed to Tiffany if she owned the copyright and transferred it to Tiffany? _____

161. Retired lawyer Peter assists his friend, Lawyer Dan, in a case. Ultimately, Dan arranges a settlement in which his fee will be $300,000. Dan wants to split this fee with Peter, but since Peter no longer has his license, this would be unethical under the rules of the state in which Peter and Dan live. Not needing the money, Peter says to Dan, "Just make a $50,000 gift to my favorite charity, and we'll call it even." If they go forward with this plan, who will be taxed on the legal fee, and why? Is there a charitable deduction to be had, and if so, who is entitled to it? _____

162. Sam is Peter's grandfather. Peter's parents are living. Sam owns a number of bonds and regularly receives interest payments on these bonds. Sam directs the company that issued the bonds to pay Peter, rather than Sam, the interest on the bonds for two years. The company does so. Who is taxed on this interest, and why? _____

163. Assume the same facts as in the previous question, except that the bonds are tax-exempt private activity bonds. Why would it matter who is taxed on these interest payments if they are tax exempt? _____

164. Barbara is George's mother. Barbara owns a ranch in Texas. In Year 1, she transferred an undivided 50% interest in the ranch to George, as a gift. In Year 10, a buyer purchases the ranch for $2,000,000. Barbara and George each report one-half of the gain on the sale. Is this correct? _____

165. Brian files a lawsuit against Rob alleging defamation of character. Prior to trial, Brian's health starts to fail. He assigns his rights in the action to Steve for a payment of $500,000. The trial and subsequent appeals result in an award of $5,000,000. Who, if anyone, must include this amount in gross income? _____

166. Kayla sues her employer for race discrimination. She hires an attorney on a contingent fee basis to represent her. Ultimately, the court enters a judgment of $500,000 against the employer. The lawyer's share of that is $165,000 for fees and $35,000 for costs, and Kayla receives $300,000. How should she treat this transaction for tax purposes? _____

167. Assume the same facts as in the previous question, except that the action was for slander rather than discrimination. What changes, if anything? _____

168. Spencer is age 12. He has a paper route, from which he makes $3,600 per year. He also has investment income of $3,000 per year from stocks and bonds given to him by relatives over the years. Spencer's parents are living. How will Spencer be taxed on his income? _____

169. Spencer's brother, Corbin, is age 20. He is a student at the local community college and has a part-time job at a local coffee house. He has investment income of $5,000 per year. How will Corbin be taxed on this income? _____

CHAPTER 15

TIME VALUE OF MONEY

170. Why should (and do) taxpayers care about the time value of money? _____

171. What is the present value of a promise to pay you $10,000 in five years, if the appropriate interest rate is 5%? What if the interest rate were 9%? _____

172. How much would you have to invest today to have $10,000 in eight years, if interest rates held steady at 6%? At 12%? _____

173. If you had $3,000 to invest today, and interest rates held steady at 4%, how much would you have at the end of 10 years? 15 years? 30 years? _____

174. Your rich aunt gives you a choice of receiving a gift of $50,000 today or a gift of $70,000 five years from now. Interest rates are holding steady at 8%. Which should you choose, assuming you are a rational taxpayer? _____

175. Grandmother is considering making a gift to her granddaughter, who is heading for college in a few years. She could either give the granddaughter $5,000 or contribute the same amount to a 529 plan for the granddaughter's benefit. From a tax perspective *only,* which plan would be better for Grandmother to implement? _____

176. Beverly is a doctor with a large income taxed at the highest federal and state tax rates. She tells you about an interesting offer that she heard about from her broker. She has an opportunity to invest in a venture to locate and communicate with alien life forms. This has dazzling commercial potential. Start-up costs would be large, and she would have to invest $75,000, but this would result in over $300,000 of losses, which would serve as deductions to her over the next five years. She could use them to offset her salary income. Beverly consults you about this idea. What do you say? _____

177. Of the following, which one is *not* an income deferral strategy?

    (a) Investing in real estate
    (b) Use of the cash method
    (c) Categorizing payments to a former spouse as alimony rather than child support
    (d) Engaging in a like-kind exchange

178. Identify two methods the Code and/or courts and the IRS use to combat inappropriate income deferral strategies. _____

179. Ronald owned the Flying Z Ranch. Due to failing health, he sold the ranch to his good friend James for $900,000. The contract called for payment in a single lump sum in five years, with no provision for interest. Ronald's basis in the ranch was $400,000, so he simply reported $500,000 of capital gain in the fifth year when he received payment. At the time the contract was entered into, the applicable federal rate was 6%. Was Ronald's reporting position correct? What is James's basis in the ranch? _____

180. Joe's mother wants to lend Joe $10,000, interest-free. What will be the tax consequences of this loan? What if the loan were $100,000? $1,000,000? _____

181. Elmo purchases a bond from Monster Cookies, Inc., in the face amount of $15,000. In five years, it will pay him a lump sum of $21,037. Elmo thinks he doesn't have to report any income until he receives it; after all, he is a cash method taxpayer. Is Elmo correct? _____

ANSWERS TO SHORT-ANSWER QUESTIONS

1. In order to avoid the substantial understatement penalty of §6662, the taxpayer might choose to fully disclose the details of a transaction. A preparer might advise a taxpayer to disclose in order to avoid the penalties of §6694 if the preparer thought that there was only a reasonable basis for the position and not substantial authority.

2. "Precedential value" means, in the tax world, that authorities can be cited as precedent in the Tax Court and that, if they are administrative guidance, the IRS will be bound by such rulings. Court opinions, temporary and final regulations, revenue rulings, and revenue procedures all have precedential value, and all bind the IRS except for some court opinions. (The IRS is bound by the Supreme Court's opinions and appellate courts' opinions for tax controversies appealable to that circuit.) Authorities that do not have precedential value and do not bind the IRS include private letter rulings and Technical Advice Memoranda addressed to other taxpayers; Chief Counsel Advice; proposed regulations; the Internal Revenue Manual; and forms and instructions issued by the IRS. Also (need it be said?) *Time* magazine—while possibly a source of tax information—does not generate opinions with precedential value.

3. Willie has two alternatives. He can file a petition in the U.S. Tax Court, if he files within 90 days of the date of the Statutory Notice of Deficiency. If he does so, he won't have to pay the tax unless and until the Tax Court decides against him. But he might want to consider coming under the wing of the Bankruptcy Court—this will stay enforcement proceedings. There is no guarantee that the taxes will be dischargeable in bankruptcy, but he could potentially keep his guitar, truck, and maybe even a few records.

4. In a U.S. District Court, a taxpayer has the right to a jury trial, while cases in the U.S. Tax Court are tried to a judge, not a jury.

5. In both private letter rulings and Revenue Rulings, the IRS addresses the application of the tax laws to a particular set of facts. But a private letter ruling is a form of written determination by the IRS, which is addressed to a particular taxpayer in response to the taxpayer's request. It is binding only with respect to that taxpayer. It cannot be used or cited as precedent. A Revenue Ruling is a statement of the law issued by the IRS, is not addressed to any particular taxpayer, and has precedential value if a taxpayer's facts are the same as those in the Revenue Ruling.

6. The standards applicable to tax preparers have changed in recent years. A preparer must have a reasonable basis for any position taken, and if the position isn't disclosed, an even higher standard applies: the substantial authority standard (for nontax shelters or transactions that are not reportable transactions). It appears that the tax preparer is concerned that the tax return position previously taken would not pass muster under the new standards of §6694. The position was supported by a reasonable basis (or else the tax preparer could not take the position at all), but the preparer appears concerned that the higher standard might not be met.

7. Taxpayers are not expected to have the same access to or experience with the various administrative interpretations of the Code as are tax professionals, so taxpayers would not be able to evaluate whether a particular position met the "reasonable basis" or "more likely than not" standards. However, taxpayers are expected to determine if the positions they are taking are frivolous, a relatively low standard to meet.

8. In advising the congressman, you would focus on the fairness, administrative practicality, and economic effects of this provision.

Fairness: Does it treat persons similarly situated, as to their ability to pay, in a similar fashion? Doubtful. Certainly the good congressman is correct: Many people getting a divorce have extra expenses associated with the divorce, and this reduces their ability to pay. But the proposal has two faults (at least) in the fairness arena. The first problem is the reach of the statute. It is not limited to people who really have extra expenses, nor does it distinguish the year in which those expenses actually occur. Second, divorce expenses are clearly personal expenses. While some personal expenses are deductible (such as certain medical expenses and casualty losses), in all of these cases, you can be pretty sure that the taxpayer is really "out" a significant amount of money. Not so with divorces—in fact, some people (those married to compulsive shoppers, for example) may be saving money by getting a divorce.

Administrative practicality: It seems to be easy to administer, at least in its current form. The year of divorce is easy to identify, and the people getting a divorce are also easy to identify. However, one might wonder how to distinguish between real divorces and those designed to take advantage of this deduction (see below).

Economic effects: Here is where you tell your congressman that "this dog won't hunt." Not only does it appear that he is supporting divorce, he may in fact appear to be creating an economic incentive for people to get a divorce. It's a political dead end because of these effects.

9. There are two principal criticisms of the Haig-Simons approach to measuring income. First, there are practical concerns. This approach would require, for example, that a taxpayer's net change in the value of property rights be measured each year. So a taxpayer who owned real estate would have to obtain an appraisal each year or rely on some other measure of value to report gain or loss. Moreover, taxpayers would not necessarily have cash with which to pay taxes on gains that accrue without a sale or exchange (i.e., a realization event). The second criticism is theoretical. These criticisms include it being tautological (it states the obvious) and that it does not measure a taxpayer's ability to pay more accurately than other approaches.

10. "Income" is the theoretical concept of inflows to a person that could make up the tax base, and the parameters of income will differ depending on which approach one adopts. "Gross income" is the statutory term used in §61 to mean "all income, from whatever source derived." It is the beginning place for the calculation of taxable income, defining the tax base on which the income tax is levied.

11. Under the Haig-Simons definition of income, Bev's income is the sum of (1) all rights she exercised in consumption, plus (2) the change in the value of her property rights from the beginning to the end of the taxable period. Bev exercised $80,000 in consumption rights. She also had a net increase in property rights of $10,000 (the CD), plus whatever interest accrued on that amount during that year. Thus, her total income (under this theory) is $100,000, plus interest, for the year, exactly the same as what she earned.

12. Bev started with a property right worth $10,500 and ended with a property right worth $1,000. In the Haig-Simons definition of income, the net decrease in property rights ($9,500) is a reduction in her income for that year.

13. When Nick is relieved of the obligation of paying the loans, this is an economic benefit to him, and so he has income. See ELO, Chap. 4 (IV).

14. The economic benefit theory of income does not include in gross income nontangible, personal benefits. The value of Nick of being near the ski slopes does not result in income to him.

15. Even though loan proceeds flow into his checking account, Ken does not experience an economic benefit from taking out the loan because he has an offsetting obligation to repay it.

16. Imputed income is the value of the use of property one owns, or the services one performs for oneself. The value of all of Martha's activities that she performs for herself and her family (child care, decorating, cooking, etc.) constitute imputed income. Also, one-half of the rental value of her home is imputed income to her. (The other one-half is imputed to her co-owner, her husband.) The advice she gives to others is not imputed income, as it is not services she provides for herself (nor does she appear to be receiving income for this activity). However, under our system of taxation, imputed income is not included in gross income and therefore is never taxed. This avoids the difficult question of how to value these services.

17. Don's income from the sale of the real estate is $250,000, the difference between the sale price ($750,000) and his cost of the property ($500,000). Don is entitled to recover his capital investment in the property tax-free and be taxed only on the gain he experiences on the sale.

18. Both have income. This is a barter transaction, in which the value of the services exchanged will be income to both parties. It will probably be easier to value the services based on the standard fee for boarding dogs, so each will have income equal to that fee.

19. No. Lana has simply transformed money into property; she has had no increase or decrease in income under any theory. However, if she receives dividends on the stock, or if she sells the stock, that would be income to her.

20. Heidi has income in the amount of the rebate check given to her by the broker. Income from an illegal source is still "income." *Rickard v. Commissioner,* T.C. Memo 2010-159.

21. Section 61(a) provides that gross income includes all income from whatever source derived, including income from services. Income can be in the form of cash or the value of property received. Diane has gross income of $3,500, which is the value of the car she received from her employer as payment for services.

22. Michael must include some of each payment in his gross income. Section 72 determines the amount to be included. Michael must multiply each payment by the exclusion ratio, the numerator of which is his investment in the contract and the denominator of which is the expected total return of the contract. The resulting number will be the nontaxable amount (his capital recovery), and the rest he must include in gross income. The expected total return is calculated by taking Michael's life expectancy and multiplying it by the annual payment on the contract ($40,000 × 20 years = $800,000). In Michael's case, the exclusion ratio produces the following result for each payment:

First, calculate the exclusion ratio:

$$\frac{\text{Investment in the Contract}}{\text{Total Expected Return}} = \frac{\$500,000}{\$800,000} = 62.5\%$$

Then, apply the exclusion ratio to each annual payment:

$40,000 \times 62.5\% = \$25,000$

Finally, subtract the excluded amount from the total payment:

$40,000 - \$25,000 = \$15,000$

Include this amount in gross income

23. Michael's death after receiving three payments of $40,000 results in the estate or beneficiary being entitled to claim an exclusion of $425,000 of the total amount received. This is Michael's unrecovered investment in the contract at the time of his death. (Total contract cost was $500,000, and he had recovered $75,000 tax-free.) Thus, of the $680,000 received, only $255,000 is includable in the estate or beneficiary's gross income. Taking all payments into consideration, the right result is reached: The total contract cost of $500,000 is recovered tax-free (Michael claimed $75,000 and the estate/beneficiary claimed $425,000), and the $300,000 of income is reported ($45,000 by Michael and $255,000 by the estate/beneficiary).

24. These payments appear to meet the requirements of alimony: They are made in cash and are received under a divorce decree; the parties aren't living together; the payments stop if the recipient dies; and they are not disguised child support. Thus, they should be included in Bill's gross income. However, because the payments vary by more than $15,000 per year, they will be considered "front-end loaded" and be subject to the special rules of §71(f). This section requires that the amount of so-called excess alimony payments be included in the income of the payor in the third post-separation year. To determine the excess alimony payment, a rather complex calculation must be completed, as follows:

Step 1: Compute the excess payment for the second post-separation year. (§71(f)(4))

Alimony paid Y2 − (Alimony Y3 + $15,000)

$50,000 − ($25,000 + $15,000)

$50,000 − $40,000 = $10,000 + excess payment for second post-separation year

Step 2: Compute the excess payment for the first post-separation year. (§71(f)(3))

$100,000 − ($32,500 + $15,000)

$100,000 − $47,500

$52,500 = excess payment for first post-separation year

Step 3: Add the two excess payments together.

   $10,000 second year
+ 52,500 first year
   $62,500 total

The total amount is the amount that will be included in Cindy's gross income and deducted from Bill's gross income in computing adjusted gross income (AGI) in the third post-separation year.

25. It is tempting to label this as alimony: It is payable in cash, pursuant to the divorce decree, and presumably the couple are living separately. However, there is no indication that the payments will stop upon the death of the recipient. If they do not cease at that time, the payments will not be alimony. The parties will look first to the terms of the decree for guidance, and if the decree is silent, state law will apply to determine whether the payments cease or are paid to Debi's estate.

26. Greta has rental income, which she must include in gross income. §61(a)(5). But how much? Focus on the exchange: Greta is providing a home for Harrison, and thus what she receives in exchange is properly considered rental income. This would be $200 per month plus the fair market value of the services Harrison agrees to perform. The best way to measure this is to determine the fair rental value of the house, or, if that is not possible because there simply isn't a rental market for dilapidated mansions, to determine the hourly rate for carpenters.

27. Marc did not have income in the year of the loan because of the offsetting obligation to repay it. However, in the year it is forgiven (written off by the bank), he has discharge of indebtedness income in the amount of $1,000,000 (plus any accrued interest left unpaid). §61(a)(12).

28. Marc does not have discharge of indebtedness income if his mother repays the loan. This is a benefit to him, which would be income, but it would probably be considered a gift that would be excluded from his gross income.

29. Frieda has $15,000 of discharge of indebtedness income that must be included in her gross income unless she can fall within any of the exceptions of §108(b), such as the insolvency exception. If Frieda had a legitimate basis for disputing any of these charges, however, the discharge attributable to those amounts would not constitute discharge of indebtedness income under the disputed liability doctrine. Allocation of the discharge among disputed and accepted items is a question of fact.

30. It appears that Greg paid for the disability insurance premiums personally, with after-tax dollars. Therefore, the amounts received would be excluded from his gross income. If instead Greg's employer had paid the premiums, and these premiums were not included in Greg's gross income, the amounts received under the policy would be includable in Greg's gross income.

31. Bea may exclude the prize from her gross income: She didn't do anything to enter the competition, she need not perform any services, and she immediately transferred the award to charity.

32. Carlotta must include the $50,000 in her gross income. Her promise to repay the funds does not affect this result. In fact, it is very unlikely that any embezzler will be able to meet the four requirements of *James v. United States,* 366 U.S. 213 (1961). Further, income from an illegal source is still "income." *Rickard v. Commissioner,* T.C. Memo 2010-159.

33. The correct answer is (e). The receipt of loan proceeds is not income because of the offsetting obligation to repay the debt. All of the other types of income listed are included in gross income.

34. Section 102(a) excludes from gross income bequests and inheritances. Rikki can exclude from her gross income the value of the carvings. (Her basis in the carvings will be their fair market value as of the date of her grandfather's death. See ELO, Chap. 9; CT, p. 81.)

35. Brenda may exclude the amounts paid for the visits to the psychologist, but the rest of the award must be included in her gross income. The injury was not physical in nature: all of her claims were for emotional distress. In order to exclude an award for damages for personal injury, there must be a direct causal connection between a physical injury and the resulting damages. See *Stadnyk v. Commissioner*, 367 Fed. Appx. 586 (6th Cir. 2010).

36. The adjustment in the amount of its indebtedness results in $700,000 of discharge of indebtedness income to DotComInc. However, because it is insolvent (liabilities exceed assets), it may exclude the discharged amount from gross income under §108(a), up to the amount of insolvency (which, in this case, is greater than the discharged amount). However, it must reduce its net operating loss to zero as a result of this discharge.

37. Under §102(c), any amount paid by an employer to an employee is not considered a gift. Therefore, the face value of the gift certificate cannot be excluded from gross income as a gift. It also does not qualify for exclusion as a de minimis fringe benefit because gift certificates are treated as cash equivalents, and cash equivalents can never be de minimis fringes. Therefore, the value of the gift certificates must be included in the staff members' gross incomes.

38. Sheri may exclude from gross income the medical insurance premiums paid by her employer for her and her family (§106) and may exclude as a no-additional-cost fringe benefit (§132) the value of standby flights.

39. If the meals are provided for the convenience of the employer, the value of the meals is excluded from gross income. In this case, the employer's explanation does not support a "convenience of the employer" argument in the usual sense, and no facts suggest that the associates and staff are "on call" during these meal times, as in the *Benaglia*, 36 B.T.A. 838 (1937), acq. 1940-1 C.B. 1. case. The concierge service will be included in the gross incomes of the associates and staff who use the service, and the amount included (unless the use is de minimis) will be the fair market value of such services (presumably valued by reference to the cost of such services in the market).

40. Section 121 requires the taxpayer to own and use the home as a principal residence for at least two of the past five years in order to exclude the gain on sale from gross income. Travis's use of the home qualifies, and therefore, he may exclude the $75,000 of gain from his gross income. (This assumes that he has not used the exclusion during the past two years.)

41. Bob has discharge of indebtedness income of $40,000. However, because the discharge relates to principal residence indebtedness—Bob's mortgage was to acquire his home— §108(a)(1)(E) applies to exclude this discharge of indebtedness income from Bob's gross income. However, he must reduce the basis of the home by $40,000. A related question, which would change the result, is whether Bob's friend intended the discharge as a gift; if so, the discharge would be excluded under §102.

42. Lisa may exclude the value of her employer's provision of insurance (both health and disability) from her gross income. §106. She also may exclude the $25,000 of insurance reimbursements because they were for medical expenses. §105(b). (The excess $5,000 not reimbursed by the insurance company may be deductible under §213. See ELO, Chap. 6 (VIII); CT, p. 74.) The disability payments she receives will be included in her gross income because her employer paid the premiums, which were not included in Lisa's gross income. §105(b).

43. The payments from Hamm to Brenda should have been bifurcated into alimony ($250/month) and child support ($750/month). The latter is child support because it is tied to the child reaching age 18. Assuming the other requirements for alimony are met, the amount allocable to alimony should have been included in Brenda's gross income. The amount that is child support is excluded from her gross income.

44. The correct answer is (e). Section 117 provides an exclusion for the scholarship, and §136 excludes the subsidy from the local utility. Although some employee achievement awards are excluded from gross income, this amount of a cash award exceeds the limits of §274(j).

45. Section 262 disallows a deduction for all "personal, living, and family expenses" unless they are deductible under a specific statute. Most of Lee's living expenses (food, rent, etc.) will not be the subject of any statute allowing deduction. In any event, personal expenses (if deductible) would not be deductible on Lee's Schedule C as part of his business expenses, but elsewhere on his return (Schedule A). They also would be subject to all of the restrictions associated with these deductions. Incidentally, this is the kind of unreasonable return position that could result in penalties, even fraud charges, against Lee. See ELO, Chap. 1.

46. Dan is entitled to deduct either the standard deduction or the itemized deduction, but not both. In his case, because his itemized deduction is greater than the standard deduction, he should have deducted only the itemized deduction.

47. A deduction is a subtraction from income in computing taxable income, and its benefit to a taxpayer is equal to the taxpayer's tax rate multiplied by the amount of the deduction. A tax credit is a dollar-for-dollar reduction in a taxpayer's tax liability. Neither is absolutely "better" than the other, but a deduction does benefit higher-income taxpayers (who are in a higher tax bracket) proportionately more than lower-income taxpayers. By contrast, a tax credit generates the same dollar benefit for all taxpayers who are entitled to it.

48. Jodi's purchase of equipment is a capital expenditure, not a deductible expense. Therefore, she cannot deduct it in the year of acquisition, but instead must recover the cost over time, through MACRS deductions, although §179 may apply to accelerate these deductions. See ELO, Chap. 7; CT, pp. 76–77.

49. In theory, the standard deduction, when combined with the personal exemption, creates a floor of income that will not be taxed because the taxpayer has no ability to pay (to contribute to the national tax obligation) until his or her income rises above that amount. Claiming the standard deduction is substantially simpler than claiming the itemized deduction, so it contributes to the goal of a straightforward, easily administered tax system.

50. Adjusted gross income (AGI) is the amount computed by subtracting certain items from gross income. Tax is not imposed on AGI, but instead on taxable income, which is the amount computed by subtracting certain items from AGI. Because AGI serves as a measurement for many other tax computations, such as phaseouts for certain tax benefits (e.g., personal casualty losses or medical expenses; see ELO, Chap. 6; CT, pp. 73–74), reducing AGI tends to increase the likelihood that a taxpayer will benefit from these other reductions.

51. *Deductible in computing AGI:* Moving expenses, retirement savings, capital losses, and alimony. *Deductible in computing taxable income:* personal exemption, standard deduction, personal casualty losses, charitable contributions, medical expenses, and net personal casualty losses.

52. Section 215 allows Tom a deduction for alimony paid during the taxable year; this is a deduction from gross income in computing AGI. The child support is not deductible.

53. Dorothy's loss on her home is a personal casualty loss, in the amount of $250,000 (the lower of basis or value). Personal casualty losses are deductible, subject to two limitations. First, in computing the deduction, each loss is reduced by $100. Second, personal casualty losses are deductible only to the extent they exceed 10% of AGI. Dorothy's AGI is $200,000, so the personal casualty loss of $249,900 is deductible to the extent it exceeds $20,000. Thus, her personal casualty loss is $229,900. This is a deduction on Dorothy's itemized return, i.e., available to her only if she itemizes, and therefore as a deduction from AGI in computing taxable income.

54. The theft of the shoes and receipt of the insurance proceeds is a constructive sale of that item, so Dorothy realizes $80,000 of gain on that transaction. This is a personal casualty gain. Personal casualty gains offset personal casualty losses, so that the net result is the net personal casualty gain (income) or the net personal casualty loss (deduction). The net loss is $249,900 minus $80,000, or $169,900. To the extent this exceeds $20,000 (10% of Dorothy's AGI), it is deductible. Thus, $149,900 is deductible on Dorothy's itemized return, i.e., available to her only if she itemizes, and therefore as a deduction from AGI in computing taxable income.

55. Assuming that the property secures the debt, the interest on the acquisition indebtedness, up to $1,000,000 of debt, is deductible. Molly also may deduct the interest on an additional amount of debt ($100,000) as home equity indebtedness. The remaining interest will be nondeductible.

56. Sam is attempting to take a charitable deduction under §170. Normally, a deduction for the fair market value of the property would be available to him (and it would be his burden to prove the value by appraisal). However, in this case, Sam appears to be receiving something of value. Without the burn, he would be in violation of the land use laws and would have to remove the older home in some way to make way for the new home. By donating the home, he avoids this cost and places his property in compliance with local law. Although this is a close case, Sam probably is not entitled to a deduction for this donation. However, if Sam could show that the costs of removal were nominal, he may be able to claim a deduction for the property donation.

57. The answer is (a)—federal income taxes. State income and property taxes are deductible, and a taxpayer may, until 2012, choose to deduct sales taxes in lieu of income taxes.

58. The amount Pete received as reimbursement for medical expenses is not included in his gross income (see ELO, Chap. 3; CT). The $10,000 distribution from the HSA is not includable in his gross income. The remaining $15,000 is deductible as an itemized deduction as medical expenses to the extent it exceeds 7.5% of his AGI. This limit—7.5% of AGI—is $18,750, and because his remaining expenses are less than that amount, Pete may not deduct any amount as medical expenses as an itemized deduction.

59. The amounts Tom received as reimbursements of travel expenses are not included in his gross income. The excess amount ($27,500) is potentially deductible on his return. However, unreimbursed employee business expenses are deductible by the taxpayer only to the extent that they—along with all other expenses in this category of miscellaneous expenses—exceed 2% of the taxpayer's AGI. This amount is $2,800 ($140,000 × 2%).

Thus, combining the $500 of miscellaneous expenses and $27,500 of unreimbursed expenses produces $28,000 of expenses. These are deductible only to the extent that they exceed $2,800. Therefore, $25,200 of these expenses is deductible. This is a deduction on Tom's itemized return, i.e., available to him only if he itemizes, and therefore as a deduction from AGI in computing taxable income. (These deductions might be limited in computing Tom's AMT; see ELO, Chap. 13; CT, pp. 93–94.)

60. In order to claim a personal exemption for any of these people, they must qualify as Janet's "dependent," which requires that they either be a "qualifying child" or a "qualifying relative."

Janet may claim an exemption for her daughter as a "qualifying child," assuming that the daughter lives with Janet for at least half the year and Janet provides over half of her daughter's support. The stepdaughter will likely not qualify because Janet no longer is married to the stepdaughter's father. None of the others qualify as a "qualifying child" because of the residence test (the son) and the relationships test (everyone else).

The foster child and the boarder are not "qualifying relatives" because of the lack of formal family relationship to Janet. However, her son, brother, mother, and even her niece may qualify, assuming that their gross incomes are less than the exemption amount ($3,800 each in 2012) and that Janet provides over half of their support. Although it would appear that Janet's mother's income is greater than the exemption amount, only a certain amount of her Social Security benefits will be included in gross income, and it is not clear how much that would be; further investigation is necessary. Even though Janet's niece may be a nonresident alien, she is domiciled in Mexico, and therefore she could be a qualifying relative.

61. Usually, the cost of tuition, room, and board would be a nondeductible personal expense, even if part of the program involves treating a medical disorder. This is because the taxpayer is purchasing education, not medical care. See *Barnes v. Commissioner,* T.C. Memo 1978-339. If, however, the taxpayer can show that a portion of the fees paid are directly connected to remediation of the child's condition and would not be paid but for that condition, this portion would qualify as a medical expense.

62. Catherine may establish either a Roth IRA or a traditional IRA. She may contribute an amount to it that is established by Congress and the IRS each year. (For example, in 2012, she may contribute up to $5,000 to it unless she is age 50 or older, in which case her contribution could increase to $6,000.) If Catherine establishes a regular IRA, she may be able to deduct contributions to it. However, because she participates in her employer's qualified retirement plan, if her AGI exceeds a certain threshold, her deduction will be reduced or eliminated. Most taxpayers seem to prefer to establish and contribute to a Roth IRA because even though there is no current deduction, distributions from the Roth IRA, unlike a traditional IRA, are not includible in the taxpayer's gross income upon withdrawal.

63. If Catherine contributes to a regular IRA, the contribution will grow tax-free until it is distributed to her after retirement. Distributions from the regular IRA will be included in her gross income, but she may believe that the combination of tax-free growth in the IRA and her anticipated lower tax rate in retirement still makes the regular IRA a good deal.

64. Maurice may deduct (but only if he "itemizes"—i.e., claims the itemized deduction) the following: $10,000 of legal fees, $1,500 in job search expenses, and probably the $500 in moving costs to remove his items from Donald's office. All of these will be miscellaneous itemized deductions subject to the 2% floor. The $5,000 in counseling will be a medical expense, which will be deductible as an itemized deduction to the extent it exceeds 7.5% of Maurice's AGI. Maurice's job search expenses will be deductible only if he is looking for a position in his current occupation. Expenses for looking for a position "in a completely different profession" will be capital in nature and nondeductible.

65. Section 162 allows a deduction for all of the ordinary and necessary expenses of carrying on a trade or business. Are Chris's travel expenses "ordinary and necessary"? While it may be ordinary and necessary to test products and discuss them with consumers in order to develop advertising, this kind of expenditure probably would be viewed as personal (a vacation) rather than sufficiently related to business. A court would likely invoke the ordinary and necessary standard to deny the deduction. See *Brown v. Commissioner*, 446 F.2d 926 (8th Cir. 1971). (Even if these expenses were deductible, they would be miscellaneous itemized deductions, subject to the 2% floor of §67, and nondeductible for AMT purposes.)

66. Section 162 allows a deduction for all of the ordinary and necessary expenses of carrying on a trade or business. Win's expenses for wages to employees, waxes, soaps, etc., and advertising would certainly fit within this category. The legal fees incurred in the dispute with a car owner would also qualify; even though they might be unique in Win's experience, legal fees are of the usual type of expenses incurred by businesspeople and therefore are considered "ordinary." Similarly, license fees are usually deductible, although there may be some question of when these are deductible. (We don't know Win's method of accounting.) Parking fines are not deductible because §162(f) prohibits a deduction for fines or illegal payments. The fees for the séance are almost certainly not deductible; although courts generally don't substitute their judgment for those of businesspeople, in this case, the expenditure would probably not be considered "ordinary" or "necessary." The legal fees to settle the dispute about title to the parking lot are properly capitalized; they are not deductible, but instead become part of the basis in the asset (fee title or lease). Similarly, the van is a capital asset that must be capitalized. However, a portion of the expense may be deducted under §179, which allows up to $500,000 (in 2012) to be deducted instead of capitalized.

67. Jody's basis in the rental home must be adjusted downward to account for MACRS deductions allocable to it. Residential real property is depreciable under MACRS on a straight-line basis over 27.5 years. Therefore Jody's annual depreciation deduction is $2,000 ($167 monthly). She is entitled to the following depreciation (MACRS) deductions:

Year 1	5½ months	$918*
Year 2	12 months	$2,000
Year 3	12 months	$2,000
Year 4	½ month	$83
Total		**$5,001**

*Jody is subject to the mid-month convention, in which a purchase of real property is deemed to have occurred on the fifteenth day of the month of purchase, regardless of the actual day of purchase.

As a result, her basis is $49,999 ($55,000 cost basis − $5,501), and the gain on sale is $30,001 ($80,000 sale price − $49,999 adjusted basis).

68. The promise from Adam is a "covenant not to compete," one of the so-called §197 intangibles that must be amortized over 15 years—regardless of the actual term of the promise. Therefore, Grant will take a deduction of $2,000 per year for 15 years attributable to the covenant.

69. Kaitlin is in the trade or business of being a teen idol. The lawsuit arises from that business, and the expenses of it are deductible as ordinary and necessary business expenses, but only to the extent that they are attributable to income that would be included in gross income. Because the settlement agreement allocates the damages between physical injuries (payment for which would be excluded from Kaitlin's gross income) and emotional damages (payment for which would be included in her gross income), Kaitlin will have to divide her legal fees and expenses accordingly. On her Schedule C for this trade or business, 75% will be nondeductible for her physical injuries and 25% will be deductible resulting from her emotional injuries.

70. The amount that Baxter paid for equipment is a capital expenditure that, except for amounts properly deductible under §179, must be capitalized and depreciated under MACRS. Of his $10,000 of pre-opening expenses ($5,000 to his assistant and $5,000 of miscellaneous expenses), only $5,000 is deductible in the year of opening. The rest is amortizable over 15 years. The expenses incurred after opening are deductible, assuming that they otherwise meet the requirements of being ordinary and necessary.

71. Section 179 allows a taxpayer to elect to claim a deduction for the cost of certain tangible personal property placed in service in the taxpayer's business during a taxable year. However, there are limitations on the election that may cause some taxpayers not to make the election for otherwise qualifying property. First, there is an overall annual limit on the amount of property for which the election has been made, and a taxpayer exceeding that limit would obviously not qualify for the election. Second, the deduction can be claimed only to the extent of the taxpayer's taxable income (not counting this deduction), so a taxpayer that did not have taxable income would not make the election. Finally, a taxpayer can carry forward the election for property that is subject to the election in a year in which the income limitation applies, so a taxpayer with sufficient carryforward would not make the election for property purchased in that year.

72. When a taxpayer acquires real property, he or she is deemed to have acquired it on the midpoint of the month it is acquired, regardless of the day on which it is actually acquired. The function of these conventions is to simplify MACRS calculations. Therefore, Lenore will be able to claim 11½ months of depreciation for Year 1, not a full 12 months.

73. Xavier would like to take a deduction for the bad debt. Ideally, he would like the debt to be a business bad debt because that leads to an ordinary deduction rather than a capital loss.

- If Xavier is Zena's father, the first question is whether there is a debt at all or, if there were a debt, whether the "badness" of it is really the father making a gift to the daughter. If the debt is bona fide, and it really is a bad debt, it would be a nonbusiness bad debt, as it is family oriented, not related to the business (absent other facts).
- If Xavier is Zena's employer, there is a possibility that this could be considered a business bad debt if Xavier's primary motivation in making the loan was to further the business. If his primary motivation was to be a "nice guy," the debt is a nonbusiness bad debt.
- If Xavier is in the business of making loans, the debt is a business bad debt.

The distinction between a business and a nonbusiness bad debt is important because business bad debts are deductible from gross income in computing AGI, while a nonbusiness bad debt is deductible only as a short-term capital loss. (See ELO, Chap. 12).

74. The best answer is (e), all of the above. A capital expenditure is an expenditure that creates a separate asset, or that creates a benefit expected to last beyond the taxable year. Each of the expenditures creates an asset or has a benefit beyond the close of the taxable year. However, (d) is a second-best answer because the IRS takes the position that these expenses are deductible, despite the fact that under *Indopco, Inc. v. Commissioner*, 503 U.S. 79 (1992), advertising in general, and this kind of advertising in particular, could easily be expected to generate benefits beyond the taxable year.

75. Wendy may probably deduct this expenditure as an ordinary and necessary business expense under §162. Although *Welch v. Helvering*, 290 U.S. 111 (1933), is often cited for the proposition that payments to restore reputation are capital expenditures, Wendy's situation is distinguishable. Her payments are not to restore a ruined reputation but are instead to maintain her good reputation. She would argue that her payments are similar to having a roofing company periodically check and repair damage to a roof, or having a painting company repair dings and scratches in the paint on her building. She would rely on *Jenkins v. Commissioner,* T.C. Memo 1983-667, where Conway Twitty's payments to investors to restore a somewhat tarnished reputation were deductible, as support for her position.

76. If Richard's job required him to earn a law degree, he would be able to deduct the costs of his law school education. However, if his employer did not require it, the cost would not be deductible because it would qualify him for a new profession. In the latter case, Richard's argument that his information would help him better carry out his current duties would probably fall on deaf Tax Court ears. See *Galligan v. Commissioner*, T.C. Memo 2002-150.

77. Of five less-than-perfect answers, the best answer is (d). Sara cannot deduct these expenses because they are properly capitalized. However, because the application fee qualifies her to join a bar, in theory it is amortizable over some period, perhaps her expected years of practice as a lawyer. See *Sharon v. Commissioner*, 66 T.C. 515 (1976), aff'd, 591 F.2d 1273 (9th Cir. 1978), cert. denied, 442 U.S. 941 (1979) (costs of admission to bar amortizable over lifetime of attorney).

78. Bonbon must report the rental income as part of her gross income but may deduct the expenditures for repairs, property management, and taxes as ordinary and necessary expenses of the production of income under §212. Thus, her net income, not considering MACRS deductions, will be $3,000. She will not be able to deduct the costs of the addition, as this is a capital expenditure because it creates a benefit that is expected to last beyond the taxable year. She will be able to claim MACRS deductions of some amount for the home and the addition, but these cannot be determined from the facts given.

79. Depreciation is allowed for capital assets, i.e., those that will last more than one year. To allow a deduction in the year of acquisition would result in a mismatch of income and the costs of producing the income over time—accelerating the deductions while the income would be reported over a number of years. Depreciation deductions match the "using up" of the asset to the income it produces over time. However, the schedule for depreciation (or amortization, for that matter) does not necessarily match up with the actual fall in value of the asset (if any); it is an approximation at best.

80. This will be the proper reporting position for the transaction if her dominant motive in making the loan was to protect her employment relationship. If the motive was to protect her stock value, the debt will be a nonbusiness bad debt. However, even if it is a business debt—and the business is the employment relationship—it would be deductible as an employee business expense and therefore subject to the 2% floor of §67. See *Graves v. Commissioner*, T.C. Memo 2004-140, 220 Fed. Appx. 601 (9th Cir. 2007).

81. Educational expenses are deductible if they either (1) maintain or improve skills required by the individual in his employment or other trade or business, or (2) allow the taxpayer to meet the express requirements of the taxpayer's employer or applicable law or regulations as a condition of retention in a job or occupation. Treas. Reg. §1.162-5. In Marco's case, the two initial courses would likely be deductible, as they would help him improve skills required in his trade or business of being employed as a litigation attorney. However, Treas. Reg. §1.162-5 also disallows educational expenses that prepare a person for a new trade or business, so Marco's courses toward a degree in clinical psychology would not likely be deductible in full, although some courses would likely qualify as related to his current trade or business.

82. Some portion of every meal is a personal expenditure; after all, everyone has to eat. If sufficiently connected to a taxpayer's trade or business, a portion of a meal expense might not have been incurred but for a business purpose. (Consider a person who would normally eat a peanut-butter-and-jelly-sandwich at her desk, but who takes a client out to lunch instead.) It would be impossible to determine what portion of a meal is personal and what portion is related to business in every case, so the 50% disallowance is an administratively feasible estimate.

83. The IRS will likely object to all of these deductions as personal expenditures that are not deductible under §262. First, with respect to the skybox, the IRS may have an early win. It is clear that only the cost of tickets (at face value) is deductible. §274(l)(2). If the skybox has 12 seats, Tom may be able to preserve the deduction for the cost of 12 tickets (at face value), if certain tests are met, but he will certainly not receive the additional amount attributable to the cost of the skybox itself.

Meal and entertainment expenses must run a gauntlet of requirements in order to be deductible. First, they must be "ordinary and necessary business expenses" as determined under §162. In this case, these are obviously ordinary expenses, as they are frequently incurred by business owners. They are of the type most business owners view as appropriate to their ability to obtain and retain business, and thus are "necessary." Tom is clearly carrying on a trade or business so there is no problem with pre-opening capitalization, and meal and entertainment expenses do not create a specific benefit beyond the close of the taxable year, so they should not be capitalized under principles of *Indopco*.

Section 274, however, will impose additional requirements. First, with respect to meals, these must not be lavish or extravagant. Lavishness or extravagance depends on the facts and circumstances of the situation. Second, for the meals and tickets, the requirement of §274 that may create the most problems is the "business connection" test. Tom may be able to meet the "directly related" test with respect to meals more easily than with respect to the sporting events because sporting events provide the kind of significant distraction that would preclude the event being directly related to his trade or business. However, Tom may be able to meet the less stringent "associated with" standard, and if so, he will be able to preserve the deduction for meals and/or entertainment. However, even if Tom can meet either business connection test, the amounts expended will still be subject to the 50% limit: Only 50% of the amount expended will be deductible. §274(n). It is not clear from the facts whether the amounts deducted are the full costs or represent 50% of the amounts expended.

As to the conference expenses, the costs of professional conferences are typically an ordinary and necessary business expense, but Tom will have to show that the travel and other costs incurred while away from home were incurred "primarily for business" in order to support this deduction.

84. Billie should be aware that the IRS may well challenge the deduction of losses from the horse farm as "hobby losses" under §183 of the Code. This provision denies a deduction for expenses in excess of income for activities not undertaken "for profit." Whether an activity is engaged in for profit depends on the taxpayer's intention, as evidenced by the nine factors outlined in the regulations. No one factor is determinative. However, a number of factors may work against Billie, including:

- *Time and energy spent on the activity:* As a surgeon, Billie probably has limited time to devote to the business. Relying on teenagers to handle the business is probably not a sound business plan in the long run. She would need to engage a manager to handle the farm business.
- *Similar success:* Billie apparently has no experience in these matters.
- *Financial situation:* Billie has substantial income from other sources and doesn't need income from the farm to support her family. In fact, she could be expected to seek tax benefits from this activity.
- *Personal enjoyment:* Billie "longs for the country life." She seems to want to support her daughters' wish to ride horses, which would suggest a personal, not profit, motive. On the other hand, she is allergic to hay, which would suggest little pleasure in a horse farm.

If Billie is to make the best possible case for deducting any loss, she should ensure that she takes a businesslike approach to this endeavor, researching best practices and getting the professional help she needs to run the operation. She should be able to show that the farm will increase in value and that these operations can and do produce profits, even if her particular farm does not. It would be helpful to not have many years of losses in a row.

85. Rudy has been reporting the results of the summer home incorrectly. He is correct in including all of the income from the rental of the property. However, because the property is used partially for personal purposes, the expenses must be allocated between personal and business use. The deductible expenses attributable to the rental (other than expenses deductible without regard to the rental) cannot exceed the total expenses (other than expenses deductible without regard to the rental) multiplied by the percentage of the year the home is rented. While Rudy will be able to deduct all of the property taxes, because these taxes are deductible regardless of rental activity, the rest of the expense will be limited.

86. Susan would like to deduct the expenses of her home office, and it appears that she can do so. She uses the home office exclusively, on a regular basis, as the principal place of business for her practice. A home office qualifies as a taxpayer's principal place of business if (1) the taxpayer uses the office to conduct administrative or management activities of the taxpayer's trade or business, and (2) there is no other fixed location of the trade or business

where the taxpayer conducts substantial administrative or managerial functions of the business. This would appear to be the case for Susan: Although she travels to trials, her administrative work is done at the home office and there is no other *fixed* place of business for her practice. As to which expenses are deductible, Susan can already deduct (regardless of the home office) the interest on her mortgage and her property taxes on the property. But because it is a home office, she may also deduct repairs made to that portion of the property and, perhaps most important, she can depreciate that portion of the dwelling. Of course, when she sells the home, she will not be entitled to the exclusion of §121 on the gain from the sale of a principal residence for the portion used as a home office and depreciated.

87. The fact that Jeff spends most of his time playing poker, studying poker, and entering tournaments suggests that he is a professional gambler. If so, he may deduct the poker losses for the year against the poker winnings for the year. He would report the winnings and losses on a Schedule C. However, the net loss for the year would not offset other income, nor may it be carried back to the profitable prior year. If Jeff is not a professional gambler, he may still deduct the poker losses, but again the loss would be limited to the poker winnings. In that case, Jeff would include his winnings as gross income and would deduct the gambling loss as an itemized deduction.

88. As Gerry's new tax adviser, the first question for you to analyze is whether Gerry's travel from City A to City B is commuting (nondeductible) or business travel away from home (deductible). Even though he seems to have deducted the cost of this travel for years, it is always worthwhile to confirm the accuracy of this reporting position, especially when the client is considering a major change such as purchase of the plane. Gerry's travel is first to his business location in City A, and then to City B. His travel to City B qualifies as business travel, not commuting. If Gerry's only location were in City B, then his travel would be considered as commuting.

When Gerry purchases the airplane, he is expecting that he will be able to either claim the §179 expense for the entire cost of the plane, or to depreciate it using an accelerated method of depreciation under MACRS. However, the airplane is "listed property," which means that it is of the class of assets about which Congress was especially concerned in terms of use for personal purposes rather than business purposes. In order to depreciate listed property using an accelerated method or to claim a §179 deduction, the property must be used at least 51% in business. If the property doesn't meet this standard, it can only be depreciated using the straight-line method and no §179 deduction is allowable. In Gerry's case, it is not clear from the facts whether he intends to use the airplane primarily for business (travel between Cities A and B), or whether his primary use will be personal (travel to see his grandchildren and to see his favorite college football team play). As his tax adviser, you will need to explain that the use of the airplane in terms of hours will determine its initial treatment, and then even if it qualifies, if later its business use falls below 51%, Gerry will be forced to recapture the prior deductions.

89. To answer this question fully, you may want to review the materials on barter, ELO, Chap. 2 (III); CT, p. 63. Steve and Mike have "bartered" their homes, i.e., traded in-kind use of the homes. Steve and Mike would be required to include in gross income an amount equal to the fair market value of the rental. If they did so, then each would be able to deduct expenses associated with that rental, subject to the limitations of §280A. Without including this amount in gross income, it is not possible to take the corresponding deduction.

90. Probably not. According to the IRS, the cost of clothing is deductible only if it is not suitable for general use. Although the fashions that Roma purchases would likely not be suitable for general use for the average working person, she certainly wears them in her everyday life, and they probably appear in fashion magazines as suitable for a certain group of society. Roma's argument that, left to her own devices, she would wear ratty sweatpants and T-shirts is not likely to be successful, as the courts employ an objective test for suitability for general use, not a subjective test of what a taxpayer would do "but for" the requirements of her job.

91. You can tell Carolyn to relax. Although her shares have gone up in value, she has not "realized" any gain because there has been no transaction that qualifies as a realization event. If she sells or trades the shares, she will realize and recognize income at that time.

92. In a transaction involving a sale or other disposition of property, realized gain is the difference between the amount realized and the taxpayer's adjusted basis in the property transferred. Recognized gain is the amount of gain that the taxpayer must include in gross income as a result of that transaction. The two numbers might not be the same.

93. This trade is a realization event to both Al and Sal. What they received was different, qualitatively, than what they had before; they have different legal rights after the trade, and therefore, this qualifies as a sale or exchange. Each has realized gain in the amount of the difference between the fair market value of what was received and the basis of what was transferred. That gain will be recognized unless they can find a nonrecognition statute that applies. (See ELO, Chap. 10; CT, p. 172.)

94. Taylor has used appreciated property to satisfy a debt, and she will be treated as if she had sold the sports car and paid the debt with cash. Therefore, she will realize and must recognize gain on that transaction equal to the difference between the fair market value of the sports car and its adjusted basis. The amount of the debt may be easier to determine than the value of the sports car, so that amount will be the amount realized.

95. Basis represents the initial economic investment a taxpayer has in an item of property (or his or her deemed investment, as in the case of property received from a decedent or by gift). §1012. Adjusted basis reflects the initial basis, plus and minus, respectively, improvements made to the property after acquisition and the capital recovery claimed with respect to the property. In both cases, basis or adjusted basis is the starting point for measuring the capital recovery deductions a taxpayer may claim and is the way of measuring gain or loss on ultimate disposition of the property.

96. It appears that Jessica has simply divided the purchase price by the recovery period (39.5 years) for this kind of property to produce the first year's MACRS deduction. There are two problems with this approach. First, Jessica must allocate a portion of the purchase price to the land. The land is not depreciable, and her basis in the depreciable office building will be the total purchase price minus the amount allocated to the land. Second, the mid-month convention will result in Jessica not receiving a full year's MACRS deduction in the first year, even if she purchased the property on January 1 of that year.

97. Dick has a realized and recognized gain of $200,000, which is equal to his amount realized ($300,000) minus his adjusted basis in the property of $100,000 ($140,000 initial basis − $40,000 depreciation deductions).

98. Dick has a realized and recognized gain of $200,000, which is equal to his amount realized of $300,000 ($200,000 in cash plus assumption of the $100,000 mortgage), minus his adjusted basis in the property of $100,000 ($140,000 – $40,000). Jerry's basis is $300,000, which is equal to his purchase price: $200,000 in cash plus the assumption of the mortgage.

99. First, note that this is a *nonrecourse* loan. A nonrecourse loan exists if the debtor is not personally liable; rather, the debt is secured by the asset. Courtney is incorrect. Courtney is thinking that her loss is equal to the difference between the fair market value of the property ($600,000) and her adjusted basis ($750,000). But this is incorrect. She should have reported a *gain* of $200,000. Under *Commissioner v. Tufts,* 461 U.S. 300 (1983), Courtney is deemed to have sold the property and the amount realized is equal to the amount of the outstanding loan ($950,000). Her adjusted basis in the property is $750,000 ($1,000,000 – $250,000 of MACRS deductions). This produces a realized and recognized gain of $200,000. So, Courtney will have gain even though she will have no cash from the transaction with which to pay the tax.

100. First, note that this is a *recourse* debt. The debtor is personally liable for recourse debt. Linda has experienced two transactions. First, in the foreclosure sale, she realized a $200,000 loss. The motel was sold for $200,000, and Linda had an adjusted basis of $400,000 in the property (her cost minus her depreciation deductions). This results in a $200,000 loss to her, which should be deductible under §165(c). Second, Linda also experienced $250,000 of discharge of indebtedness income as a result of the bank writing off the loan. This may be excludable from Linda's gross income; however, if she meets any of the exceptions of §108(a), such as the insolvency exception.

101. The result would be the same, assuming that the value of the motel was $200,000 on the date of transfer.

102. If the property were Linda's principal residence, the exclusion of §108(a)(1)(E) would likely apply to exclude from gross income the $250,000 of discharge of indebtedness income. She would not have depreciated a residence, so her basis would be her original cost of $500,000 (assuming no improvements). The sale for $200,000 results in a $300,000 loss, but this loss is not deductible under §165(c).

103. Craig's property is worth $400,000, and he and the lender are negotiating to reduce the total loan balance to this amount, which results in discharge of indebtedness income of $100,000. This question focuses on the exclusion from gross income for discharge of debt attributable to qualified principal residence indebtedness under §108(a)(1)(E). Only acquisition indebtedness qualifies for this exclusion (not the HELOC), so a reduction in the original mortgage (scenario B) is more favorable for Craig. He will have to reduce his basis in the residence, but that won't matter because if he ultimately sells it, he will presumably enjoy the exclusion of §121.

104. Fred is not correct: He actually has a $50,000 loss. Because Fred used the plane for both business and personal purposes, he had to bifurcate the purchase price of $1,000,000 based on use, so that the purchase price for the business portion of the plane was $600,000. The MACRS deductions are attributable to this portion, reducing the basis to $250,000. Then, on sale, the purchase price must again be bifurcated, into business (60%, or $300,000) and personal (40%, or $200,000). He has a gain of $50,000 on the business portion of the plane ($300,000 amount realized minus $250,000 adjusted basis) and a $200,000 personal (nondeductible) loss attributable to the personal portion of the plane ($200,000 amount realized, minus $400,000 adjusted basis). See *Sharp v. United States,* 199 F. Supp. 743 (D. Del. 1961), aff'd, 303 F.2d 783 (3d Cir. 1962).

105. When a taxpayer receives property and must include its fair market value in gross income, the basis of the property is its "tax cost," or the amount included in gross income. An example of tax cost basis is when a taxpayer is paid for services with property. The taxpayer includes the fair market value of the property in gross income and takes the property with a basis equal to the amount included in gross income.

106. The correct answer is (b), the fair market value of the painting at the grandmother's death. §1014(a).

107. This familiar question (it's the same as Question 93) has a different answer now that we know about §1031. Al and Sal have realized gain attributable to the trade. However, assuming that these properties are held by Al and Sal "for investment," §1031 will probably apply to defer recognition of the gain. The football and baseball are properties of a like kind and appear to be investment properties potentially eligible for like-kind exchange treatment (unless Al or Sal are in the business of collecting and trading memorabilia, in which case these items would be inventory to that person and thus ineligible). If §1031 applies, Al and Sal will not recognize the gain associated with the trade and will take a basis in the new item (the "replacement property") equal to the basis in the old item (the "relinquished property").

108. All of the nonrecognition provisions of the Code are about deferring the time at which gain or loss will be toted up and will appear on an income tax return. For like-kind exchanges, involuntary conversions, and divorce transfers, there is a sense that the time is not ripe for taxing gains and allowing losses: The taxpayers have stayed in the same investments or kind of investments and no cash has changed hands (and if it does, recognition of gain does occur). For like-kind exchanges, there is the added rationale that nonrecognition combats the "lock-in effect"—the tendency to hold on to property to avoid the adverse income tax consequences. (Perhaps this rationale could be extended to divorce transfers as well—a different kind of "lock-in.") For involuntary conversions and divorce transfers, there is the added rationale of not kicking someone when they are down—waiting until a better time, when property is actually sold (and cash is available), to assess the taxpayer's true gain or loss.

109. Spencer and Katherine's tax consequences are analyzed separately.

- *Katherine's tax consequences, assuming qualification as like-kind exchange:*

Realized gain:	$60,000 ($90,000 + $10,000 − $40,000)
Recognized gain:	$10,000 (the value of the sports car)
Basis in Blueacre:	$40,000

- *Spencer's tax consequences, assuming qualification as a like-kind exchange under §1031:*

Realized gain:	$60,000 ($90,000 − $30,000)
Recognized gain:	-0-
Basis in Blueacre:	$40,000 ($30,000 + $10,000)

The fair market value of the sports car must be $10,000 if the transaction is to involve a trade of value-for-value. If Spencer's basis in the sports car were different from its fair market value, he would realize gain or loss on the transfer of the car. Realized gain would be recognized, but it is doubtful that loss would be recognized. Katherine's basis in the sports car would be $10,000 (its fair market value).

110. If Spencer did not hold Blueacre for investment, all of his realized gain would be recognized because the transaction would not qualify as a like-kind exchange under §1031. This does not affect Katherine's ability to qualify for like-kind exchange treatment.

111. If Katherine and Spencer are married, §1041 prevents the recognition of *any* gain on the transaction for either party. Katherine will take any property she receives with the same basis as it had in the hands of Spencer. Thus, §1031 is not necessary to achieve nonrecognition.

112. If Jim trades Wineacre for Squashacre, his loss will not be recognized. Therefore, he should not trade properties; he should *sell* Wineacre, recognize the loss, and *purchase* Squashacre.

113. This is a qualifying like-kind exchange. Therefore, the parties' tax consequences are as follows:

- *Tony's tax consequences:*

Realized gain/loss:	$140,000 ($330,000 − $160,000)
Recognized gain:	$120,000 ($150,000 − $30,000)
Adjusted basis in Egypt Tower:	$160,000

- *Cleo's tax consequences:*

Realized gain/loss:	($20,000) ($330,000 − $350,000)
Recognized gain/loss:	-0-
Adjusted basis in Egypt Tower:	$320,000

114. Notice in this case that because the "equity" in each property is the same ($120,000), there will be no transfer of the additional $30,000 from Tony to Cleo. The tax consequences to Tony and Cleo are summarized in the chart below.

Tax Consequences to Tony and Cleo

	Tony	**Cleo**
Realized Gain/Loss	$140,000 Gain	$80,000 Gain
Recognized Gain/Loss	$120,000 (net relief from liability)	-0- (no net relief from liabilities)
Basis of New Property	$160,000 Old basis + 120,000 Gain recognized − 180,000 Cleo's A/L + 60,000 Tony's A/L $160,000	$100,000 Old basis + 0 Gain recognized − 60,000 Tony's A/L + 180,000 Cleo's A/L $220,000

	Tony	**Cleo**
Is this correct?	If sold for FMV ($180,000), using this basis, Tony would recognize the realized gain that was not recognized: $20,000.	If sold for FMV ($300,000), using this basis, Cleo would recognize all of the gain that went unrecognized: $80,000.

115. The transfers of property are almost certainly incident to a divorce, and therefore §1041 applies to defer recognition of any gain or loss. Neither Harry nor Sally will have income or deductions as a result of these transactions, and each will take the property he or she receives with the basis it had immediately prior to the transfer. Therefore, Sally will receive the marital home with a basis of $150,000 and the ABC stock with a basis of $175,000.

116. Steve is probably right. Remember that §1041 applies as between the parties to a divorce, not to sales to third parties. Who owns the property is a legal and factual question, and in this case, Steve has a strong case that Ivanna was the owner of the property, so its sale to a third party generated income to her, not to Steve. The division of the proceeds of the sale would probably be governed by §1041, however, resulting in no income or a deduction to either party. Ivanna would probably be able to claim an exclusion under §121, which Steve would not be able to do because he did not live in the home or own it for the time periods required. See *Suhr v. Commissioner*, T.C. Memo 2001-28.

117. The destruction of the fishing boat is a constructive sale of the fishing boat in which Don realizes a gain of $400,000, which is the difference between the amount received from the insurance company ($600,000) and his adjusted basis in the boat ($200,000). However, he may defer recognition of this gain if he meets the requirements of §1033. In order to qualify, he must reinvest the proceeds in similar property within two years. In this case, he probably qualifies, as he has purchased a commercial fishing boat within the requisite period. However, he did not fully invest the proceeds. Therefore, he will recognize $100,000 of gain, and his basis in the boat will be his old basis ($200,000) plus the gain recognized ($100,000), minus the amount not reinvested ($100,000), or $200,000. If he reinvests in a tourist fishing boat, he runs the risk that this will not be considered property similar in use, and therefore he may have to recognize all of the gain. This is a close case, and the IRS would be likely to assert that commercial fishing and tourist deep sea fishing tours are not "similar" uses.

118. The government needs some way to measure a taxpayer's income and collect the tax at predictable, objective, and fairly frequent intervals. The taxable year concept provides that technique.

119. Income averaging per se is not possible, but Jerry may carry back his net operating loss of $30,000 in Year 4 to Year 2 (applying $25,000, reducing taxable income to zero) and Year 3 (applying $5,000, reducing taxable income to $20,000). He does this by filing amended returns, and this carryback has the result similar to "averaging" his income.

120. In this case, Sandy had a colorable legal claim to $100,000 and must include that amount in income in the year of receipt. In the next year, she can invoke §1341 to pay the lower of the tax resulting from (a) computing the tax in Year 1 as if the $15,000 had never been included; or (b) including the income in Year 1 and deducting the repayment in Year 2.

121. Because Tom is a cash-method taxpayer, he will include the payment in gross income in the year he receives it, Year 2. When he performed the services and sent his bill is irrelevant.

122. Tom would probably be in constructive receipt of payment because he had access to the money and refused to take it.

123. These questions address the proper timing of deductions for a calendar-year, cash-method taxpayer. A cash-method taxpayer deducts amounts when paid.

  (a) For tax purposes, a timely mailing is a timely payment, so unless other factors exist that would prevent a deduction, Pamela may deduct payments made by check and mailed in Year 1 for otherwise deductible personal income taxes.

  (b) By postdating the check January 1, Year 2, Pamela prevents the check from being presented for payment until Year 2, and so the payment is not deductible until Year 2.

  (c) If the taxpayer is aware (or should be aware) that there are insufficient funds in the account on which the check is drawn, the mailing of the check does not constitute payment.

  (d) If the taxpayer had no knowledge (or no reason to know) of the levy, mailing constitutes payment even if the check is dishonored.

  (e) Because the alimony isn't due until Year 2, Pamela cannot accelerate the deduction by prepaying it in Year 1.

124. Opie will deduct $5,000 for payments made, and it doesn't matter if they are made by check or credit card. He cannot deduct amounts owed at the end of the year because he has not yet paid them.

125. Oils R Us is required to account for inventories because it sells merchandise. It has $50,000 of gross income. Its cost of goods sold is computed by taking beginning inventory ($10,000), adding purchases ($25,000), and subtracting ending inventory ($12,000). Its cost of goods sold is $23,000. Therefore, its net income, considering only inventory costs, is $27,000 ($50,000 − $23,000).

126. Adam has received property for services, a transaction that generates compensation income to him. However, this property is "restricted": Adam cannot sell it and may forfeit his rights to the stock. Under §83, Adam will include the fair market value of the stock in his gross income (and the employer, BigCo, will take a deduction) on the first date at which the stock is transferable or the forfeiture provisions lapse. For example, if Adam receives 500 shares on January 2, Year 1, the transferability and forfeiture provisions will lapse on January 2, Year 6, and Adam would be required to include in his gross income the fair market value of the shares in his gross income in Year 6 (at their value in that year). Adam can make a §83(b) election to include the value of the shares in his gross income when he receives them, which would be a good choice if he expects the value of the BigCo shares to increase greatly in value.

127. As an accrual-method taxpayer, GoTown generally deducts expenses when all events have occurred that determine the fact of the liability and the amount of the liability can be determined with reasonable accuracy. This test would normally lead to GoTown deducting the expense in Year 1. However, the economic performance rules are an overlay on the all-events test. They provide that deduction cannot occur prior to economic performance. For the purchase of services, economic performance occurs when the services are provided. Therefore, GoTown may not deduct the payment until Year 2, when Soundbites provides the services.

128. Unless Samantha elects out of the installment method, she will report the gain realized on the transaction over the five-year period of payments. The portion of each payment that is income is determined by multiplying the payment ($200,000) by a fraction, the numerator of which is the gross profit ($1,000,000 − $300,000) and the denominator of which is the total contract price ($1,000,000). Thus, 70% of each payment, or $140,000, will be income. Moreover, Samantha must include the interest paid by Darin in gross income in the year it is received, assuming she is a cash-method taxpayer.

129. Under §111, the refund of the state income taxes is a recovery that may lead to inclusion of amounts in Sara's gross income. The exclusionary amount—the amount of the total $2,000 recovery that can be excluded from gross income—is the amount of the original deduction that did not reduce tax in the prior year. Since the entire amount was used to reduce tax, the entire amount of the recovery is included in gross income.

130. This is probably a passive activity loss, as it is produced from the activity of rental real estate. Therefore, Bev may deduct it against passive income, and depending on her AGI, Bev may be able to claim $25,000 of it as a deduction (§469(i)). If she cannot deduct the loss, it will be suspended and will carry over to the future until she can use it against passive income or she sells the apartment building.

131. Harry's basis in the XYZ shares is his cost: $10,000. The gain or loss that he would recognized in each of the offered scenarios is as follows.

   (a) **$90,000.** Harry's realized gain is $140,000 ($150,000 − $10,000). But because Harry's father's loss of $50,000 was disallowed on the sale to his son, Harry's gain is reduced by the amount of the previously disallowed loss. His $140,000 gain is reduced to $90,000.

   (b) **-0-.** Harry's realized gain of $50,000 is reduced by the previously disallowed loss to eliminate the gain entirely.

   (c) **-0-.** Although Harry might be tempted to report a loss, he cannot do so under the rule of §267(d). A portion of Harry's father's disallowed loss is gone forever.

   (d) **-0-.** Harry has no realized gain or loss on the transaction. Again, Harry's father's disallowed loss is gone forever.

   (e) **($5,000).** Harry has a realized loss of $5,000, and absent some other provision of the Code that would prevent recognition, such as the capital loss restrictions, he may recognize this loss.

132. Tell her (gently) that she's got it backwards: Taxpayers seek to characterize income as capital and loss as ordinary. Capital gain income is eligible for preferential tax rates, which save the taxpayer significant amounts of money as compared to the rates on ordinary income. On the deduction side, there are restrictions on the ability of taxpayers to take deductions for capital losses, while ordinary losses offset ordinary income. Therefore, taxpayers try to characterize income as capital and losses as ordinary.

133. The wood is part of his inventory or supplies and is therefore not a capital asset.

134. Several courts (see *United States v. Maginnis,* 356 F.3d 1179 (9th Cir. 2004)), have held that a taxpayer who sells his or her right to lottery payouts does not qualify for capital gain treatment. If Laura had not sold the rights, she would have received ordinary income over

25 years; selling the rights is merely an acceleration of that income and does not transform it from ordinary to capital.

135. *Of course* Lee has a capital gain. Distinguishing this from the sale of lottery winnings isn't difficult. Owning the stock grants Lee more rights than just the right to dividends; the owner of stock has a collection of rights, including the right to dividends, possibly the right to vote, and the right to share in liquidation proceeds on dissolution. So, the value of the stock incorporates all of these rights. By contrast, the sale of the right to lottery winnings is *only* the sale of the right to what otherwise would be ordinary income.

136. The loss on the sale of the van is a §1231 loss because it is attributable to the sale of a depreciable asset used in Wally's trade or business. If §1231 losses exceed gains, the net loss is deductible as an ordinary loss. If §1231 gains exceed losses, they are taxable as capital gain. In this case, if there is only a loss on the sale of the van, it will be an ordinary loss for him. If gains on the sale of the displays exceed the loss on the sale of the van, the gain will be considered capital gain (probably 15%/0% gain).

137. The easy answer is that John has an $80,000 gain on the sale of the instruments. This would be considered §1231 gain, which would normally be taxed as a capital gain, since there is no reported §1231 loss. However, §1245 requires recapture of the depreciation of $30,000 as ordinary income. The rest would be capital gain, and probably would be considered 15%/0% gain. However, if these are collectibles, the gain would be taxed at 28%. This becomes more difficult to analyze, however, because if they were collectible, John may have been incorrect in claiming MACRS deductions; they may not be subject to "wear and tear" and therefore would be nondepreciable.

138. The capital gains tax rate is supposed to be less than the rate for ordinary income. For taxpayers in the 15% or 10% bracket, a 15% capital gains rate would not be lower. Therefore, the 0% rate is available for taxpayers in brackets up to 15%.

139. The question for Michael is whether he has capital gain or ordinary income on the sale of the property, i.e., whether the property is a capital asset. If the property is inventory in his hands, it is not a capital asset, and he would have ordinary income on its sale. If he sells the parcel as a whole, he probably would not have ordinary income; he probably has a good argument that the parcel is an investment, not inventory. However, the more activity he engages in—installing services, plotting the lots, etc.—the closer he gets to the edge. When he subdivides and sells the lots individually, he likely has crossed the line into the world of inventory, especially if he takes all the usual steps to sell the lots, such as advertising, meeting with customers, etc. However, there is no bright line in this area. Section 1237 would have provided him with a bright line, but it appears that it is too late for Michael to take advantage of it.

140. Tillie's analysis is not exactly correct. The Code provides for a 25% rate on unrecaptured §1250 gain, which is the lesser of the taxpayer's §1231 gain or the depreciation deductions previously claimed with respect to the property. So, upon sale, it is likely that a portion of the gain will be taxed at the 25% rate, while the rest (as Tillie had hoped) will be taxed at the lowest rate.

141. Andrea's gains and losses must first be categorized. The sale of land generates a $5,000 long-term capital loss in the 15%/0% category. The sale of ABC stock generates a long-term 15%/0% capital gain in the amount of $15,000. The sale of NOP stock was held for less than one year, so it generates a short-term capital loss of $25,000. The sale of the stamp collection generates long-term capital gain of $20,000 in the 28% (collectibles) category.

Next, the gains and losses in each category must be netted. The only category that has both gains and losses in the long term is the 15%/0% category, so the $15,000 gain is netted against the $5,000 loss to produce a net long-term 15%/0% capital gain of $10,000.

In the next step, net capital losses in each category are applied against net capital gains in each category. The short-term capital loss is applied first to reduce the gain in the 28% category to zero, and then the remaining amount ($5,000) is applied to reduce the capital gain in the 15%/0% category.

Andrea's net result is a $5,000 long-term capital gain in the 15%/0% category.

142. All of these assets appear to be §1231 assets: They are depreciable property (equipment) used in a taxpayer's trade or business. Bev's casualty losses exceed casualty gains, so the net loss is excluded from the computation of §1231 gains and losses (this loss is considered an ordinary loss). The gain on Property B is netted against the loss on Property C, but only $35,000 of the gain on Property B is included in the computation because the recapture income is ordinary income and cannot be §1231 gain. The netting process produces a net gain of $20,000, which is considered capital in nature.

143. If Bev had experienced in the previous year a $5,000 loss that was characterized as an ordinary loss under §1231, a portion of her gain in the current year—up to that amount of loss—would be considered ordinary. Thus, $5,000 of her gain would be ordinary and the remaining $15,000 would be capital.

144. There are several principal arguments for having a capital gains preference (a lower tax rate on capital gains income). (1) A reduction in the tax rate on investments will increase savings, investment, and economic prosperity. (2) A capital gains preference is said to reduce lock-in (the tendency to hold on to assets rather than putting them to their best economic use) by reducing the tax associated with sale. (3) Because capital gains often accrue over many years, requiring the gain to be recognized in a single year (the "bunching" effect) can result in the taxation of gain at the highest marginal rate in the year of recognition, even though the incremental gains might have been taxed at lower rates had they been recognized in the years they accrued, so a capital gains preference reduces the bunching effect. (4) Because the recognized gain upon sale of a capital asset may not represent real gain but instead may represent inflationary gains, the capital gains preference mitigates the impact of inflation by lowering the tax in the year of sale.

The principal arguments against a capital gains preference is that it introduces new heights of complexity into the tax code, and of course, that it may not have the effects described above.

The rationale for a limitation on capital losses is that allowing a taxpayer to deduct capital losses without limitation would arguably give the taxpayer too much discretion to lower his or her tax rate by selling capital assets that have declined in value in years in which the taxpayer has significant ordinary income.

145. Brian is thinking like a tax lawyer: He would prefer an exclusion from gross income, but if he must have income, he'd like it to be taxed at a lower capital gains rate, rather than as ordinary income. Unfortunately for Brian, several courts have held that the sale of plasma and other body parts generates income, and no one has (yet) been successful in claiming that the sale is of a capital asset, as it is more likely to be considered inventory. See *Green v. Commissioner*, 74 T.C. 1229 (1980) (taxpayer claimed "depletion allowance"—a kind of capital recovery—to offset ordinary income on the sale of her rare blood, but the court rejected her claim).

146. With the proliferation of categories, some ordering rule is necessary to prevent chaos. The long-term loss/gain ordering rules are relatively taxpayer friendly, allowing losses to be applied to reduce gains, first, on the kinds of capital gain subject to the highest rates (28% and 25%). Thus, the overall rate of tax on capital gains should be lower than if the reverse applied—if losses were first applied to the 15%/0% category. The ordering rule that puts short-term capital losses at the end of the line—they cannot be applied against long-term capital gain until all long-term losses have been applied—makes it more difficult for taxpayers to use (or generate) short-term losses to offset long-term gains. The ordering rules work against taxpayers who have long-term losses and short-term gains, as the former cannot offset the latter.

147. A tax credit is a dollar-for-dollar reduction in the amount of tax due, while a deduction is a reduction in the amount of gross income or AGI, upon which the tax is calculated. An exclusion ensures that some amount of what would otherwise be income never becomes part of the tax calculation at all. A deduction or exclusion potentially saves the taxpayer the amount equal to his or her rate multiplied by the dollar amount of the deduction or exclusion, while a tax credit potentially saves the taxpayer one dollar for every dollar of tax credit. Moreover, some tax credits are refundable; i.e., they generate a refund if the credits exceed the tax, which is not a characteristic of deductions or exclusions.

148. The rationale for the AMT is that every taxpayer—even those with activities that generate significant tax benefits in the form of deferred or excluded income or significant deductions—should pay some tax. For example, certain kinds of tax-exempt interest (from private activity bonds) are included in gross income for AMT purposes, while exempt for regular tax purposes. Also, depreciation on equipment is required to be claimed on a longer, slower schedule for AMT purposes than for regular tax purposes. Thus, taxpayers whose activities generate significant amounts of MACRS deductions, which reduce their taxable income and tax for regular tax purposes, will have larger alternative minimum taxable income (AMTI) in the early years of capital recovery.

149. The answer is (c). State income taxes and miscellaneous expenses (miscellaneous itemized deductions) are deductible for regular income tax purposes, but not when computing AMTI. The other answers include items that are both treated differently and not treated differently under the two tax systems.

150. To determine whether Catherine is subject to the AMT, first compute taxable income and tax for regular tax purposes, as follows.

Salary income:	$97,200
Plus taxable interest income:	$3,000
Gross income:	$100,200
Minus alimony payments:	−$12,000
AGI	**$88,200**

Minus itemized deductions

Home mortgage interest:		$ 5,000
State income tax:		$ 9,000
Medical expenses in excess of 7.5% of AGI:		$ 1,000
Charitable deductions:		$ 2,000
Miscellaneous itemized deductions in excess of 2% floor:		$ 3,000
Total itemized deductions:		−$ 20,000
Minus personal exemption:		−$ 4,000
Taxable income for *regular* tax purposes:		**$ 64,200**
Tax on regular taxable income:		**$ 10,200**

To determine whether Catherine will have to pay AMT, her taxable income is adjusted as follows to produce AMTI.

Taxable income for *regular* tax purposes:		**$64,200**
Plus:		
Tax-exempt interest on private activity bonds:	$ 2,000	
State income taxes:	$ 9,000	
Miscellaneous itemized deductions:	$ 3,000	
Medical expenses:	$ 1,000	
Personal exemption:	$ 4,000	
Total adjustments:		+$19,000
AMTI		**$ 83,200**
Minus exemption amount		−$ 50,000
Tax base for AMT		$ 33,200
Multiply by tax rate for AMT (26%)		× .26
AMT		**$ 8,632**

Because Catherine's regular tax liability ($10,200) is more than her AMT liability ($8,632), she will not pay AMT. (However, this does not excuse her from calculating the AMT liability to determine if she is subject to this surtax.)

151. No, elimination of the deduction for alimony won't increase Catherine's chances of being caught in the AMT net. It is not one of the tax preference items that trigger AMT concerns.

152. All of the award must be included in Becky's gross income, and her $100,000 of attorneys' fees is deductible on Schedule A as a miscellaneous itemized deduction for regular tax purposes, to the extent that these fees, plus any other miscellaneous itemized deductions, exceed 2% of her AGI. She cannot claim these as an above-the-line deduction because the award was not pursuant to the relatively limited category of claims that generate attorneys' fees eligible for such a deduction. See ELO, Chap. 6 (X); CT, p. 94. For purposes of calculating her AMTI, however, none of the attorneys' fees are deductible because they are a miscellaneous itemized expense. This can generate significant AMT liability.

153. Candace can't deduct these personal expenses. §262. However, she may be entitled to a nonrefundable tax credit for dependent care expenses. She appears to qualify: She

maintains a household with children; they are under the age of 13; and she incurs expenses to care for them while she works. The amount expended for child care while she works as a volunteer ($500) would not be eligible for the credit. The amount of the credit will be a percentage of the lesser of her earned income, child care expenses, or the specified dollar amount of the statute based on the number of children ($6,000 for two children). The percentage is based on AGI. In Candace's case, she will be entitled to claim 23% of her actual expenses of $3,000, or $690, as the child care credit.

154. For 2012, the earned income amount for a single person with one child is $9,320 and the phaseout amount is $17,090. Assuming that the myriad requirements of the earned income tax credit are met (and other facts are needed to make this determination), Jordan is entitled to claim the earned income credit because his income is within the earned income limitation. He has one qualifying child, and thus he will be entitled to a credit of $3,162, computed as follows:

Credit Percentage: $34\% \times \$9,320$	$= \$3,095$
Less Limitation: $-15.98\% \times (10,000 - 17,090)$	$=$ -0-
Jordan's Earned Income Credit	$= \mathbf{\$3,095}$

155. For 2012, the earned income amount for a couple with three children is $13,090 and the phaseout amount is $22,300. Assuming that the myriad requirements of the earned income tax credit are met (and other facts are needed to make this determination), Kara and Jim may claim an earned income credit of $1,532. This is computed as follows:

Credit Percentage: $45\% \times \$13,090$	$=$ $\$5,891$
Less Limitation: $21.06\% \times (43,000 - 22,300)$	$=$ $-\$4,359$
Kara and Jim's earned income credit	$=$ $\mathbf{\$1,532}$

156. The difference between these two categories of credits is whether they are refundable or not. Some tax credits are refundable; i.e., they generate a refund if the credits exceed the tax, which is not a characteristic of deductions or exclusions. The taxes-paid credit, the earned income credit, and, potentially, part of the child credit are refundable. If these credits exceed taxes due, the taxpayer may receive a refund. The child care credit is not refundable; if the taxpayer has more credit available than taxes, the excess credit goes to waste.

157. No, David is not correct. First, David and Li must decide if they want to take the deduction or the credit, because they can't take both. If they decide that a credit is more favorable to them, they must allocate expenses first to the HOPE/American Opportunity tax credit ($4,000) for the tax credit of $2,500. The remaining $6,000 can be allocated to the Lifetime Learning credit, for a tax credit of $1,200 ($6,000 × 20%). If David and Li decide to opt for the deduction under §222, the maximum deduction will be $4,000. We have no facts on which to determine if these amounts (credit or deduction) will be limited or eliminated based on David and Li's income, but this should also be investigated.

158. Taxpayers "assign" income in order to direct it to a person in a lower tax rate than their own and to avoid paying gift taxes. If a father is in the 33% bracket for ordinary income and his son is in the 15% bracket, it makes sense for the father to try to direct income to the son, as the family as a unit will save 18% in taxes if the attempt is successful. As tax rates become more progressive (i.e., there is a larger gap between the lowest and highest rates), there is a greater incentive to engage in assignment of income strategies.

159. Danielle has probably engaged in an inappropriate assignment of income. She transferred income from services (transformed into "property"—the intellectual property that gives rise to the income) to her daughter, who did not perform the services. However, she would argue that there is no impermissible assignment because she transferred all of the income stream. However, without also transferring the intellectual property that gives rise to the income, she retains power over that income stream, which would defeat her argument.

160. If Danielle can transfer the intellectual property (the copyright) to Tiffany, she will be able to direct the income to Tiffany as well. Of course, the transfer of the copyright to Tiffany will be a gift (not includible in Tiffany's income for income tax purposes (§102), but a gift for gift tax purposes).

161. In these circumstances, only Dan could legally receive the legal fee under the rules of the state bar. Therefore, he would be required to include the entire $300,000 fee in gross income. His transfer of $50,000 to the charity would not likely generate a charitable deduction for him, as he would be making the contribution as a quid pro quo for Dan's services. The more likely characterization is that Peter would be deemed to have paid Dan a $50,000 fee for services, which Peter would be required to include in gross income. The charitable deduction would inure to Peter, who is deemed to make a donation of the amount received. (Whether this arrangement is ethical is a separate question.)

162. Sam is taxed on the interest. He cannot give away just the interest element. If he wants Peter to be taxed on the interest, then Sam must give Peter the bonds.

163. If the income is tax-exempt interest, it won't matter who is deemed to own it for regular tax purposes. But this kind of interest income may be included in AMTI, and therefore, the assignment of income doctrine will apply.

164. It is probably correct. Although the *Salvatore* 29 T.C.M. 89 (1970) case might raise questions, in this case (1) the length of time between gift and ultimate sale; and (2) the absence of facts suggesting that Barbara's share was uncertain supports the taxpayers' position that the transfer was bona fide and that the substance of the transaction is a sale by both Barbara and George of the property.

165. Brian's assignment of his claim will probably not result in an assignment of income because the claim is contingent and doubtful at the time of transfer. Thus, the transferee will properly include the amount in gross income. Because Steve has a basis in this action of $500,000, he will include only $4,500,000 in gross income; the rest will be a return of capital. Steve will argue that this is capital gain, but he is unlikely to prevail. See ELO, Chap. 12 (III); CT, p. 89.

166. Under *Banks v. Commissioner*, 543 U.S. 426 (2005), Kayla must include the entire amount of the award ($500,000) in her gross income when she receives it. (Section 104(a) doesn't apply to exclude this award because this is a nonphysical injury.) However, Kayla will be allowed an above-the-line deduction (a deduction from gross income in computing AGI) for her attorneys' fees and costs.

167. In this case, Kayla must still include the $500,000 in her gross income but is not allowed an above-the-line deduction in computing AGI for her attorneys' fees and costs. Instead, she can claim these as a miscellaneous itemized deduction, subject to the 2% floor of §67.

168. Spencer will probably file his own tax return, but he does have the option of filing with his parents for his investment income. His regular tax rate (10%) will apply to his earned income and up to $1,900 of his investment income. But the remaining amount of investment income will be taxed at his parents' marginal rate.

169. Corbin's situation is a little more difficult to analyze than Spencer's. At his age, for the kiddie tax to apply, Corbin must be a full-time student for at least five months of the year and must not provide more than one-half of his support during the year in question. If those two conditions apply, the kiddie tax will apply to Corbin, and all of his investment income in excess of $1,900 will be taxed at his parents' rate. If not, Corbin's regular tax rate will apply to all of his income, earned and investment.

170. Taxpayers should (and do) care about time value of money principles because these principles affect the amount of tax they owe—specifically, by affecting the timing of taxes. Taxpayers seek to defer income as far into the future as possible (while still having access to it) in order to defer the tax on this income. Taxpayers want to contribute money to tax-deferred savings vehicles such as IRAs for this reason. A tax-deferred vehicle may be a tax never paid (consider the impact of §1014), and the present value of that future tax is less than its face amount. Taxpayers also want to accelerate deductions as much as possible because these deductions reduce the taxes owed now.

171. The present value of a promise to pay you $10,000 in five years if the appropriate interest rate is 5% is $7,840. If the appropriate rate is 9%, the present value is $6,500. The appropriate interest rate should take into account the riskiness of the promise. A promise by the U.S. federal government (as in a savings bond) is essentially risk-free and would have a low interest rate. By contrast, a promise by a deadbeat (high risk) would carry a higher interest rate.

172. This is just another way to ask for the present value of a future sum. If you know you have a debt of $10,000 to be paid in eight years, you might set aside the present value of that debt (assuming an interest rate) and let that sum grow during the term so that you would have just the right amount to pay off the obligation. This is often how people save for college educations for children or for their own retirement, although they generally do that through periodic savings rather than putting aside a lump sum. At 6%, the amount you would have to put aside is $6,270. At 12%, you would have to put aside only $4,040.

173. If interest rates held steady at 4%, you would have amounts as follows:

10 years:	$4,437
15 years:	$5,405
30 years:	$9,740

174. To answer this question, you must compare the present values of the two gifts: the present value of $70,000 five years in the future, or $50,000 today. Because gifts are not included in gross income, there are no taxes to figure into the equation on the gift itself. You should take the gift today because the present value of the future gift is $47,670, less than the current gift. The present value is calculated as follows:

$$PV = \frac{FV}{(1+i)^n}$$

$$PV = \frac{\$70,000}{(1+.08)^5}$$

$$PV = \$47,670$$

This can also be calculated by using a present value table: Multiply the future gift by the number at the intersection of 8% and five years, or 0.681. This produces the same number. (It's a relatively close case. You should also consider whether the stated interest rate doesn't reflect the riskiness of this gift—your rich aunt might "forget" to make it! The riskier the promise, the higher the interest rate properly used in calculating present value, and the lower the present value of the future gift.)

175. Putting aside nontax issues, such as whether the granddaughter is mature enough to handle a $5,000 gift, Grandmother should seriously consider using the 529 plan. If the granddaughter invests the money, she will be taxed (perhaps at her parents' rate) on the income from the gift. If the money is placed in a 529 plan, it can grow tax-free, and this income will never be taxed if the money is used for educational purposes. However, in making that decision, Grandmother should consider any fees associated with the plan and the likely rate of return in the plan.

176. Beverly should run—not walk—away from this so-called opportunity. Leaving aside the wisdom of such a venture, she will not be able to use the losses from the venture to offset her income from private practice. This would constitute a passive activity because it is certain that Beverly, a doctor, will not be actively involved in the business of contacting alien life forms. (Plus, the structure of the investment will probably ensure that it is a passive activity for her.) The passive loss rules prevent a taxpayer from using "passive losses" to offset nonpassive income, so that the deductions from the venture would be useless to her until she disposes of the activity.

177. The correct answer is (c), which is not an income deferral strategy. Investing in real estate takes advantage of the realization principle: Increases in the value of the real property are not taxed until the property is disposed of in a realization event. Use of the cash method can defer income until it is received. A like-kind exchange defers the gain on the exchange of property until the replacement property is sold. But the characterization of a payment to a former spouse as alimony results in a deduction to the payor (thus, a deduction strategy) and the payee spouse must include it in gross income when received.

178. Each Code section that allows for potential deferral (e.g., like-kind exchanges under §1031) contain myriad rules to confine the technique to its intended scope. The doctrine of constructive receipt is an example of a non-Code method of preventing inappropriate use of the cash method to defer income. A cash-method taxpayer cannot exclude income if he or she has the right to it, even if he or she does not claim it.

179. No. The Code will impute interest to this transaction. There are three potentially applicable Code provisions (§483, §7872, and §1272, and its related statutes). Of these, §483

applies because this involves a sale or exchange of property for which the purchase price is less than $1,000,000.

Section 483 provides that the unstated interest must be calculated by subtracting from the total deferred purchase price the present value of the future payments, using the applicable federal rate. In this situation, the AFR is 6%. Using present value formulas (or a calculator), the unstated interest is calculated to be $227,700, and therefore, the purchase price for the ranch is $672,300. Ronald's gain on the transaction is $272,300 (the sales price minus his basis). James's basis in the ranch is $672,300, the same as Ronald's selling price.

180. Joe's mother may lend him a total of $10,000 without interest because of the de minimis exception for gift loans. §7872(c)(2)(A). If the loan is $100,000 or less, the transaction will be cast as a gift of the forgone interest (calculated at the applicable federal rate for long-term obligations), but the amount treated as included in the mother's income will be limited to Joe's investment income (i.e., his total of dividends, interest, etc.). If the loan is $1,000,000, neither of these exceptions applies. In that case, each year, Joe's mother will be deemed to have made a gift of the forgone interest to Joe, who in turn transfers it to his mother as interest, which she must include in her gross income.

181. Elmo is incorrect. He must include in his gross income a proportionate amount of the interest on the bond each year, and this will be ordinary income to him. The interest rate is 7% on this bond.

ESSAY EXAM QUESTIONS
AND ANSWERS

ESSAY EXAM QUESTIONS

QUESTION 1

Oh, it's good to be the president of the United States. Sure, you have to deal with wars, looming deficits, natural disasters, and Congress, but there is a nice salary and some *very* nice perks. For example, the president has the use of Camp David as a private retreat and the use of Air Force One for travel. Five chefs at the White House (and three at Camp David) provide meals to the First Family, on demand, 24 hours a day. In addition, U.S. Code, Title 3, Chapter 2, §§102, 103, and 104 (*as edited or invented*) provide as follows:

§102. Compensation of the president

The president shall receive in full for his or her services during the term for which he or she shall have been elected compensation as an employee of the United States in the aggregate amount of $400,000 a year, to be paid monthly, plus health insurance, life insurance in the amount of $500,000, and disability insurance and in addition an expense allowance of $50,000 to be used exclusively in defraying expenses relating to or resulting from the discharge of his or her official duties. He or she shall be entitled also to the use of the furniture and other effects belonging to the United States and kept in the Executive Residence at the White House and have unrestricted access without charge to all National Parks, National Monuments, and National Museums.

§103. Traveling expenses

There may be expended for or on account of the traveling expenses of the president of the United States such sum as Congress may from time to time appropriate, not exceeding $100,000 per annum, such sum when appropriated to be expended in the discretion of the president.

§104. After leaving office

After leaving office, the president shall be entitled to an annual stipend of $250,000 for his or her lifetime, as well as health insurance. Personal protective services shall be provided as requested or as recommended by the Secret Service.

Mrs. X has just been elected president of the United States, after serving two terms as a senator from a southwestern state. She is married to Mr. X, and they have two children, ages eight and ten. Mr. X recently retired as a corporate executive in order to assist his wife on the campaign trail. The couple has just attended the obligatory human resources orientation, where they learned about the compensation package. You have been the longtime tax adviser to the Xs, and they have come to you for advice as to the federal income tax consequences of their "new job." Please advise them.

QUESTION 2

Several recent tax reform proposals have suggested the repeal or scaling back of IRC §163(h). Please comment, from a tax policy point of view, on how such proposals might be structured and whether they are a "good idea."

QUESTION 3

Brian owns Whiteacre, an apartment building, which he holds for investment. He has an adjusted basis of $400,000 in Whiteacre, and it is subject to a mortgage of $260,000. Anita owns Blueacre, a commercial office building, which she also holds for investment. It is worth $800,000 and is subject to a mortgage of $350,000. Anita has an adjusted basis of $400,000 in Blueacre.

A. Brian and Anita exchange Whiteacre for Blueacre, and Brian transfers a painting worth $10,000, in which he had a basis of $2,000, to Anita as well. Each assumes the other's liabilities. What are the tax consequences of this exchange to each taxpayer?

B. Would your answer change if Anita had recently acquired Blueacre as an inheritance?

QUESTION 4

Spencer, a single taxpayer, is the owner of an Internet research business organized as a sole proprietorship. He uses the cash method of accounting. Last year, he recorded on his books $150,000 in sales of information to customers. As of December 31, he had received $125,000 in payments and $25,000 in oral promises from clients to pay within 30 days. He also incurred the following expenses:

Compensation to employees	$25,000
Advertising	$5,000
Rent	$12,000
Telephone & Internet	$2,500
Taxes	$2,000
Business entertainment	$1,000
Insurance	$3,500

He purchased a computer for $5,000 for exclusive use in the business and sold a used computer that had a basis of zero for $1,500. He had originally purchased the computer for $10,000. Spencer also had a theft this year of some office equipment, with a fair market value of $1,500 and basis of $2,500. He received no insurance proceeds for this, as it was below his deductible amount. A flood destroyed some of his office art, which had a basis of $5,000 and a fair market value of $8,000. His insurance company paid him $8,000 for this loss.

Please advise Spencer on the tax consequences of these transactions. Do you have any suggestions for him to reduce next year's taxes?

QUESTION 5

Big Law Firm has a dress code, which is strictly enforced. Much to the delight of attorneys and staff, the Big Law Firm managing board issued the following edict on January 2:

> Commencing this week and throughout the rest of the year, attorneys and staff may wear jeans to the office on Fridays (and only on Fridays), but only if such jeans-wearing person makes a donation to the Big Firm Charitable Fund by 10 a.m. of the Friday on which jeans are worn. Donations may be made at the Human Resources Office.
>
> Attorneys are encouraged to donate to the Fund not less than $10, and staff are encouraged to donate not less than $5, for each Friday that the person wears jeans. At the end of the year, the Big Law Firm Charitable Fund will be donated, on behalf of the

participating attorneys and staff, to a variety of public charities from nominations by the participating staff members.

Ragged jeans, jeans with holes, jeans bedecked with rhinestones, denim miniskirts, and the like will not be tolerated. The Board would like to take this opportunity to remind attorneys and staff of our established dress code, which remains in effect for all other days (excepting Sundays) or for persons who have not made an appropriate donation.

This year, Attorney G wore jeans on 50 Fridays and contributed $800 to the Big Law Charitable Fund. On December 31, the entire fund was donated to a qualifying §501(c)(3) charity. Big Firm gave Attorney G a report showing his $800 deduction. Attorney G wishes to claim a charitable deduction on his tax return for the year. May he do so?

QUESTION 6

Peter and Gabrielle divorced in Year 1. Their divorce decree provided that Peter was to pay Gabrielle the following amounts:

$40,000	Year 1
$20,000	Year 2
$10,000	Year 3 and each year thereafter

In addition, Peter transferred to Gabrielle the following assets:

100 shares of XYZ stock, in which Peter had a basis of $50,000.
The family home, for which the couple paid $200,000. It was worth $175,000 at the time of the divorce, subject to a mortgage of $150,000.

Peter was obligated to pay the mortgage on the home each month until it was repaid or until Gabrielle sold the home or ceased to use it as her principal residence, whichever came first.

A. In each year, Peter deducted the amount he paid to Gabrielle, including the amount paid under the mortgage and the value of the XYZ stock. Gabrielle included these amounts in her gross income. Is this treatment correct?

B. In Year 6, Gabrielle moved out of the home and gave it to her daughter, Trendee. At that time, the property was worth $160,000 and was subject to a mortgage of $90,000. What is Trendee's basis in the home?

ESSAY EXAM ANSWERS

SAMPLE ANSWER TO QUESTION 1

This is obviously a compensation question, in which the focus is the taxpayer's compensation package. **See Figures 2 (Analyzing Income) and 3 (Personal Deductions).**

Who is the taxpayer?

As an initial matter, we are talking about a married couple who will likely file a joint return. No facts indicate income or deductions for Mr. X or the children, so the primary focus will be the tax consequences to Mrs. X of her compensation package.

Income issues

Of course, Madam President and her family will experience the thrill of being president and the First Family. This thrill may be offset, perhaps, by the continual demands of the job, not to mention the hassles of the constant presence of the Secret Service. Fortunately, however, neither of these needs to be measured because noneconomic benefits are not considered ''income'' in our federal income tax system, and noneconomic detriments do not generate deductions. **Figure 2, Box [1] → [2] →[3].**

Madam President will receive several items that constitute an ''economic benefit'' to her, which do constitute income in a theoretical sense. These include (1) salary; (2) meals and lodging at the White House and Camp David; (3) health, life, and disability insurance premiums; (4) an expense allowance; (5) use of the property of the United States at the White House; (6) an annual pass to the national parks, etc.; and (7) use of Air Force One, plus up to $100,000 in traveling expenses. In due course, when she leaves office, Mrs. X will enjoy (1) the annual retirement stipend, (2) health insurance, and (3) protective services. All of these items constitute gross income in the sense of Code §61. They must, at some point in time, be included in Madam President's gross income, unless a specific statutory provision excludes them. **Figure 2, Box [1] → [2] →[4] → [5].**

There is no exclusion for salary and the retirement stipend, even for the president of the United States. However, various fringe benefit provisions may be available to exclude other items, as discussed next (**see Figure 2, Box [6] → [10] → [11] → [12 or 13]**).

Meals and lodging: Section 119 allows an employee to exclude the value of meals and lodging provided to the employee on the business premises of the employer, if those meals and lodging are provided for the convenience of the employer. The locations where the president and her family will reside are the White House and Camp David, both of which are owned by the employer (the United States) and are places where the United States conducts business. The ''convenience of the employer'' test should be met, for two reasons. Like the hotel manager in *Benaglia*, the president is on call 24 hours a day, 7 days a week. Plus, it is more convenient for the United States to protect its president and First Family by having them live in a place that has already been secured. Although there is no specific statutory language supporting this, the lodging exclusion is considered as including the use of the employer's furnishings at the lodging. Therefore, the First Family's use of the White House property, such as the famous dinnerware, is likely included in the meals and lodging exclusion.

A related question is whether the meals and lodging exclusion extends to the meals and lodging provided to the family of the employee. Section 119(a) fortunately answers this question in the affirmative, so that the value of such benefits provided to the employee's "spouse or any of his dependents" is excluded from the employee's gross income.

Therefore, the value of the meals and lodging provided at the White House and at Camp David should be excluded from the gross income of the president.

Health, life, and disability insurance: Sections 79 and 106 of the Code allow an exclusion from gross income for premiums for life, health, and disability insurance provided by an employer to an employee. However, there is a $50,000 limit on life insurance, and it must be group term life insurance. Therefore, the premiums for health and disability insurance should be excluded from the president's gross income. All or a portion of the life insurance premium will be included in her gross income because only $50,000 of group term life insurance is excluded from gross income under §79. (More facts are needed about the type of insurance.) In addition, post-employment health insurance coverage can be excluded from gross income because it will be provided in connection with previous employment.

$50,000 expense allowance: If the $50,000 is provided as part of an accountable plan, the amount can be excluded from the president's gross income. An accountable plan requires that the employee account to the employer for the expenditures, and that any excess amount advanced be returned to the employer. If there is no accountable plan, then the employee must include the amount in gross income. (See "Deduction Issues," below.)

Use of Air Force One, traveling expenses, and protective services: The use of Air Force One, the $100,000 in traveling expenses, and the protective services would likely be excluded as a working condition fringe benefit under §132 of the Code. If the president were self-employed, these are the kind of expenses that would be deductible and therefore qualify as working condition fringe benefits.

Annual national park/museum pass: There is no specific exclusion in the fringe benefit Code sections for a pass to the national parks and museums. However, this might be considered either (1) a de minimis fringe benefit, as its value is de minimis in connection with the overall compensation package; or (2) a working condition fringe benefit, if part of the president's job is to visit and support these national institutions. If so, the amount would be excluded from Mrs. X's gross income. If not, the value of the pass must be included as part of her compensation income. See §132.

Deduction Issues

See Figure 3, Box [1] →[3] →[5].

Moving expense deduction: The president and the First Family will be moving into the White House. Mrs. X has served two terms as a senator from a southwestern state, and it is likely that her tax home was in that state. If so, she will be moving more than 50 miles to a new place of employment and may claim an above-the-line deduction for her moving expenses (19 cents per mile, and the cost of moving her belongings). If, however, her tax home had been in Washington, D.C., she would not qualify under the 50-mile rule, and the moving expense deduction would not be allowed.

$50,000 expense allowance: If the expense allowance is included in gross income, amounts expended for legitimate employee business expenses may be deducted, but only as miscellaneous itemized deductions subject to the 2% floor. For example, assuming that the president's AGI were $500,000, any amount of employee business expenses would have to exceed $10,000 to be deductible as an itemized deduction. See §67.

Other deductions: There are no other facts to suggest other deductions, such as mortgage interest on a principal residence in the president's home state, or real estate taxes, but these should be explored. The president will likely claim the itemized deduction and will be entitled to an exemption amount for herself, her husband, and her two children.

Timing issues

Like most individuals, Madam President is a cash method taxpayer who will include her items of gross income when she receives them. In particular, the retirement stipend will likely be included as she receives it. It is unclear whether the stipend qualifies as deferred compensation that would be subject to §409A, but this is an item that bears further scrutiny when more facts are available.

Character

The income that the president includes in her gross income will be ordinary income because it is compensation income, not income from the disposition of property.

Rates

Because the income is ordinary income, it will be subject to marginal rates of 35% (in 2012).

Credits

The First Family includes two children under the age of 13, and so the question arises of whether the president and Mr. X will be entitled to claim a dependent care credit for expenses incurred in caring for their children while they work. The dependent care credit is available even at high income levels, and it is a nonrefundable credit equal to the applicable percentage (here 20%) multiplied by the earned income of the lower-earning spouse. It appears that Mr. X will not be earning a salary, as he is retired and there is no mention of a salary for anyone but the president. If that is the case, no dependent care credit can be claimed, even if the couple must engage a child care provider to care for their children while they both work—after all, both of them will have significant public duties. If, however, Mr. X becomes part of the president's staff, and is therefore employed, a dependent care credit will be allowed to the extent described above for child care expenses.

SAMPLE ANSWER TO QUESTION 2

Author's Note: There is no one "right" answer to this policy question. An answer to a policy question should show that the student (1) knows what the affected Code section does; (2) can speak to what reform might look like; and (3) can analyze the potential effects of tax reform in terms of raising revenue, the three major tax policy concerns, and practical politics. (If you are reading this after Congress has already acted with respect to §163(h), check the book's website at www.aspenlawschool.com/books/tax_outline for an alternative question/answer.)

See Figure 18, Box [1] → [3] →[8].

Section 163(h) allows taxpayers who claim the itemized deduction to deduct interest on debt that qualifies as acquisition indebtedness (up to $1,000,000 of debt) and home equity indebtedness (up to $100,000 of debt). Without going into detail, this allows a taxpayer who takes out a mortgage to purchase a home a deduction for the interest paid each year (plus, in certain cases, points paid and even mortgage insurance premiums). It also allows a taxpayer who accesses the equity in his or her home by taking out a home equity loan to deduct the interest on this loan.

A repeal of this provision would eliminate this itemized deduction, making mortgage and home equity line of credit (HELOC) interest nondeductible like most other kinds of personal interest. Possibilities for scaling back §163(h) could include, for example, reducing the amount of debt that could qualify, eliminating home equity indebtedness but keeping some amount of acquisition indebtedness, or (the perennial congressional favorite) reducing the benefit of the deduction as AGI rises.

The deduction for home mortgage interest of §163(h) is a major tax expenditure, with estimated revenue loss of $62 billion annually. Recalling that the income tax code is how the U.S. government raises money, repealing or even scaling back §163(h) could result in a significant increase in tax revenues. However, given the issues discussed below (see "Economic effects"), Congress can expect major pushback if it tries to repeal this Code section.

Apart from a tax provision's ability to raise revenue, a tax provision can be evaluated in terms of its effect on fairness of the Code, its effect on administrative practicality, and its expected economic effects, as compared to current law.

Fairness: The tax code is intended to tax people based on their ability to pay, and a proposed change can be evaluated based on whether it makes the system more or less "fair." Fairness is typically described in terms of horizontal equity: taxpayers with similar abilities to pay should pay similar amounts of tax. So, a provision that would make the tax system fairer would (1) more accurately measure ability to pay more accurately; or (2) result in a greater degree of horizontal equity (a better fit between tax and ability to pay) than current provisions of the Code.

Repealing or scaling back the deduction for acquisition indebtedness could lead to greater fairness in the tax system. Consider "twin" taxpayers A and B, who have identical salaries and live in identical houses on the same street. Taxpayer A purchased the home, taking out a $200,000, 30-year mortgage at 5%, and makes a monthly mortgage payment of about $1,000. Taxpayer B rents her home for $1,000 per month. Allowing A to deduct the interest portion of the loan reduces A's taxable income as compared to B, but they are in precisely the same situation in terms of salary and housing. Allowing the deduction, therefore, appears to violate principles of horizontal equity. Its repeal could lead to greater fairness between renters and owners. The problem with this analysis is that it is often difficult to determine if A and B are really "similarly situated." An argument can be made that they are not, as A has undertaken the commitment desired by society to home ownership, but this begins to bleed over into economic effects, as discussed below.

From a fairness point of view, the deduction for the *home equity indebtedness* interest is almost unsupportable. Consider twin taxpayers C and D, alike in every way, including a desire to buy a $50,000 boat, but without ready cash. C has access to a HELOC, secured by a home, and D has access to an unsecured line of credit at the bank. C can borrow to buy the boat, and that purchase will be subsidized by a tax deduction for the interest, making the boat cheaper for C to buy. D also borrows to purchase the boat, paying for it with a practically identical line of credit, except for security, but the purchase is not subsidized. Both C and D have equal abilities to pay, but the tax system draws a distinction between them, suggesting that C's ability to pay is less than D's. This obvious glitch in the tax system makes at least this aspect of §163(h) a ready target for the chopping block.

Administrative practicality: The desirability of a tax provision can be measured in terms of how practical it is to administer and the costs of administration. An outright repeal of §163(h) would likely reduce the complexity of the Code and thereby reduce overall compliance and administrative costs because fewer taxpayers would likely itemize; i.e., if they could not claim this deduction, they might opt for the standard deduction. Therefore, repeal would not create an administrative burden and would probably create an administrative benefit. Scaling back §163 could increase complexity, however, because at least some of the solutions (eliminating the deduction as AGI rises, for example) would draw finer lines between taxpayers as to eligibility for the deduction.

Economic effects: Any proposed tax provisions should be evaluated based on the expected economic effects of the provision. In this analysis, we make the assumption that taxpayers respond to tax incentives by taking certain actions. Section 163(h) is an important component of a larger group of tax and other federal law provisions that benefit the U.S. housing market and encourage taxpayers to purchase and own homes. The theory is that a nation of homeowners is likely to be more stable than a nation of renters. The economic effects of acquisition indebtedness and home equity indebtedness are likely different, however, and must be analyzed separately.

Acquisition indebtedness: Presumably, the deduction for interest of §163(h) factors into taxpayers' decisions to purchase homes. (However, whether it is a deciding factor would be a good question for economists to answer.) Specifically, §163(h) makes purchasing a home less expensive than if the deduction were not available. Therefore, as compared with a tax system without §163(h), a tax code with this provision is likely to result in (1) more taxpayers purchasing homes, and (2) taxpayers purchasing more expensive homes than they would otherwise desire because the after-tax cost of a home is less than its price without a tax subsidy. Given the recent housing meltdown and the continuing foreclosure crisis, one can question the policy of encouraging "home ownership by all" through the tax code or any other means. So, repealing the provision could implement a policy decision to remove a subsidy to home ownership.

However, that is not the end of the story. A repeal of §163(h) could lead to fewer people willing to purchase homes and could accelerate the decline in value of homes (with fewer buyers engaged in the market and less willing or able to pay high prices for homes due to the absence of the tax subsidy). This could lead to a decline in home prices. Obviously, the suggested repeal of §163(h) would elicit some political pushback from the construction industry, realtors, and even regular folks who would expect to see their home values dropping even further. That said, some scaling back of the deduction might not have adverse economic effects. The current limit of $1,000,000 on acquisition indebtedness seems high, given that the average home price in the United States is about a quarter of that amount. Presumably, people purchasing million-dollar homes are not motivated solely by tax considerations, and there just aren't that many million-dollar homes. At the other end of the scale, the elimination of the deduction for mortgage insurance premiums (already scheduled for 2012) could have the desirable economic effect of causing home purchasers to increase their down payments.

Home equity indebtedness: The policy foundation for the deduction for interest on home equity indebtedness is not as strong as for its cousin, acquisition indebtedness. The deduction for interest on home equity loans is left over from a time when all personal interest was deductible, and perhaps it is designed to boost consumer spending at a time of rapidly rising home prices. This provision arguably contributed to the foreclosure crisis, by encouraging taxpayers to take out "second mortgages" on their homes. These factors suggest that it is ripe for repeal or scaling back.

SAMPLE ANSWER TO QUESTION 3

This is a question that involves a transaction in property, in which the major issues will be the realization and recognition of gain and loss to the taxpayer. **See Figures 12 (Gain/Loss on Property Dispositions), 14 (Like-Kind Exchanges of Property (IRC §1031)), and 15 (Character of Gain or Loss as Capital or Ordinary).**

Who is the taxpayer?

This question focuses on the tax consequences to both taxpayers. In property transactions, each taxpayer's consequences are usually independent of each other and must be analyzed separately.

Part A

Will Brian and/or Anita recognize income as a result of this transaction?

In exchanging Whiteacre and Blueacre, Brian and Anita have each experienced a realization event. Section 1001 measures their realized gain or loss as the difference between their amounts realized and their adjusted bases in the property transferred. (See calculation below.) Section 1001 requires recognition of this gain (which is includable in gross income under §61) unless another Code section excludes or defers it. There is no applicable exclusion statute for commercial property, but potentially, §1031 will allow deferral of gain if its requirements are met. **See Figure 12, Box [1] → [3] → [4] → [5] → [6] → [8].**

A taxpayer will not recognize gain or loss on an exchange of property if the requirements of §1031 are met: an exchange of qualifying property of like kind, when the taxpayer has held the surrendered property for investment or for use in a trade or business and intends to hold the property received for investment or in a trade or business. **See Figure 14, Box [1] → [2] → [3] → [4] → [5].**

The two properties are like kind (real property for real property, regardless of use) and this kind of property qualifies for a like-kind exchange. Assuming that each of these taxpayers held the properties for investment or for use in a trade or business and intends to hold the acquired properties for either of these uses, these requirements are met. If so, neither taxpayer will recognize gain or loss, except to the extent of nonlike-kind property received (boot). **Figure 14, Box [7] → [8] → [9] → [10].** Net relief from liabilities is treated as boot. The basis of the property received in the transaction is equal to the basis of the property transferred, plus the gain recognized on the transaction, minus the fair market value of the boot received, plus the fair market value of the boot given. **See §1031(d) and Figure 14, Box [11].**

Anita's equity in Blueacre is $450,000 (its fair market value of $800,000, minus the debt of $350,000). Therefore, Whiteacre must be worth $700,000 because Brian will trade Whiteacre (with equity of $440,000) for Blueacre plus a painting worth $10,000. Therefore, the tax consequences to the two taxpayers are as follows:

	Brian	Anita
Amount Realized	$ 800,000 Blueacre + 260,000 A/L **$1,060,000**	$ 700,000 Whiteacre + 350,000 A/L + 10,000 Painting **$1,060,000**
Basis in Property Surrendered	$ 400,000 Whiteacre +350,000 A/L + 10,000 Painting **$ 760,000**	$ 400,000 Blueacre +260,000 A/L **$ 660,000**
Realized Gain or Loss	**$300,000**	**$400,000**
Recognized Gain or Loss	**$8,000** gain on painting	$ 10,000 Painting + 90,000 Net Liab. Relief **$100,000**
Basis of Property Received	$400,000 Basis of W/A + 10,000 Painting − 260,000 A/L + 350,000 A/L **$500,000 Basis of Blueacre**	$ 400,000 Basis of B/A +100,000 Gain Recognition −350,000 +260,000 − 10,000 **$ 400,000 Basis of Whiteacre** **$ 10,000 Basis of Painting**

Will Anita and Brian have any deductions associated with this transaction?

As described above, both Anita and Brian realized gain on the transaction, not loss. They will undoubtedly have expenses associated with the sale, which will be included as part of their basis in the properties transferred. In addition, there are real estate taxes and mortgage interest to be allocated and deducted in the year of sale. Each will be entitled to his or her share of real property taxes as a deduction.

When will Anita and Brian recognize gain?

The essence of §1031 is that it requires recognition of gain in the year of the transaction to the extent that the taxpayer "cashes out" of the investment, but it defers any other gain to future years. The recognized gain described in the table above must be recognized in the year of sale. If Anita or Brian sells Whiteacre or Blueacre in a future year, the seller will compute the amount realized based on the property's values as of that date, and the adjusted basis will be computed based on the exchanged basis rule described above, adjusted further for depreciation.

What is the character of the gain recognized by Anita and Brian?

Both Anita and Brian held their respective properties (including the painting, in Brian's case) for investment, rather than as part of a trade or business. Each property constitutes a capital asset with respect to its owner under §1221 because the property does not fall within any of the excluded categories of that section. The exchange by the taxpayers qualifies as a "sale or exchange," and thus the recognized gain will be capital in nature. The gain recognized by Brian on the transfer of the painting will be classified as 28% capital gain. The gain recognized by Anita will be either 25% or 15%/0% capital gain. **See Figure 15, Box [1] → [3] → [4] → [5] → [8].**

What are the tax rates to be paid by Anita and Brian?

As noted above, the capital gain that each recognizes will be taxable at different rates because of the nature of the gains. Each taxpayer must take the gain into account in computing net capital gain.

Are Brian and Anita able to claim any tax credits?

This kind of transaction does not typically generate any tax credits.

Part B

If Anita had received the office building as an inheritance, the theoretical question arises of whether she held it for investment or for use in a trade or business. There is no definitive answer to this; it depends on her intentions as revealed by her use, the period of time she held the property, and similar factors. However, it may not matter (or matter much) to Anita because if she had recently received Blueacre as inheritance, her basis would be the fair market value on the date of death, and therefore she would have little if any gain or loss in the property. Anita's situation does not affect Brian's ability potentially to qualify his side of the transaction as a §1031 exchange; each taxpayer's situation is analyzed independently.

SAMPLE ANSWER TO QUESTION 4

This question raises issues relating to business income and expenses.

Who is the taxpayer?

Spencer is a sole proprietor of a business. Sole proprietors report the income and deductions attributable to their businesses on Schedule C of their tax returns. Net income from business is includable in gross income (§61(a)(2)), and net loss generates a deduction (§165(c)(1)), subject to some limitations.

Does Spencer have income? If so, what is its character?

Spencer begins by including in his gross income his receipts from sales of information. **See Figure 2, Box [1] → [2] → [4] → [5] → [13].** In addition, Spencer has had several property transactions during the year (both voluntary and involuntary), and he may have net gain or loss from these. Because the character of this income or loss is so closely tied to its computation, these two major issues are considered together. Spencer's information sales are ordinary income, but the character of the gain or loss on the property transactions is a more complicated issue. Whenever there is a sale of real or depreciable property held for use in a trade or business (a §1231 asset), the taxpayer-friendly rules of §1231 must be consulted, along with the usual rules governing character of gain or loss.

Sale of computer: Spencer's sale of the computer used in his business is the sale of a §1231 asset. However, we must first apply the recapture rule of §1245 to recast as ordinary income any amount of accelerated depreciation claimed on the computer. It is not clear from the facts how much that would be, but let us assume for purposes of illustration that the recapture amount is $100. That amount is treated as ordinary income. The rest ($1,400) is §1231 gain. **See Figure 15, Box [1] → [3] → [4] → [10].**

As such, we must add up the §1231 gains and losses for the year, netting the two. Spencer had a theft loss of the equipment, with a basis of $2,500 and a fair market value of $1,500. If property used in a trade or business or for the production of income is totally destroyed, and if the fair market value of such property immediately before the casualty is less than its adjusted basis, the adjusted basis of such property is the amount of the loss. Reg. §1.165-7(b)(1)(ii). Therefore, Spencer's casualty loss is $2,500 on the theft. He also had a casualty gain of $3,000 due to the flood. Because Spencer's casualty losses are not greater than his casualty gains, all of the gains and losses are included in the computation of §1231 gains, as follows:

Sale of computer:	$1,400 gain
Theft loss:	$2,500 loss
Flood gain:	$3,000 gain
Net	**$1,900 gain**

This gain would be capital in nature. There is no indication that Spencer has unrecaptured losses in previous years that would treat any of this as ordinary income. This capital gain income would be taxed at 15%, or 0%, depending on Spencer's income. Because Spencer's net income from business (ordinary income) exceeds the amount that would be subject to the 15% rate, this capital gain will be taxed at the 15% rate. **See Figure 16, Box [1] → [3a] & [3b] → [4a] & [4b] → [5] → [6].**

Which deductions may Spencer claim?

In order to qualify for any deduction, an expenditure must meet the specific requirements of a deduction statute. Potential deduction statutes are discussed below.

Ordinary and necessary business expenses: Section 162 allows a deduction for all "ordinary and necessary business expenses." This requires that the expenditure be usual in the trade ("ordinary"), have a reasonable likelihood of generating profit ("necessary"), be incurred for business and not personal reasons, be incurred while the taxpayer is engaged in a trade or business ("trade or business"), and not be a capital expenditure ("expense"). Spencer's expenditures for compensation (if reasonable in amount), rent, advertising, and telephone/Internet would all seem to meet this requirement. **See Figure 4, Box [1] → [3] → [5] → [7] → [8] → [9] → [10] → [12] → [13] → [14].**

Business entertainment: While business entertainment may also seem to fall within the category of §162 expenses, special rules limit deductions for business entertainment. First, Spencer must establish that the entertainment item was "directly related to" the active conduct of his trade or business, or if the activity immediately preceded or followed a bona fide business discussion, it was "associated with" the active conduct of his trade or business. IRC §274(a). Even if he meets this requirement, only 50% of the amount expended will be deductible. IRC §274(n). Spencer must substantiate his deductions for entertainment expenses, and additional information would be necessary to determine if he is eligible for any deductions. **See Figure 4, Box [12] → [4] & [13].**

Purchase of computer: The purchase of the computer is an outlay for a capital expenditure because the computer is likely to generate benefits beyond the close of the taxable year. IRC §263. Thus, Spencer cannot take a deduction under §162 for this outlay. He may, however, deduct the cost of such items up to the lesser of $500,000 (in 2011) or the net income of the business disregarding this expense. §179. If he elects to deduct the cost of the computer under §179, its basis will be reduced by the amount of the deduction (if he fully deducts the amount, the basis will be zero). **See Figure 10 (Basis) and Figure 11, Boxes [1] → [3] → [5] → [6] → [10] → [11].**

Taxes: Section 164 allows a deduction for income, real property, personal property taxes, and sales taxes, at least in some years. It is not clear what kind of tax Spencer paid, and further information is necessary to determine the deductibility of this expense.

Retirement planning: To generate an additional deduction in future years, Spencer might consider establishing some sort of retirement plan for his business to defer income to future years, or prepaying some expenses (within the limits imposed on prepayments) to accelerate deductions to earlier years.

When must Spencer include items in gross income, and when may he claim deductions?

Since Spencer uses the cash method of accounting for his business, he will include income in the year he receives it and claim deductions in the year they are paid. Therefore, he will include $125,000 in gross income, not including the $25,000 of promises. For deductions, "payment" includes payment by credit card, even if Spencer does not pay the balance to the credit card company. Thus, he should deduct those expenses that have been paid during the year and include income that he has received, but not the promises to pay from clients.

To what tax rates will Spencer be subject?

Spencer's net ordinary income will be taxed at rates ranging from 5% to 35% (in 2012). His capital gain will fall into the 15% category and will be taxed at 15% unless his other income is subject to tax at 5%, in which case the capital gain will escape tax altogether.

Will Spencer be entitled to claim any tax credits?

None of the facts suggest Spencer's entitlement to any kind of tax credit.

SAMPLE ANSWER TO QUESTION 5

This is a question tightly focused on personal deductions, specifically the charitable deduction. For that reason, only the "deduction" question of the seven major tax issues will be discussed. **See Figure 3 (Personal Deductions).**

A charitable deduction is allowable as part of the itemized deduction for donations by individuals of cash and property (within specified limits) to qualifying §501(c)(3) public charities.

In this case, a preliminary question is whether Attorney G made a donation to the qualifying charity, or whether the donation properly belongs to Big Law Firm. Although Attorney G did not directly donate to the charity or select the charity himself, the edict says that the Fund will be contributed "on behalf of participants" to qualifying charities, and the Firm did give Attorney G a statement of his donation. Therefore, Attorney G should be viewed as the donor. **See Figure 3, Box [1] → [3].**

The second question is whether the donation is available when it directly results in a benefit to the donor, which in this case is the privilege of a day of exemption from the firm's strict dress code. A charitable deduction is allowable for a donation only if the donor does not receive a "quid pro quo" for the donation. In *Ottawa Silica Co. v. United States*, 699 F.2d 1124 (Fed. Cir. 1983) for example, a donation for the value of land to the local school district was denied because the donor received the benefit of significant improvements to surrounding land through public improvements. In that case, the benefit was economic and substantial. **See Figure 3, Box [3] ➔ [5] ➔ [9].**

In this case, Attorney G made an $800 contribution, when the "suggested" contribution was only $500 for 50 weeks of jeans-Fridays. There is no question that the $300 "additional" contribution is not for a quid pro quo.

Moreover, the managing board's edict included only a "recommended" donation. In theory, Attorney G could have donated just a penny every Friday for the privilege of wearing jeans because only a "donation" was required. Whether Attorney G succumbed to peer pressure, sensibly decided to exceed expectations, or simply wanted to give more out of a sincere charitable impulse, the fact remains that he exceeded what was required as a condition of wearing jeans.

Finally, this should not be viewed as a quid pro quo in the same sense as in *Ottawa Silica* and similar cases because it is not the kind of economic benefit usually taken into consideration in the tax code, and whether it is "substantial" depends on the subjective view of the donor. It could be likened to the naming of a building for a major donor to a college, for example, which is not viewed as a disqualifying quid pro quo for a charitable deduction.

Although charitable deductions are subject to limits based on AGI, this $800 donation should not begin to reach that limit for Attorney G. This is an itemized deduction for Attorney G. **See Figure 3, Box [10] ➔ [13].**

In conclusion, Attorney G should be entitled to the charitable deduction of $800 if he itemizes.

SAMPLE ANSWER TO QUESTION 6

This question focuses on a specific kind of intrafamilial transfer, i.e., transfers that occur as part of a divorce situation. In this situation, the primary questions are (1) the income to a former spouse; (2) the deductions available to the other former spouse; and (3) the basis of any property that changes hands in the divorce.

Part A

In general, the payor of alimony may deduct it from his or her gross income, and the recipient must include it in gross income. However, for this treatment to occur, the payments must qualify as alimony under the federal definition of alimony (state law labels don't matter). Alimony must be paid in cash, must be pursuant to a divorce decree or written instrument pursuant to divorce, must not be designated as nondeductible and nonincludable in the decree, must not be paid while the couple are living together, and must terminate upon the death of the payee spouse. In addition, the payments cannot be disguised child support. **See Figure 3, Box [1] ➔ [3] ➔ [5] ➔ [6] ➔ [10] ➔ [12].**

The question in this situation is whether the payments deducted by Peter and included by Gabrielle are "alimony" as defined in §71.

XYZ stock: Because alimony must be paid in cash, the transfer of the XYZ stock does not qualify as alimony. So this amount cannot be deducted by Peter, nor must it be included in Gabrielle's gross income. Instead, it is a transfer of property incident to a divorce and is governed by §1041.

Mortgage payments: It is possible for payments made to a third party to qualify as alimony (see Treas. Reg. §1.71-1T, Q-6). These payments require some scrutiny to see if they would terminate upon Gabrielle's death. The decree provides that they will continue until the earlier of the sale of the home, the payoff of the mortgage, or when Gabrielle ceases to use the home as her principal residence. Peter has a good argument that the payments qualify because, upon Gabrielle's death, she will no longer be using this residence as her principal residence. The parties would have been better off to state explicitly in the decree that the payments do or do not end upon Gabrielle's death.

Cash—front-end-loaded alimony? The cash payments appear to meet the definition of alimony, but the question is whether there is front-end-loaded alimony. If so, the excess alimony payment will be included in the payor's gross income in the third post-separation year and will be deductible by the payee spouse in that year. See §71(f).

Step 1   Calculate the excess alimony payment for the *second* post-separation year.
$20,000 − ($10,000 + $15,000) = -0-

Step 2   Calculate the excess alimony payment for the *first* post-separation year.

$$\$40,000 - \left[\left\{ \frac{\$(20,000 - 0) + \$10,000}{2} \right\} + \$15,000 \right] = \$10,000$$

Step 3   Calculate the excess alimony payment—the sum of steps 1 and 2:
-0- + $10,000 = $10,000

Step 4   Determine the consequences to payor and recipient in the third post-separation year:
$10,000 deduction from AGI to Gabrielle
$10,000 inclusion in gross income for Peter

Part B

The transfer of the family home to Gabrielle in the divorce is governed by §1041. That section provides that she receives this as a gift (and therefore does not include any of this value in gross income) and takes the basis of the home equal to the couple's basis in it immediately before the divorce, i.e., $200,000. When Gabrielle gives it to her daughter, Trendee, she takes the home with a basis equal to the donor's basis ($200,000), except that for purposes of determining loss on any sale by Trendee, her basis will be the fair market value on the date of the gift, i.e., $160,000.

Glossary

Above the line: A deduction obtained by subtracting from gross income in computing adjusted gross income. See §62.

Accrual method: A method of accounting that many businesses use, which requires taxpayers to include income when they have a right to it (whether or not it is received) and to deduct expenses when they become obligated for them (subject to certain restrictions).

Adjusted basis: The taxpayer's initial basis in an asset, adjusted downward for MACRS or other capital recovery. See §1016.

Administrative practicality: A criterion for evaluating the merits of a tax statute, which focuses on how a tax statute would be administered by the IRS. Would administration be easy or difficult? Would it require more or less intrusion into taxpayers' lives? Would the cost of administration be worth the advantages of the statute, whether increased fairness, certain economic behaviors, or increased revenue?

Alimony: A payment made by a former spouse to the other former spouse that meets the requirements of §71, regardless of how it is labeled for state law purposes. See §71.

Alternative minimum tax: Known as the "AMT," this is a surtax designed to ensure that taxpayers that enjoy special tax benefits that reduce regular taxable income do pay some tax. See §55.

American opportunity credit: Formerly known as the "Hope Scholarship Credit," a tax credit allowed for certain expenditures for higher education. See §25A.

Amortization: The common term for capital recovery for intangible assets used in a trade or business or held for investment.

Amount realized: With respect to the disposition of an asset, the sum of the amount of money received, the fair market value of property received, and the liabilities of the taxpayer assumed by a buyer in the transaction. See §1001.

Amounts at risk: For purposes of determining whether a taxpayer may claim a loss with respect to an activity, the amount of money or property that the taxpayer could lose if the activity fails. See §465.

Annual accounting: The principle that income and deductions are to be reported on an annual (12-month) basis and that taxpayers report the tax results of activities on the last day of such annual period, even if circumstances change later.

Assignment of income: A strategy employed by taxpayers to attempt to direct income to related persons in a lower tax bracket.

Barter: The exchange of goods and/or services without a cash payment.

Basis: The taxpayer's economic investment in an item of property.

Below-market loan: A loan that does not include a market rate of interest, as established from time to time by the IRS, and with respect to which interest may be imputed. See §7872.

Below the line: A deduction that is allowable as a subtraction from adjusted gross income in computing taxable income. See §63.

Bonus depreciation: "Extra" depreciation that Congress sometimes allows taxpayers as a method of encouraging taxpayers to make purchases of capital equipment. See §167.

Calendar year: The 12-month period for reporting income and deductions that begins on January 1 and ends on December 31.

Capital asset: Any asset other than those listed in §1221.

Capital expenditure: An expenditure incurred by a taxpayer that creates a separate asset or the benefit of which is likely to extend beyond the close of the taxable year. See §263.

Capital gain: Recognized income from the sale or exchange of a capital asset. See §1222.

Capital loss: Recognized loss from the sale or exchange of a capital asset. See §1222.

Capital recovery: With respect to an asset, the process by which the taxpayer is allowed to recoup his or her investment in the asset in order to be taxed only on the income on the disposition of that asset. Capital recovery may be allowed upon acquisition (see §179), over the period that the asset produces income (see MACRS), or upon disposition of the asset (see §1001). The timing of capital recovery is a matter for Congress.

Cash method: The accounting method that most individuals use, which requires taxpayers to include income when received (actually or constructively) and deduct expenses when paid (subject to certain restrictions).

Casualty: A natural or manmade disaster or sudden event that causes loss to property. *Example:* an earthquake.

Character: The nature of income or loss as capital gain or loss or ordinary income or loss.

Charitable contribution: The donation of cash or property to a qualifying charitable organization, which potentially generates an itemized deduction. See §170.

Claim of right: The principle that a taxpayer must include items of gross income to which the taxpayer has a reasonable claim of right, even if the taxpayer must repay all or any part of that amount later. See §1341.

Collectible: A type of capital asset that generates 28% capital gain or loss upon sale or other disposition. *Example:* the sale of a coin collection.

Compensation: Income received for the performance of services, whether as an employee or otherwise, and whether received in the form of cash or property. See §61(a)(1).

Constructive receipt: An overlay on the cash method of accounting principle, under which cash method taxpayers must include income in their gross incomes when they have the right to receive it, even if they choose not to do so.

Cost basis: A taxpayer's initial purchase price for an item of property, including the cash paid for the item, the fair market value of property transferred to obtain the property, and the liabilities assumed by the taxpayer. See §1012.

Deduction: A subtraction from gross income in computing adjusted gross income, or a subtraction from adjusted gross income in computing taxable income.

Deference: The principle that a court should defer to the IRS's prelitigation, published position on a tax matter.

Deferral of income: A strategy employed by a taxpayer to save taxes by delaying the receipt of income until a future year.

Dependent care credit: The tax credit available for up to 30% of certain amounts paid for the care of dependents while the taxpayer earns income. See §21.

Depreciation: The common term for capital recovery of tangible assets used in a trade or business or held for the production of income. The method of depreciation currently in use is MACRS.

Discharge of debt: The action by a creditor that excuses a debtor from paying all or part of a debt, which can generate gross income unless excluded under §108.

Discount rate: The percentage rate used in determining present or future value, which is determined by a number of factors, including the expected interest rates that will prevail in the applicable period and the riskiness of the payments.

Earned income credit: The refundable tax credit available to taxpayers with low amounts of earned income, which varies with the number of children that the taxpayer claim as dependents. See §32.

Economic benefit: Any benefit to a taxpayer of a pecuniary nature, whether in cash or in another form, as opposed to a purely emotional benefit.

Economic effects: A criterion for evaluating the merits of a tax statute, which focuses on the likely effects of the statute on taxpayer behavior. Will taxpayers be likely to engage in the kind of activity encouraged by the statute? Would they engage in other, undesirable behaviors?

Would these effects justify the cost of administration of the statute, its effects on fairness of the system, and the impact on revenue?

Education savings account: An account established for savings for higher education under §530, which allow deferral and possibly the exclusion of earnings on such accounts.

Exclusion: The characteristic of an item of income that it is excluded from gross income; i.e., it never becomes part of the base on which the federal income tax is levied.

Fairness: A criterion for evaluating the merits of a tax statute, which focuses on whether the statute makes the tax system more or less able to reflect each taxpayer's relative ability to pay. If a statute increases the fairness of the system, the questions are whether such an increase justifies any increased cost of administration and whether the statute would affect revenue and taxpayer behavior in positive ways.

Fiscal year: A 12-month period for reporting income and deductions other than a calendar year.

Fringe benefit: A benefit provided by an employer to an employee. *Example:* parking. See §132.

Future value: The projected value of a sum invested today which earns interest over a stated period at a stated rate.

Gambling: Games of chance, such as poker, slots, and other games.

Gift: A transfer made with detached and disinterested generosity, i.e., without expectation of any quid pro quo. See §102.

Gross income: the starting place for the calculation of the federal income tax, i.e., all "income" from whatever source derived. See §61.

Health savings account: An account to which taxpayers may make contributions, the earnings on which accumulate tax free and may be distributed tax free to pay for medical expenses. See §223.

Hobby losses: The common term for losses incurred in activities that are arguably not undertaken for profit, even though they may generate income. *Examples:* horses; race cars. See §183.

Holding period: The period of time a taxpayer holds an asset, used for computing capital gain or loss. See §1223.

Home office: An office used in a taxpayer's trade or business that occupies a portion of the taxpayer's principal residence. See §280A.

Imputed income: The value of property that one owns and uses, or the value of services that one performs for oneself and one's family.

Individual Retirement Account: Known as an "IRA"; a savings vehicle that allows taxpayers to contribute funds to an account, the earnings on which will grow tax free. See §408. Contributions to traditional IRAs are potentially deductible, and withdrawals after retirement are included in gross income. Contributions to Roth IRAs are not deductible, but withdrawals are not included in gross income.

Installment method: A method of reporting income from the sale of property (other than inventory) in which at least one payment is received after the close of the taxable year in which the sale occurs. See §453.

Interest: the compensation that a lender receives for making a loan, which is generally taxable as ordinary income.

Internal Revenue Code: Known as the "Code"; Title 26 of the United States Code.

Internal Revenue Service: Known as the "IRS" or the "Service"; a bureau of the Department of the Treasury charged with the administration of the tax laws.

Investment income: Income from dividends, rents, royalties, and similar items.

Involuntary conversion: The condemnation of property, or its destruction by fire, storm, earthquake, or other disaster.

Itemized deduction: The sum of a taxpayer's itemized deductions, i.e., those taken on Schedule A and taken in lieu of the standard deduction. See §63.

Kiddie tax: The tax imposed on certain young taxpayers with significant amounts of investment incomes, which raises their tax rate to that of their parents. See §1.

Life insurance: A contract between a purchaser of a life insurance policy and the insurance company, in which upon the death of the named insured, the company will pay the beneficiary a stated or determinable sum. See §102.

Like-kind exchange: An exchange of qualifying properties that qualifies under §1031.

Loan: A promise to repay a sum within a certain period, with or without interest.

Long term: Referring to the holding period of assets—one year or longer. See §1223.

Loss: The excess of deductions over income, or the excess of a taxpayer's adjusted basis over the sales price of an asset, or an event that results in the theft or other casualty of property. See §165.

Matching principle: The principle that deductions should be matched in the same taxable year with the income produced by such expenditures in order to best reflect the taxpayer's income for that period.

Meals and entertainment expenses: Expenses associated with business, which are potentially subject to special limitations under §274.

Medical expense: Expenditures for the treatment, diagnosis, and amelioration of disease or injury, which are potentially deductible if the expenses meet certain requirements. See §213.

Miscellaneous itemized deductions: A category of itemized deductions, which are deductible to the extent that, collectively, they exceed 2% of a taxpayer's adjusted gross income. See §67.

Modified accelerated cost recovery system (MACRS):   The method of capital recovery in use for tangible property, whether personal or real. See §167.

Moving expenses: Expenditures to move the taxpayer, the taxpayer's family, and the taxpayer's personal effects, which are potentially deductible if the move meets certain requirements. See §215.

Net operating loss: The excess of deductions over income for a trade or business or income-producing activity, which can carry back 3 years or forward 20 years. See §172.

Nonrecourse debt: Debt for which the debtor does not have personal liability.

Nonrefundable credit: A tax credit that does not reduce the tax due below zero; i.e., it cannot generate a tax refund. *Example:* dependent care credit.

Nonrecognition provisions: A number of Code provisions that allow or require a taxpayer to defer recognition of income, or require deferral of recognition of loss. *Examples:* like-kind exchanges and involuntary conversion.

Ordinary and necessary: The requirement for deduction of business expenses that focuses on how regular and appropriate the expenditures are in the conduct of business. See §162.

Ordinary income: Income that is other than capital gain. See §64.

Origin test: The principle that it is the origin or purpose of an expenditure, not the effects, that determines its proper categorization as personal or business. See §162.

Passive loss: A loss incurred in an activity that constitutes a trade or business, but with respect to which the taxpayer did not materially participate. See §469.

Personal casualty loss: A loss incurred by a taxpayer with respect to property held for personal use, and its destruction by fire, storm, earthquake, or other disaster, or by theft. See §165(c)(3).

Personal exemption: The below-the-line deduction to which each taxpayer is entitled and which is based on a standard amount per individual. See §151.

Personal expense: An expenditure, the origin of which is the taxpayer's personal life as opposed to his or her business activity, and which is normally nondeductible unless a specific statute applies. *Example:* medical expenses. See §262.

Pre-opening expense: An expenditure incurred by a taxpayer conducting a business before the business is ready to serve customers, i.e., before it opens. See §195.

Present value: The value now of a sum or sums, to be received at a specified time or times in the future, after making assumptions as to the appropriate discount rate.

Principal residence: The taxpayer's home where he or she usually lives. See §121.

Property settlement: A transfer of property pursuant to a divorce decree, and which potentially qualifies under §1041.

Qualified dividend income: Certain dividends received from domestic companies, which qualify for the special 15% rate as opposed to the regular rates on ordinary income. See §1.

Qualified residence interest: Interest on debt incurred to acquire a principal residence and interest on certain home equity loans. See §163.

Realization event: A transaction in which a taxpayer receives something qualitatively different than what he or she transferred. See §1001.

Recapture: Upon the sale of an asset held for use in a trade or business or for the production of income, the casting of what would otherwise be capital gain as ordinary income in order to reverse the benefit of previous deductions against ordinary income by the taxpayer with respect to the assets. See §1245.

Recognition: Including an item of income on a tax return or deducting a loss.

Recourse debt: Debt for which a taxpayer is personally liable.

Refundable credit: A tax credit that can reduce the tax due below zero, i.e., generate a tax refund. *Example:* earned income credit.

Relinquished property: In a like-kind exchange, the property that the taxpayer transfers in the exchange.

Replacement property: In a like-kind exchange, the property that the taxpayer acquires in the exchange.

Restricted property: Property received in exchange for the performance of services, which is subject to a substantial risk of forfeiture. See §83.

Revenue Ruling: A publication by the IRS, which applies the law to a stated set of facts, and upon which a taxpayer may rely.

Section 179 expense: A deduction for the purchase of tangible personal property to be used in a trade or business or income-producing activity, subject to certain requirements. See §179.

Section 529 plan: An account established for the funding of a taxpayer's higher education expenses in which earnings from the account are deferred or excluded from gross income. See §529.

Short term: Referring to the holding period of assets for purposes of calculating capital gain and loss—less than one year.

Section 1231 asset: Real or personal depreciable property used in a taxpayer's trade or business. *Example:* equipment.

Section 1231 gain or loss: gain or loss from the disposition of tangible assets used in a taxpayer's trade or business and described in §1231.

Standard deduction: Taken in lieu of itemized deductions, the sum of the taxpayer's basic standard deductions and certain other standard deductions. See §63.

Tax cost basis: A method of determining a taxpayer's basis in property, which relies on the amount of income a taxpayer included in gross income.

Tax credit: A tax benefit that reduces tax on a dollar-for-dollar basis, such as the dependent care credit.

Taxable income: The base on which the federal income tax is imposed, i.e., gross income minus all available deductions. See §63.

Taxable year: The 12-month period during which a taxpayer reports income and deductions, which can be a calendar year or a fiscal (non-calendar) year.

Tax rate: The percentage defining the tax on an item of net income. *Examples:* 10% or 28%.

Time value of money: The principle that a sum of money is more valuable the sooner it is received. A dollar to be received in the future is worth less than a dollar received today because a dollar invested today can earn interest or other appreciation.

Timing: The principle that income and deductions must be assigned to the correct year. Taxpayers try using timing strategies to defer income and accelerate deductions.

Trade or business: The activity of holding oneself out as providing goods and services to customers or engaging in gambling as a profession. See §162.

Unrecaptured §1231 loss: For purposes of §1231, a loss in a previous year that would otherwise have been a capital loss, but that was characterized as ordinary because of §1231. Net §1231 gains are classified as ordinary to the extent of such losses.

U.S. Tax Court: The court assigned to adjudicate tax cases, to which a taxpayer may make a petition without first paying the tax.

Table of Cases

213

Table of Internal Revenue Code Sections

Table of Administrative Authorities

Index

Page numbers are used for references to the Flow Charts, Capsule Summary, and Exam Tips. References to the Short-Answer Questions and Answers are indicated by "S" plus the question number. References to the Essay Questions and Answers are indicated by "E" plus the question number.

Study hint: Use this index to test your recall of tax concepts. Do you know what each term means? Can you match the concept with its Code section?